THE NETSCAPE INTRANET SOLUTION

Deploying the Full-Service Intranet

THE NETSCAPE INTRANET SOLUTION

Deploying the Full-Service Intranet

Shanen Boettcher

WILEY COMPUTER PUBLISHING

John Wiley & Sons, Inc.

New York • Chichester • Weinheim • Brisbane • Singapore • Toronto

Publisher: Robert Ipsen

Editor: Marjorie Spencer

Managing Editor: Micheline Frederick

Text Design & Composition: SunCliff Graphic Productions

Designations used by companies to distinguish their products are often claimed as trademarks. In all instances where John Wiley & Sons, Inc., is aware of a claim, the product names appear in initial capital or ALL CAPITAL LETTERS. Readers, however, should contact the appropriate companies for more complete information regarding trademarks and registration.

This text is printed on acid-free paper.

Published by John Wiley & Sons, Inc.

Published simultaneously in Canada.

Library of Congress Cataloging-in-Publication Data

Boettcher, Shanen, 1970–
    The Netscape Intranet solution : deploying the full service
Intranet / Shanen Boettcher.
       p.   cm.
    Includes bibliographical references and index.
    ISBN: 0-471-19225-2 (pbk. : alk. paper)
    1. Intranets (Computer networks).   2. Business enterprises-
-Computer networks.   3. Netscape Communications Corporation.
I. Title.
HD30.385.B64   1998
650'.0285'46--dc21

                                       97-37941
                                           CIP

Printed in the United States of America
10 9 8 7 6 5 4 3 2 1

CONTENTS

Chapter 7 Intranet Personnel Infrastructure 173

Chapter 8 Intranet Site Structure and Information 179 Architecture

Chapter 9 Application Development 221

INTRODUCTION

The intranet has come in on the second wave of Internet technology, following the tide created by the Internet and World Wide Web. Companies began posting sites on the Web and advertising their sites on television with the now all too-familiar "Visit our Web site at *http://www.acme.com*". Thus, the current wave which is marked by the flow of Internet technology inside the corporation, represents a paradigm shift in the traditional corporate information systems; in fact, by enabling new and faster ways of sharing information, it is likely that the intranet will have as great an effect on corporate communications as the telephone.

In the wake of the potential offered by corporate intranets, comes the media hype, which makes it seem that every company on the planet has already fully adopted and implemented intranet technology. Further, the press would have company executives believe that if they have not implemented an intranet, their company is hopelessly behind in corporate computing and that their competitors will leverage this to their advantage. The message is not entirely inaccurate, but it is well out of proportion. Reality check aside, most Fortune 1000 companies do have small implementations or a mixture of grassroots intranets within their organizations, and now is a great time to implement an intranet. The technology has matured, and there is enough experience from which to learn and improve your implementation of an intranet.

This book focuses on the experiences of companies implementing intranets using Netscape technology, distilled into a collection of best practices and guidelines for intranet implementation and deployment. Because this is a rapidly evolving technology, the most difficult aspect of writing this book was to ensure that it be meaningful by the time of publication. Several sections had to be revised prior to publication to reflect advances in technology that occurred during the writing. For this reason, it is important that, while reading, you concentrate on the techniques used in mapping the technology to user requirements and strategies used in the deployment process rather than on the specifics of the latest versions of products, as these techniques will transcend the inevitable change in technology and prove useful for companies deploying intranets today and in the future.

Who This Book Is For

This book is intended for IT managers, executives, or anyone in the process of deploying business solutions using Netscape technology. It assumes a moderate knowledge of Internet technology including the vocabulary and the basic building blocks of intranet systems. It discusses strategies and techniques for rolling out intranet technology both from a technical and functional perspective, based on experiences with Fortune 1000 companies. It concentrates more on the *how* of deploying an intranet rather than on the *what* or *why* addressed by many other publications. It therefore assumes that a decision has been made to pursue Netscape intranet technology. Further, it does not compare and contrast intranet product offerings from Netscape's competitors. Nevertheless, although the content centers around Netscape technology, the concepts presented can be applied more generally to intranet product architecture and deployment.

This book provides the building blocks to deploy intranet technology and defines a starting point for large-scale intranet installations. In addition, we pay close attention to deployment issues and offer strategies for their resolution. You will find practical advice on translating the information needs of a company's user community to user and network services of the intranet.

Conventions Used in this Book

It is important to clarify at the outset how systems and system components are addressed throughout this book. If you have found the intranet versus intranet distinction difficult to keep straight, we complicate the issue further by introducing the extranet. When discussing these three inclusively, the terms *Web system* and *Web technology* are used, particularly when discussing the technology as a whole, independent of specific implementation. Otherwise, the specific terms (*intranet, Internet, extranet*) are used to address issues specific to each type of deployment. The terms *client* , *browser*, and *Communicator* are often used interchangeably when discussing Web client technology. Browser refers only to the Navigator portion of the Communicator, while client refers to the Communicator as a whole. The term *server* is used, by default, to describe a software server rather than a physical computer. When discussing hardware, the term *hardware server* is used. References to the generic *information technology* (IT) department are made throughout the book to refer to system administration and support organizations within companies, which are often called the management information systems (MIS) department or information services (IS) department.

Part I

THE NETSCAPE INTRANET

THE EVOLUTION OF THE INTRANET

The evolution of the intranet is both an IT department's sweetest dream and worst nightmare. The introduction, or more appropriately "invasion," of the intranet into corporate computing marks a paradigm shift in information technology. For the first time, users are spearheading technology and bringing it to bear on corporate computing. Grassroots efforts often lead the adoption of intranet technology within the enterprise thanks to the inexpensive nature of the products and the relative ease of installation and configuration, which have empowered end users. Departmental groups within companies often use existing hardware and their own budgets to deploy Web servers and clients within their group. Unfortunately, once the departmental users initiate the intranet, it grows quickly and soon becomes too much to handle—system administration and user support become maintenance burdens. Often, at this point, the initiating department will request that the IT department take over the maintenance of this new system.

This shift has been a difficult one for many corporate IT departments. For the first time, users are telling *them* about the technology and rolling out the system on their own. In large organizations, the IT department is left with a mixed bag of Web technologies and little in the way of standards. Enter Netscape Professional Services, which can help architect and redeploy the intranet within an organization, putting standards in place

3

to ensure maintainability and efficiency of the intranet. The challenge is to institute standards across the organization while preserving the functional level of the first round of the intranet. Necessary standards include hardware and software architectures and configurations, as well as procedural standards in the areas of information creation and publishing. We will address the development of these standards throughout this book.

Mainframe or Client/Server?

If we put mainframe, dumb terminal online/batch at one end of the computing spectrum and full client/server technology at the other, Web technology falls somewhere in the middle. The key to client/server or distributed architectures is the splitting of the processing power between the client and server machines. In the mainframe world, all processing is performed on the server side; the terminal is simply a nongraphical display device. Applications are forms-based, whereby data is exchanged one screen at a time; a form is submitted or received from the mainframe/server. In addition, for online applications, users require a direct connection to the mainframe, and sap a finite amount of valuable CPU (Central Processing Unit) time in order to display information back to the user as an application is executed. In a batch application, data is gathered from the user and stored by the mainframe for later use. Then, usually in off-hours, programs are run against this static data, considered to be a purely *stateless* environment.

By contrast, in client/server architectures, applications consume resources on both the client and the server machines. The client machine is much more than a dumb terminal; in the course of an application, it performs calculations and displays information dynamically to the user. In this model, the client and server machines share application processing. For example, an application that requires a user to enter a list of expenses for time reporting can calculate total expenses prior to submitting them to a back-end database located on the server machine. These computations are made using the CPU of the client machine rather than that of the server. In the mainframe world, all computations are performed on the singular server or mainframe machine. This distributed processing is often cited as the efficiency of client/server applications. Since users can perform most of the computations on the client machine and interact with the server only to exchange information, there is much less demand on the central server and far less chance of processing contingency at the server level.

With the distribution of processing in client/server architecture comes distributed maintenance. As complexity at the desktop level increases, system and application maintenance increases in a linear fashion. Under the centralized mainframe model, maintenance is restricted to the mainframe machine itself; desktop trouble is almost exclusively hardware-related, as all of the intelligence is contained in the central computer. In addition, application code resides in only one place in the mainframe environment. Consequently, application developers have to maintain only one copy of production code for its users. Under the client/server model, applications must be distributed to all of the desktops, thus, each client machine must have the new software installed. The first question from all help desks is, "Which version are you running?" and the universal cure-all answer is, "You need to upgrade to the newest release." Distribution and ongoing maintenance of client/server applications are two of the primary functions of many IT departments.

Web Technology: The Middle Ground

As noted, Web technology falls somewhere in the middle of mainframe and client/server system architectures. It has been designed to address the shortcomings of each of these environments, and so is indeed a hybrid. Like the mainframe environment, the user works with a light client, by comparison to many client/server applications. In addition, the Web client relies on the server to provide it with application code. This application code, whether in the form of HTML, Java applets, or JavaScript is stored on the server and distributed to the client machine upon request. This central storage of application information is analogous to the mainframe world of computing, and eliminates the maintenance associated with distributing new versions and updates to application code. Such code began as stateless forms-based HTML pages through a Common Gateway Interface (CGI), which requested data from the user, was passed to the server, and was then validated and processed on the server side. This was similar to the mainframe application architecture in that the client side was simply a display mechanism, albeit a graphical one in Web technology. As Web technology matured, more and richer client processing became available through Java and JavaScript, which approximates traditional client/server applications. Now, dynamic applications, which combine processing of client and server, can be achieved using Web technology while reaping the benefit of centralized code maintenance. In addition to advances in distributed processing, Web technologies have evolved to more *stateful* characteristics, a concept explained next.

In the early days of Web technology, applications, like the underlying protocol, were *stateless* by design, to minimize network traffic and maximize security. Under the Web's HTTP protocol, the "conversation" between a client and server consists of a requests coming from the client and responses coming from the server. This is a one-to-one relationship; one request, one response. The challenge for a programmer in this environment is to simulate a discussion or process that requires multiple steps to accomplish a task. In a stateful environment, a processing session is maintained between the client and server for the course of an application. By maintaining this session, the application is aware of multiple interactions in the sequence of a programmatic operation. In stateless environments, on the other hand, each interaction between the server and the client is singular and independent.

The infamous "cookie" is the mechanism most widely associated with state control in Web applications. A cookie is nothing more than a token or piece of information that is stored during a session to maintain the state between the server and the client, and can refer to two different pieces of information in an application. The first is a file to which the application can write information that it requires to process a multistep task. The other is information passed between the client and server via the URL, which allows the server to use that information to complete a multistep task. As with all major technological advances, Web technology has introduced new risks; specifically, the potential for misuse of client system resources; to read and write to the local disk, to run programs, and others. Users fear that malicious programs may be downloaded to the client and corrupt that machine. For this reason, Netscape developers have been careful to allow only minimal utilization of client resources from within an application: within the client browser application itself. This is consistent with the introduction of Java, which also has a very limited and secure application area, or "sandbox" as it is often called. The introduction of *trusted applets* will bring a wider range of distributed processing to Web technology. A trusted applet is a Java program that is granted permission by the user to access a specified local system resource. Further, this applet is "signed" using an x.509 certificate to identify the developer or company that produced the applet. In this way, users can make informed decisions as to granting applets local system resources, giving them the confidence to trust applications to use a greater range of client resources. These applications will closely approximate the functionality of traditional client/server applications because more processing resources will be made available to the applications, while reducing much of the resource demand of application distribution and maintenance.

Intranet Idiom

Before delving into architecture designs and deployment plans, we'll define the terms we use in this book and describe the context in which they will be used because even the most basic term, the intranet, means many things to many people. In less than two years, the questions surrounding the intranet have changed dramatically. In the early days, our group spent a great deal of effort selling the concept of the intranet; that is, we answered definition and justification questions; defined its boundaries; explained how it would, hypothetically "fit in" to existing systems; described why the intranet technology was a worthwhile investment of IT funds, and demonstrated return on investment figures associated with intranet solutions. The definition of the intranet continues to evolve, but recent studies by International Data Corporation (IDC) have shown unprecedented return on investment figures as high as 1,500 percent in as little as three months. In addition, recent surveys by Forrester Research show that 90 percent of Fortune 1000 companies have deployed intranet technology within their organizations, or plan to within nine months. With these preliminary studies in hand and the ubiquity of Internet and intranet technology, the questions on corporate executives' minds are not currently focused on why, but how intranet solutions are deployed and the strategic and long-term positioning of the intranet within the organization. To answer those questions, this book addresses the deployment strategies of intranet business solutions using Netscape technology. It assumes an acceptance of intranet technology within today's corporate environment. The book then describes what an intranet should be from a user perspective, and what that means to an IT organization in terms of technical architecture and support.

Before answering the how questions of deployment, it is important to establish a baseline understanding of the term *intranet* as well as to itemize criteria for evaluating its development. In addition, it is important to understand the state of intranet technology as it currently exists within the organization.

There are two general definitions of intranets: the technical and the functional. The technical definition focuses on the technology and its deployment; the functional on business solutions and providing user and network services to your organization. This is an important distinction and one that has caused confusion in the marketplace. It is essential to understand that there can be intranet technology without an intranet. Studies demonstrate the acceptance of intranet technology into corporate computing, but they do not answer the question of how this technology was deployed or the level of service it supplies to its users. The underlying issue is how those companies defined the intranet in terms of technology and functionality.

Technical Definition

Much of the media hype surrounding intranets is focused on the technical definition, which, simply, is *Web technology deployed behind the firewall*. This is the criterion used by many companies today to define the existence of an intranet. Under this definition, a company has an intranet if it has a Web server and some browsers behind the firewall—which of course means that nearly every company in the world has an intranet.

As stated earlier, however, there is much more to an intranet than the technology. It is important to repeat here that corporate IT groups have accepted and often embraced Internet technology. The popularity among the common user and its affordable price have brought the Internet inside the firewall to the corporate desktop. Consequently, there is the perception in corporate computing that if an intranet has not yet been deployed, then the company is significantly behind the technology curve. This is a misconception based on the fact that most Fortune 1000 companies plan to *have the technology in place*. This means that now is a great time to deploy or redeploy the intranet within your company, and to deploy more than technology, but a comprehensive solution made up of user and network services. This concept, the *full-service intranet*, is one coined by Forrester Research and developed by Marc Andreesen and the Netscape technology team in a white paper entitled "The Full-Service Intranet." It is a useful way to view the functional side of the intranet and how it fits into corporate computing. The full-service intranet focuses on providing user and network services to deliver a comprehensive solution through Netscape technology.

Functional Definition: The Full-Service Intranet

The concept of the full-service intranet provides a framework for discussion of the product offerings of Netscape Communications. Simply, it is based on the premise that an intranet must provide value to its users, that is, it must deliver utility to the desktop to help people do their jobs. Taking the concept one step further, the Netscape vision of the full-service intranet is outlined in Netscape's intranet Roadmap whitepaper, which quantifies the utility of the intranet in terms of user and network services. User services are those that engage and interface with the user directly. These include:

❑ Information sharing and management
❑ Communication and collaboration
❑ Navigation
❑ Application access

Network services make up the foundation of computing communication and include:

❑ Directory
❑ Replication
❑ Security
❑ Management

This division provides a useful model from which to describe comprehensive enterprise solutions, which are provided through the Netscape suite of intranet technology. While these criteria can be used to evaluate corporate communications using proprietary systems such as Lotus Notes or Microsoft Exchange, Netscape technology most closely maps to the goals of the full-service intranet vision.

User Services

User services are the utilities provided to the end user by the intranet. A successful intranet supplies all of the services required by its users to complete their job tasks and become, for the first time, a one-stop shop for all computing need—utilizing open standards, cross-platform operability, and the intuitive, ubiquitous nature of HTML and Web client/server technology.

Information Sharing and Management

The intranet must give the user the ability to share and manage information and easily create and publish documents online. The intranet must provide tools that enable users to create and distribute documents electronically. Although often overlooked, this function is the core competency of Web technology; that is, the distribution of information in a one-to-many paradigm.

There are three aspects of information sharing and management: information creation-authoring, information organization and formatting-publishing, and information release—distribution. Each of these is required to provide this function. Authoring today requires WYSIWYG (what you see is what you get) tools with drag-and-drop capabilities for content manipulation. Note that, here, content refers to multiple word processing formats and multimedia objects. All of these formats must be available and easy to manipulate when creating or repurposing information. Accessing and revising this content must be managed to ensure integrity of information. The Composer component of the Netscape Communicator provides all of these authoring features, as well as the information management functionality through its integration with the SuiteSpot servers.

Communication and Collaboration

Users must be able to communicate and cooperate using the intranet. This requires open e-mail and groupware throughout the organization. Internet standards now enable open e-mail and groupware capabilities that are as powerful and functional as proprietary alternatives and that can be integrated across the full-service intranet. Access control and security ensure that both e-mail and discussion groups will be private, through authentication of all parties across the network. E-mail and discussion groups can be distributed across systems or taken offline for disconnected use. Richly formatted e-mail and discussion group features, plus network calendaring and scheduling, provide a seamless collaboration environment. In addition, users can locate e-mail addresses, security keys, and Internet phone numbers by referring to a simple address book interface tied into an open directory service across the Internet.

Navigation

Hand in hand with information sharing and management comes the requirement to locate that information. Users must be able to find answers to questions or problems using sophisticated search and retrieval tools, which must be intuitive and open multiple paths along which to quickly find needed information. Further, these tools must return information instantly, because users need this information to make critical business decisions.

Application Access

A great strength of the intranet is that it can function as a singular user interface for all your business information needs. To do this, the intranet must provide seamless access to databases, applications, and legacy systems. Access to structured data is a basic requirement of all business solutions and is therefore required of the intranet.

Using the intranet, existing databases, data warehouses, and legacy applications can be accessed easily from a single interface. New applications can be authored once with JavaScript and Java, and quickly deployed on any platform, across all desktop and server operating environments and hardware platforms; all client-side application logic is downloaded when an application is accessed, and the logic is automatically updated. Applications can be interwoven with content and be deployed transparently over the Internet as well as over the intranet. All the full-service intranet services are available to applications, including content management, directories, and replication. Application access can be easily controlled, and can be built on top of business processes, enabling easy-to-use workflow capabilities across the entire enterprise.

Network Services

In addition to providing user-centric services, the intranet must provide "public utilities," or network services. These services focus on a lower level to provide the framework upon which the user services are built.

Directory

Traditionally, directories have served one of two functions in systems: as user identification (id/password) or as an application for finding phone numbers and addresses. Most client/server, database, and network operating systems maintained their own proprietary user directory, which had obvious ramifications for users with multiple logins as well as system administrators who had to maintain these multiple-user entries. In the future, these functions will come together to produce a single directory in which to store standardized user information for access privileges, along with demographic information and encryption keys for secure transmission of data.

The directory is the central point to which all applications come to find user information and to authenticate identity. This vision of the directory has a single point of access for the user and the administrator; that is, a single user login and central administration of user accounts. In addition to the traditional id/password information, the directory can be used to hold attributes about an individual—demographics, position, skills, current projects, and so on. With this information, the directory becomes more than a phone book or an access control list; it becomes a service that provides information about the people and resources that make up an organization.

Replication

Replication is the function of spreading data throughout a system to provide immediate access to information used most frequently by users. In this way replication improves performance. In a perfect world with unlimited bandwidth, all content would be stored singularly and centrally, and replication would not be needed; but, in real-world network architectures, to provide a high level of performance to users, replication, a mixture of art and science, is necessary to bring a copy of the information to the user and to manage the updates to dynamic content.

Some replication models focus on the duplication and synchronization of information, but the ultimate goal of replication is to make the information that is most pertinent to a user available locally and to transparently manage the updates to that information. There are two methods for performing replication: *on-command* and *on-demand*. The on-command method involves running an update routine periodically to refresh a specified area of content (e.g., update the entire root directory of a server). With the on-command method, decisions must be made as to when, how frequently, and how thoroughly the replication process will occur. On-command replication is often performed through custom scripts that update files that have changed. In contrast, the on-demand method of replication is driven by user requests for information. Rather than making assumptions about when and how often information is updated on an aggregate level, the content is updated only when the user requests that information or the information has changed. In this way, the information that is the most frequently used is most frequently updated in the most efficient way possible.

Security

System security is one of the most talked about topics in deployment of intranet business solutions. Often used as a barrier to entry by IS departments, security is also one of the most misunderstood areas of Internet technology. Because of the tremendous amount of hype associated with Internet computing, intranet deployments often inherit the stigma of Internet credit card theft and so-called Big Brother concerns. All of these issues become more intense inside the company and reach unprecedented levels when discussing the combined intranet and Internet solutions of extranets.

The goal, of course, is for security to be ubiquitous and easy to manage, that is, for it to be a given. In reality, security becomes a series of somewhat subjective decisions based on the value of information. The adage that no system is impenetrable and that users play a major role in implementing and maintaining a secure system holds true for intranets in these days of secure sockets layer (SSL), encryption, and certificate technology. Furthermore, decisions about the nature of information must be made to determine how wide and how thick the walls of security need to be and at what cost. Ironically, although the answer is inevitably, "We need the highest level of security available for all parts of our system because our data is invaluable," many companies will not hesitate to fax or discuss next quarter's projections on the public phone lines with no encryption or authentication. The perception of security is largely driven by the perception of the intranet as a whole, covering the spectrum from an open communications platform to a mission-critical transaction processing system.

Management

Last, but not least, someone must administer the system. To provide a full-service solution, this maintenance must be easy and centralized. System administrators require tools that are secure and can be used remotely to maintain a production information system. These tools also have to be provided by a multiplatform, standards-based, intuitive implementation. In addition to remote administration, many companies require a system maintenance model in which there is centralized control, along with distributed administration to allow company headquarters to maintain a set of internal standards, while leveraging its localized IT resources to administer the systems for remote offices.

Management also requires integration with existing system administration tools to provide a single point of contact for system administrators from which they can monitor the intranet. More than making backups and restoring files, maintenance of any distributed client/server system requires the distribution of software. In the intranet, the distribution of updates to application code is transparent to the user and the system administrator. This grants the system administrator centralized control of the distribution and installation of software and the user current, supported application functionality.

The Intranet and Your Company

As indicated earlier, the first and most important task required for the deployment of a successful intranet is to define the intranet for your company. You must determine which parts of the full-service solution will be provided as well as the mission-critical nature of the system. Corporate intranets run the gamut from pure communication tools as an extension to phones, fax, and the conversation in the hallways, to systems that run the transactions of a business. Positioning the intranet is important because it will dictate much of the deployment approach in terms of system and network architecture and the types of tools available for use in the deployment process. For each phase of development it is important to identify the users of the system, the user and network services required by those users, and the nature of the implementation of those services by those users. For example, a financial company whose traders use the intranet to communicate market research and trading strategies will have stricter requirements for the protection of information than perhaps a retail store that uses the intranet to post procedure manuals for the maintenance of their stores. Even within the same company, different departments may have different levels of data security. The human resources department often requires very strict security in contrast to the facilities department that may want to provide as much information to as wide an audience as possible. In either case, there are different users, uses, and implications for the intranet, all of which influence deployment considerations.

CHAPTER 2

INTRANET BENEFITS

Scaling Down: From Internet to Intranet

One of the most refreshing aspects of working with intranet technology is that, for the first time, technology scales down to enterprise computing. In the past, client/server technology was developed first for the desktop or workgroup, which meant that the move to enterprisewide information sharing required modifications to the original system architecture and often produced less than great performance and scalability. In addition, client/server technology was developed under the assumption that it would be run in a LAN environment with relatively high bandwidth and stable network connections. Here, too, Internet technology was designed for the worst-case scenario via the HTTP protocol to manage the transmission of data in a stateless manner to provide robust transmission of data in an extremely diverse and sometimes feeble network. Although this has introduced some challenges in managing transaction state in applications, it provides for the deployment across a diverse worldwide network and the ability to use "old iron" to run an intranet, thus reducing the overall cost and improving return on investment.

As the technology moves inside the company and applications become more prevalent, tools to manage state are being developed using the same communications protocol to maintain scalability. Intranet technology, then, first designed for the Internet and is now being scaled down to the enterprise without bringing assumptions of environment, and thus providing a uniquely scalable architecture.

Open Standards

The definition of the term *open* as it refers to intranet technology is questionable in many people's minds. The confusion stems from the fact that all software products are, at the lowest level, proprietary; the Netscape Communicator source code, for example, belongs to Netscape and no other company. The true definition of open hinges on the communication protocols and format of data used between applications. An open standards environment requires no gateways, format conversions, or redundant application development. Information on applications that are created for an open standards environment are developed only once, in one format, and can be guaranteed to appear as intended on any number of platforms. This is the core idea behind standards in Internet technology. There is, of course, always room for customized feature sets in the applications themselves, but the delivery formats and mechanisms are standardized. A good case in point are attachments to messages. Many e-mail systems require gateways to communicate with other mail systems. Lotus Notes, for example, requires a gateway from Notes mail to SMTP mail. This requires a filtering of the original content to a standardized format prior to being sent to an external mail system. Text is fairly easy to convert and send in this manner, but binary file attachments are often corrupted when sent through the gateway or e-mail filter. By contrast, in the Netscape Messaging server, the messages are stored in standard HTML and attachments in the MIME standard format. In addition, the Netscape Messaging server communicates natively in SMTP. For this reason, the mail messages and the attachments sent using the Netscape Messaging server require no filtering or transformation prior to being sent across the Internet to external systems. This reduces the processing time required to send a message and eliminates the possibility of loss or corruption of data due to a filtering process.

Many software vendors claim support for the open standards based on the introduction of filters or conversion tools from native formats to open formats. Certainly, many of these products will covert their proprietary formats to open ones, but the applications themselves were designed to operate on the original proprietary formats released with the products (e.g., RTF and Lotus Compound Document Object Format). Essentially, these products are treating the symptoms rather than the cause by forcing their proprietary formats into open ones. The Netscape product suite has been developed with the open formats in mind and takes advantage of that efficiency to provide scalable solutions.

Platform Independence

A benefit of designing products with standards in mind is portability. The standards themselves are concerned with providing solutions that are independent of any hardware architecture. As a result, Netscape products span all common platforms on both the client and the server. This makes the promise of using "old iron" to run an intranet a reality. In addition, the information and applications created for the intranet can be used by anyone on any platform. Portability reduces the effort required of content creators and application developers significantly—write once, deploy many.

The ability to run on most platforms ensures that all users will be able to participate in the intranet and that system administrators can leverage their knowledge of the existing hardware within their company by running the intranet on those preferred or standardized server platforms.

User Acceptance

The popularity of the Internet has given many users a high level of familiarity with Web technology. The advantage is that the introduction of the intranet is a little less difficult than with other systems. The disadvantage is that the sophistication of the user community can become a barrier in and of itself. As discussed earlier, often it is the user community that brings the intranet to the IT department. This theme continues with the development of one-off applications by closet Web developers. The point is, for this first time, users are embracing technology prior to the enterprise.

Netscape versus Competition

The goal of this section is to answer the questions raised to IT departments in the process of implementing Netscape technology within the enterprise. Most companies realize that intranet technology is inevitable in corporate computing, but many invoke the technical definition of the intranet and therefore view it as a point solution. When the intranet is positioned as the full-service intranet, however, many questions are raised. For running the business on the intranet, companies prefer to consider what they know; that is, usually Microsoft and Lotus. Consequently, introducing Netscape technology is often difficult. The following subsections offer the answers to some of the hard questions.

Momentum

The race to support open standards by all vendors of enterprise software indicates that standards are an important part of communicating within large organizations. Although young, Netscape has more experience in developing cross-platform, standards-based products than any of its competitors, as demonstrated by the spearheading efforts of the company to develop standards in several areas of corporate computing. The marketplace tracks Netscape's progress as a guide to developing their own product strategies. In short, Netscape's vision defines to an extant the direction of the intranet industry, which subsequently influences the groupware, document management, messaging, and publishing functions within the enterprise.

Cost Savings

With figures as high as 1500 percent return on investment in as little as three months, cost of ownership of Netscape intranet technology has redefined the way companies spend money on information systems. As stated earlier, the low initial cost of Netscape technology has shifted the paradigm in IT shops and led to internal departments piecing together their own Web sites. Netscape intranet technology costs a fraction of proprietary solutions such as Lotus Notes or Microsoft Exchange. Indeed, the demand to use the universal client has forced such companies to rethink their strategies and offering. Many proprietary solutions now offer a "light" client version that provides an HTML client interface to their servers.

Cost savings from technology are always difficult to calculate accurately, and are usually done on hard costs, which map directly to copying and shipping costs. It is clear that these figures only touch on how intranets save or make money. The next step is to estimate labor time-savings brought about by the technology and to determine how jobs are made more efficient. This is done by comparing the way things were done before the technology was introduced. Because information is made readily available via the intranet, employees are better informed and make better, more productive decisions on the job. This is both the most significant and most elusive value to calculate. The adage that information is power is more true now than ever before. That power is being brought to the desktop via intranet technology. The best news is that the already unprecedented return on investment offered by intranet technology is only the beginning.

Depth and Breadth of Solution

The full-service intranet paints the ideal picture of corporate communications by taking into account all aspects of user and network services. To date, Netscape is the only company to provide solutions that address all areas of the full-service intranet. Netscape's competitors are still playing catch-up in all areas of Web technology, many by addressing only the basic requirements of Internet technology rather than those unique to the enterprise. Netscape's product line is tailored to the enterprise and meets the special needs of security and administration in the distributed corporate environment. Netscape's full-service intranet is available today in SuiteSpot and the Communicator.

Netscape also offers a state-of-the-art intranet application development environment in Netscape ONE, which provides application developers with the tools they need to build open, cross-platform applications for their corporate users. From base-level APIs to fourth-generation user-interface development tools, Netscape ONE provides the capability to interface with existing systems and build sophisticated custom applications to solve business problems.

The full-service intranet provides a solid framework for understanding how the Netscape product family delivers business solutions. The next chapter discusses the component parts of the full Netscape solution.

CHAPTER 3

NETSCAPE PRODUCTS

The Netscape product line is made up of the client, the Netscape Communicator, and a collection of servers called the Netscape SuiteSpot. This section outlines the product offerings as of the writing of this book, which no doubt will be outdated in the near future. Nevertheless, all of the base units of an intranet are represented in these products and are likely to remain part of the Netscape line in one form or another. With that caveat in mind, the goal of this chapter is to describe the modular nature of the products and describe how each of them maps to the user and network services that make up the Netscape full-service intranet, not to give a detailed feature listing of all the products. Detailed current information on the products can be always obtained at: http://home.netscape.com.

Client Products

For many people Netscape and the Navigator are synonymous. Indeed, the Navigator put Netscape on the map and continues to be the most popular computer application of all time.

Netscape Communicator

More than just a Web browser, Netscape Communicator is a suite of client components designed to address the needs of intranet users. Available in two editions, the Standard Edition Communicator contains the Navigator, the Composer, Conference, Messenger, and Collabra. The Professional Edition includes the Standard Edition components plus Calendar, AutoAdmin, and IBM Host On-Demand. The Professional Edition is built specifically to meet the needs of the corporation, and is used most frequently in intranet deployments.

Netscape Navigator

Netscape Navigator is the leading World Wide Web browser and the most used computer application in history. It continues to lead the industry in providing users with access to information (Figure 3.1). Navigator's browsing function will continue to be the central mechanism for delivering information to users of Web systems. The following subsections describe the new features of the Navigator 4.0 release within the Communicator.

Client-side ORB

Built into the Communicator base code is a CORBA standard Object Request Broker (ORB). This enables the development of client-side object-oriented applications that make use of network-stored objects. It works with the ORB in the Enterprise Server 3. 0 to communicate to back-end systems. Both ORBs are accessible via standard object Interface Definition Language (IDL) and the Internet Inter-ORB Protocol (IIOP). (CORBA, IIOP, and ORBs are discussed further in the Application Development section.)

Layers

The inability to accurately control the position of HTML elements has become a stumbling block for producing rich HTML documents. A layer is a container within an HTML document that can contain any HTML element: text, graphics, Java applets, and more (see Figure 3.2). The properties of a layer enable the author to specify the exact horizontal and vertical pixel positions of the container, its stacking order with respect to other layers, and its initial visibility. These layer properties can then be manipulated through JavaScript to add dynamic features to an otherwise static page such as "flying" images; stacking text on top of graphics to achieve page builds; and hiding and revealing text or graphics, or executing an applet based on screen events. Layers play a major role in delivering drag-and-drop capabilities within a Web page; users are able to grab

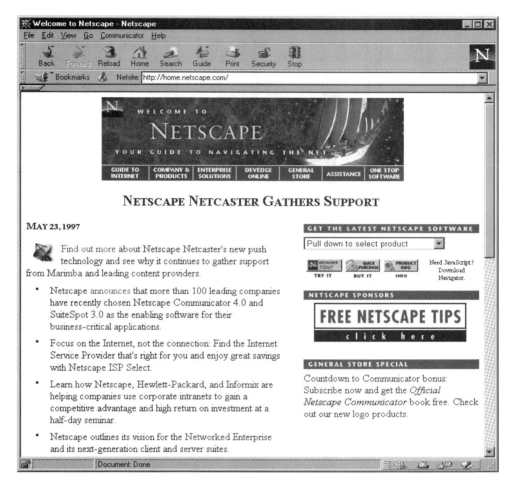

Figure 3.1 Navigator component of the Netscape Communicator.

paragraphs, graphics, and other objects, and position them anywhere on the page.

Style Sheets

Style sheets are templates that specify format information for HTML tags and provide the publisher with greater flexibility and control of the presentation of HTML documents. Their purpose is to separate the content from the format of documents. Style sheets can be used to define, for example, that the contents of top-level head will be rendered in bright red

Figure 3.2 Layers in Netscape Navigator.

and in the Times font, 48 point. The style sheets can then be linked or embedded with HTML content files to construct the pages that are displayed to the user. In this way, the appearance of the Web site can be changed independently of the content. Style sheets are implemented under the Cascading Style Sheets mechanism, level 1, which is currently under review by the World Wide Web Consortium (W3C).

HTML Fonts

HTML fonts provide designers with a new method of defining and embedding typefaces within HTML documents. HTML fonts introduce a new HTML class that can be used to define a font in a style sheet, which can then be used for referencing within any documents to which style sheets apply. HTML fonts also make it possible to embed font information in the document, provide a source location for font information not on the system, and offer ways to approximate the intended font through synthesis or substitution if the font information is not available to the document. Overall, Web page designers are given a much fuller palette for the creation of rich-text HTML documents. Figure 3.3 shows a Web page created using HTML font.

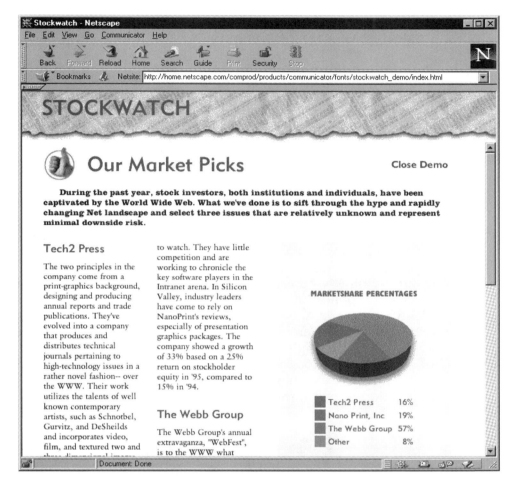

Figure 3.3 HTML fonts in Netscape Navigator.

Object Tag

The OBJECT element enables the insertion of an object such as an OLE or ActiveX object into an HTML document. The object element is the same as the body element in HTML with the addition of PARAM elements, which may be used to initialize the object.

Java Performance Enhancements

The Communicator has greatly improved the Java platform. Specifically, the loading of Java class libraries has been extensively tuned to enable faster execution of Java applets. In addition, the new Java Virtual Machine inside the Netscape Communicator has stabilized the Java platform.

Signed Applets and Plug-ins

Until the introduction of authentication and signing, applications in Web technologies were severely limited in terms of access to the resources of the client machine. A design decision was made to address the ubiquitous nature of the Internet and the concomitant concerns associated with application security, viruses, and malicious applications.

Signed applications in the form of plug-ins or Java applets refer to those that users can choose to trust or grant access to the local resources of their client machine (see Figure 3.4). The concept is that a user can agree to trust applications obtained via the Web, based on identifying the developer of the application; for example, users could choose to trust any application signed by Netscape. In this way, the application may use local client machine resources to run state-rich and more complex operations.

Signed applications use certificate-based authentication processes to identify their origin. In practice, the user interaction with signed applications is minimal. Vendors identify themselves by digitally signing their applications; the applications then request permission to perform operations that require local system resources or potentially dangerous actions at runtime. The user has the option of granting permission to access the application or not. If the user grants permission to the vendor, the capa-

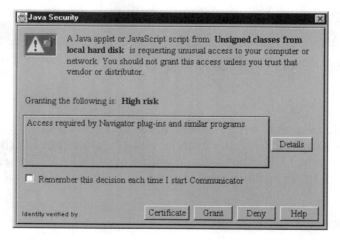

Figure 3.4 Signed applet user dialog.

bility will be granted, but will be withdrawn when the user surfs to a new Web page. If the user cancels the request for capabilities, the application will fail, but it can make the request again. If the user then denies access to the vendor, the application will be barred from requesting that capability again. For longer-term capability (either allowed or denied), the user may select *Until I quit the Navigator* or *Forever.*

In short, application signing expands the client/server distributed processing architecture by enabling the user to allow or prohibit access to client machine resources. This is especially important for intranet deployments, as many companies need to leverage client-side resources to build more complex applications while also leveraging the platform independence and distribution paradigms of Web technology.

Security API

The Netscape Communicator supplies an application programming interface (API) for the security features available in the client, based on the Crypto API specification issued by Intel Corporation. This API is intended for use by vendors writing plug-ins or for companies writing customizations to the Communicator code itself. It exposes the functions and features specific to the security features available in the Communicator including client-side certificates, SSL connections, encryption, signed applications, and others. The API can be used to programmatically configure or check security options in the Communicator client.

VRML 2.0 Rendering Engine

The Navigator now includes a VRML (Virtual Reality Markup Language) rendering engine that enables it to display three-dimensional graphical images and animation, giving content creators new ways of representing information and displaying it to the user (see Figure 3.5).

Auto Plug-in Loading

The Navigator comes equipped with technology that automates the process of obtaining and loading plug-in components. In the past, users were only notified that a plug-in was required for the display of an object in the Navigator, and told where they could find, load, and configure the plug-in component. The Navigator now has the capability to automatically locate and load the plug-in from the Internet, based on

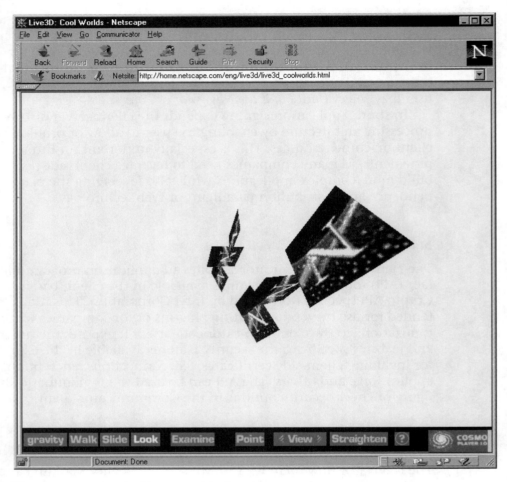

Figure 3.5 VRML in Netscape Navigator.

the plug-in's tagging information. This eases use and speeds the delivery of information.

Netscape Messenger

The Netscape Messenger is the open e-mail client portion of the Netscape Communicator. It is built on open Internet standards, and allows for rich HTML mail, encryption, directory access, and support for mobile users. The Messenger portion of the Netscape Communicator provides the following features.

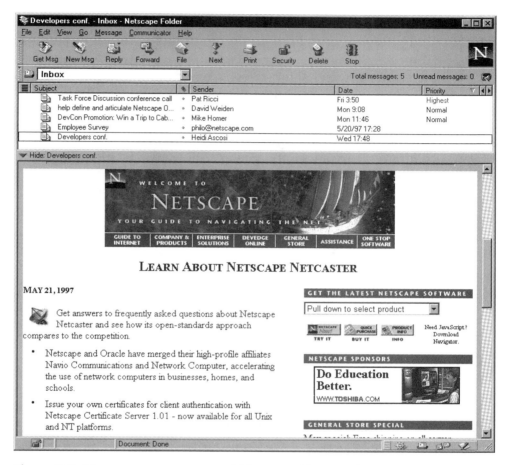

Figure 3.6 Messenger component of Netscape Communicator.

Rich HTML E-mail

The Netscape Messenger is tightly integrated with the Netscape Composer to enable the creation of rich HTML-based e-mail. This means that e-mail messages can contain the same rich font as HTML documents. Users can include graphics, links, even JavaScript applications or applets in their e-mail messages, thus introducing a new *push paradigm* workflow application environment—the inbox is now also a browser window (see Figure 3.6). Fully integrated with the rest of the Communicator components, e-mail messages can direct users to Web pages; discussion groups, directories, or applications. Previously, e-mail was used primarily as notification; now it is being used as the application itself.

Secure Multipurpose Internet Mail Extensions

Secure Multipurpose Internet Mail Extensions, or S/MIME, is a point-to-point e-mail encryption standard that makes use of client-side certificates to ensure secure e-mail between two parties. It is an open standard that defines how electronic mail messages are encrypted and decrypted. Using an open standard means that users from completely different open electronic mail systems can exchange secure messages. S/MIME also defines how electronic signatures are attached to mail messages, verifying the identity of the sender and guaranteeing that the message has not been tampered with in delivery.

Simple Mail Transfer Protocol

Simple Mail Transfer Protocol, or SMTP, is used for sending messages between servers, as well as from a user's mail client to the messaging server. Using a proven open standard (SMTP is defined in RFC 821/822, circa 1978) enables a corporation to exchange electronic mail without mail gateways. This reduces support costs and improves reliability when transmitting attachments to and from the Internet or other corporations.

Post Office Protocol

Post Office Protocol, or POP3, is a simple protocol enabling clients to download mail messages from a mail server. POP3 is considered a stateless mail protocol because it does not maintain connections with the messaging server and is therefore less aware of server operations such as delivery of sent messages.

Internet Message Access Protocol

Internet Message Access Protocol, or IMAP4, is another access method by which clients can read mail. IMAP4 maintains messages on the server, along with client mail state information so that users can access and read their electronic mail from anywhere. IMAP4 is more stateful than POP3 which means it can provide delivery status information in the form of return receipts.

Lightweight Directory Access Protocol

Netscape Messenger has a built-in LDAP client that enables it to seamlessly query LDAP Directory Servers such as the Netscape Directory Server for e-mail addresses, phone numbers, public keys, and any other information available from an LDAP server (see Figure 3.7).

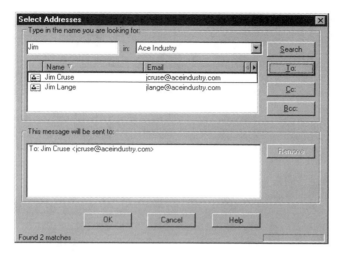

Figure 3.7 LDAP Address Book interface in Netscape Messenger.

Virtual Cards

Virtual Cards, or v-cards, are electronic business cards that can be attached to outgoing e-mail. Similar to a signature file that contains a sender's name, e-mail address, phone number, and so on, the v-card gives the user the option to add that contact to his or her personal address book (see Figure 3.8).

E-mail Filtering and Searching

Netscape Messenger gives the user the ability to screen incoming e-mail by constructing custom filters based on fields in incoming messages. For example, messages that contain the user's supervisor's name in the From field can be elevated in priority or moved to a different folder from other e-mail. Similarly, users can search across or within folders for messages based on field content within the message. Figure 3.9 shows filtering for To or CC fields.

Netscape Collabra

Netscape Collabra is the open groupware component of the Communicator client. Replacing the Netscape News client, the Collabra client, together with the Netscape Collabra Server, extends the open Network News Transmission Protocol (NNTP) to provide a feature-rich discussion

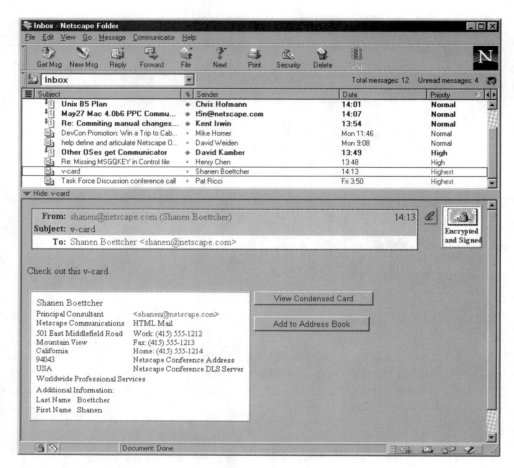

Figure 3.8 V-card attached to e-mail.

Figure 3.9 Mail filters dialog in Netscape Messenger.

and collaboration environment. The Collabra also supports the open NNTP standard of new architecture, which makes it possible for companies to give users the ability to read and participate in Internet newsgroups and discussions (Usenet). External and internal newsgroups function the same to the end user through the Collabra client.

In addition to the NNTP standard functions, Netscape Collabra provides many user-friendly features to make collaboration more efficient. For example, users can name forums with intuitive names. Rather than sports.usc.soccer.usc.edu, a user could name the newsgroup soccer. Users can also search across forums, view categories in a hierarchy of folders, and read and post offline, capabilities that make newsgroups more productive for everyone. In short, the Collabra client, together with the Messenger client, provides a one-stop-shop for ad hoc information. These tools give the user a tailored home knowledge base and portal to the organization.

Security

Along with the user capability to create and manage personal discussions, the Collabra client allows them to specify access control for these discussions (see Figure 3.10). Like the other parts of Communicator, the Collabra client supports SSL communications with servers to enable encrypted communication for secure news reading and posting. This is especially important as companies begin to use the Internet to exchange information between their intranets for collaborative projects and business-to-business communication over extranets.

Netscape Composer

Formerly associated with the functionality of Navigator Gold, the Netscape Composer is a full-feature HTML editor that lets users create and modify HTML documents and e-mail messages in a WYSIWYG environment. It is in the Netscape Composer that users formulate and publish documents to the intranet. As HTML becomes more presentation-rich through the Navigator, its tools also must advance to support rich formatting; these advances include easy manipulation of fonts, alignment, lists, and tables. The Netscape Composer has these and other features that make creating HTML documents similar to using proprietary word processing packages. For example, the Composer now has a built-in spell checker and page templates, and supports drag-and-drop of images, links, and objects such as Java applets (see Figure 3.11).

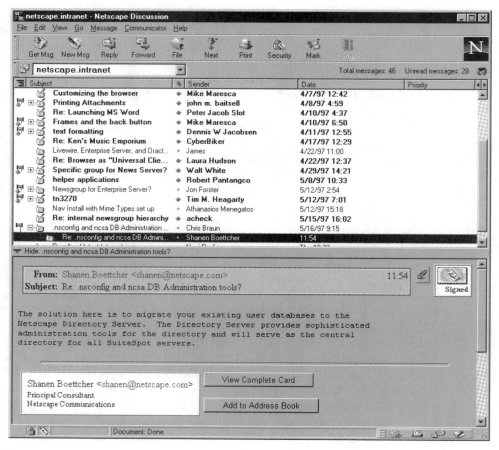

Figure 3.10 Collabra component of Netscape Communicator.

In addition, the Composer provides the user with simple, one-step/button publishing of documents to the Enterprise Server. The Composer also includes an extensive API toolkit for building custom editing functions in JavaScript, Java, and others. For example, one designer built an image map editor that enables authors to easily link various areas within an image, a capability formerly confined to the Web master. The Composer is a viable document creation tool for information sharing and management, an important point to recognize, since most companies want to distribute the publishing function to the desktop and eliminate the administration involved in converting documents to HTML.

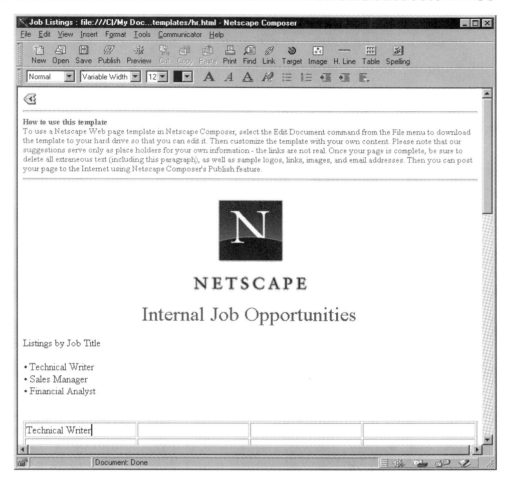

Figure 3.11 Composer component of Netscape Communicator.

Netscape Conference

Communicator's Netscape Conference component is a real-time collaboration tool for text and audio chat, whiteboarding, file transfer, and collaborative browsing. Formerly known as CoolTalk, Netscape Conference makes it possible for companies to use their existing network connectivity for real-time conferencing over the Internet and intranets. Since its redesignation as Conference, many features have been added to improve usability. For example, addressing or connecting to other users has been improved through integration with the Messenger address book, which

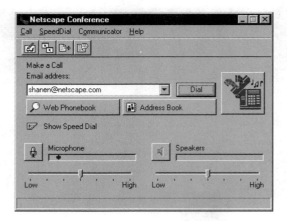

Figure 3.12 Conference component of Netscape Communicator.

allows for connections based on e-mail addresses or machine IP addressing (see Figure 3.12). Conference includes multiple compression algorithms to accommodate varying levels of bandwidth connectivity to support LAN or dial-up users with standard H.323 audio/video conferencing. Unlike most of the other components of the Netscape Communicator, there is no server portion to Netscape Conference; it is strictly a client-to-client communication and collaboration tool.

Netscape Calendar

The Netscape Calendar component of the Communicator Professional Edition is a personal and collaborative scheduling and calendaring feature (see Figure 3.13). Users can view multiple calendars simultaneously to schedule meetings, reserve facilities, work offline, synchronize schedules, and manage task lists. The component supports full-access control to schedules and entries, the vCalendar standard, and SMTP e-mail notification of meetings scheduled. Netscape is specifically directed at corporate intranet users who need reliable, scalable scheduling within the organization.

Netscape AutoAdmin

System administrators can use the Netscape AutoAdmin tool for remote configuration and management of all Netscape Communicator applica-

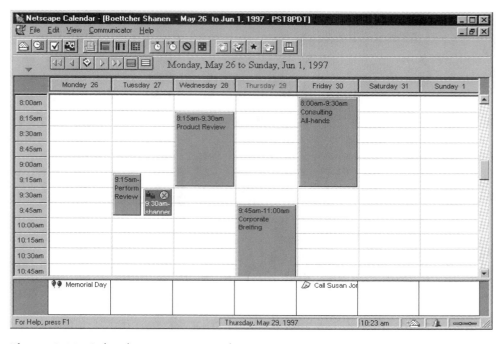

Figure 3.13 Calendar component of Netscape Communicator Pro.

tions. Used in conjunction with the Netscape Administration Kit, the ConfigURL feature permits the centralized configuration of group or individual Communicator preference options, such as e-mail, network, and security feature settings (see Figure 3.14). AutoAdmin also enables centralized management of the download, installation, and upgrade of software components, including plug-ins. Using the UpgradeURL feature, Communicator desktops can be securely "locked," so that only components authorized and signed by the administrator may be downloaded and installed.

Netscape IBM Host On-Demand

The Netscape IBM Host On-Demand component of the Netscape Communicator is a full-featured 3270 emulator to engage connectivity to existing host-based systems within the organization. IBM Host On-Demand is written entirely in Java, and supports multiple, simultaneous session runs, resizable session windows with dynamically sizable fonts, and

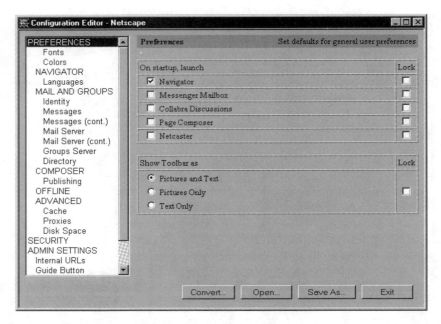

Figure 3.14 AutoAdmin component of Netscape Communicator Pro.

mapped 3270 function keys (see Figure 3.15). Many companies have extant mission-critical systems or applications involving MVS, VM, PROFS, and DB2, and IBM Host On-Demand gives them a way to achieve a thin, "browser-centric" desktop environment by providing access to these systems from the Netscape Communicator.

Netscape Netcaster

Netscape Netcaster is a cross-platform Internet/intranet desktop. Often referred to as the "Net Top," Netscape Netcaster is a fully customizable user workspace that runs one level above the windowing system, analogous to Microsoft Windows, which runs on top of DOS (see Figure 3.16). Netcaster is fully platform-independent, as it is written completely in Java and JavaScript. With Netcaster, users can create a personal workspace or homeport, tailored specifically to their information needs. Netcaster employs the concept of information *push*, or *netcast*, technology, whereby information "finds" the user, in contrast to traditional *pull* navigation methods.

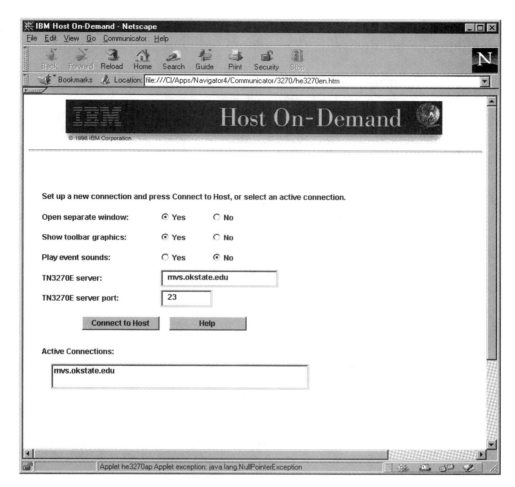

Figure 3.15 IBM Host On-Demand component of Netscape Communicator Pro.

Netcaster also features built-in sophisticated replication, which means the customized homeport information can follow a user across locations and platforms with identical look, feel, and functionality. Netcaster is implemented by companies to provide a dynamic, proactive information environment for their users, by broadcasting job-specific information to the desktop. Netcaster is an important step toward achieving true location and platform independence by further separating the user from the details of the operating system via a standard interface across multiple operating systems.

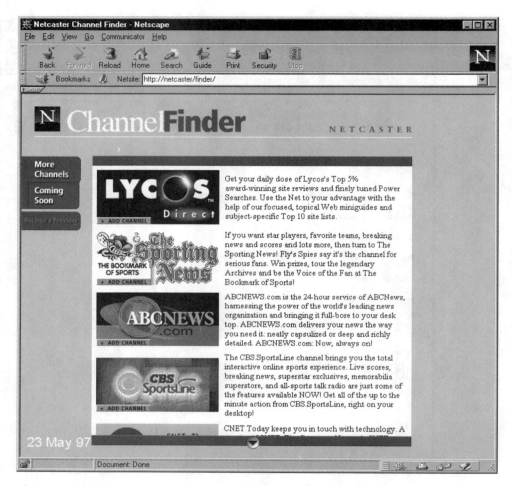

Figure 3.16 Netcaster component of Netscape Communicator.

Server Products

Netscape SuiteSpot

The server side of the Netscape Product line called SuiteSpot is often misunderstood. Currently it includes nine separate products that make up the user and network services comprising the full-service intranet. These servers are distributed in a modular fashion so that companies can deploy only those required for their respective intranet. This flexibility, however, raises a question that must be answered in the deployment process, specifically, which servers are required to provide which of the services. And, the days of the simple choice between the Communications Server and the Commerce Server are long past. One of the goals of this book is to give some insight into the tailoring of an intranet system using these products, exemplified by examples of their implementation. Many of the SuiteSpot servers map directly to the Netscape Communicator in their modularity; others provide network services that are transparent to the user.

Enterprise Server

The Enterprise Server, the flagship of SuiteSpot, is a central content management and application management server. It is an open Web server that can leverage existing resources to connect employees to network-based applications with powerful information management services, and is the backbone of any intranet providing these essential services. The Netscape Enterprise Server 3.0 features advanced document management and publishing capabilities that support HTML and other document formats including Microsoft Office. Users can assign and track document attributes, check in and out version documents for collaborative authoring, and remotely access and manage documents.

The Enterprise Server also has user agents, processes that run on the server to alert users of events on the intranet or to perform functions on their behalf. For example, users can configure an agent to notify them when specific documents change or when new documents of a specific type are added to the server. For administrators, the Enterprise Server supports LDAP, which means it can use a central user directory for access control. And new performance-monitoring and load-balancing tools ease management tasks. For developers, the Enterprise Server includes the LiveWire development environment for access to databases, ODBC, Oracle, Sybase, and Informix. The Enterprise Server also includes Internet Foundation Services and Classes for building applications for the Netscape ONE development platform.

Media Server

The Netscape Media Server enables streaming audio across the intranet so that companies can include recording of speeches or meetings in Web pages as an alternative method of distributing information within the organization. Audio can be synchronized with the content of HTML documents, plug-ins, Java applets, and JavaScript to create multimedia information sharing. Designed for use over the Internet, the Media Server automatically delivers the highest quality audio over various connection speeds based on available bandwidth. Future versions of the Media Server are likely to be included as a component of the Enterprise Server.

Proxy Server

Originally developed as a server to work with firewalls and manage secure access to the Internet from within a company, the Proxy Server has matured into a key replication tool for distributing information and maximizing the value of network bandwidth. Netscape Proxy Server lowers network costs by locally caching or copying documents so that subsequent requests for the same document are fulfilled without traversing the network. This server also allows selective access to internal as well as external Internet data, and can scan passing files for viruses.

The Proxy Server caches or makes local copies of files on the Internet or intranet accessed by users. Caching the document locally precludes the need to access the original document server for subsequent requests for that document; thus, bandwidth is saved and performance improves. This is an example of *on-demand replication*, whereby a user request populates the Proxy Server. The Proxy Server can also be stocked periodically with documents per a replication schedule (*on-command replication*). Companies often use the Proxy Server with a combination of on-demand and on-command replication to distribute information efficiently around the world within the organization.

In addition to caching, the Proxy Server supplies many tools for managing intranet content, such as filtering to prevent access to inappropriate content, built-in virus protection, and encrypted transmission for secure information. The Enterprise and Proxy Servers form the basis of the information management and sharing services; specifically, the Proxy Server enables replication and content management.

Messaging Server

Netscape Messaging Server is the third generation of the open standards-based client/server messaging system. As stated earlier, using the Netscape Messenger, users are equipped with an inbox that is fully integrated with the intranet, and supports rich composition and formatting of messages.

The Netscape Messaging Server gives companies a new choice when implementing intranets. In the past, they had to choose between low-cost, moderately featured, open standards-based messaging systems, and high-cost, feature-rich, proprietary messaging networks. For most companies, the choice was clear: proprietary message systems were chosen because of the features required to make messaging a viable business application. Unfortunately, communicating with other, different, proprietary mail systems required gateways for translation and retranslation of messages between systems, which often rendered messages garbled and attachments dropped.

Netscape Messaging Server 3.0 offers a combination of a feature-rich messaging environment and standards-based protocols and file formats to ensure interoperability and communication with outside systems, without the use of gateways. Standards supported by the Netscape Messaging Server include: Lightweight Directory Access Protocol (LDAP) services, Simple Mail Transfer Protocol (SMTP), Internet Mail Access Protocol (IMAP4), Simple Network Management Protocol (SNMP) management, and x.509v3 client certificates.

The Messaging Server also includes many administration features such as message quotas for managing mail storage; and Simple Network Management Protocol (SNMP) support and conversion tools from Microsoft Mail and Exchange, Lotus cc:Mail, Notes, and others. For developers, the Messaging Server includes an API for building mail transport and workflow applications that can combine Java, JavaScript, and HTML and Enterprise Server functionality for rich mail-enabled workflow applications.

Migration Toolkit

The Netscape Migration Toolkit provided with the Netscape Messaging Server helps companies move from their existing proprietary mail systems to the Netscape Messaging Server. The toolkit converts and imports messages, attachments, folders, folder hierarchies, distribution lists, aliases, address books, and other messaging system information to the Netscape Messaging Server and the Netscape Directory Server. The Netscape Migration Toolkit currently converts Lotus cc:Mail (see Figure 3.17) and Notes, Microsoft Exchange and MS Mail, and Eudora to the Netscape Messaging Server.

Collabra Server

The Netscape Collabra Server combines the features of Collabra Share and the open standards base of the Netscape News Server, giving companies the scalability and feature set required for corporate use. Many com-

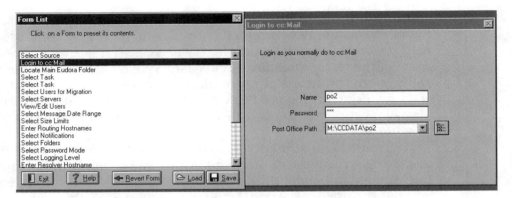

Figure 3.17 Messaging Server Migration Toolkit.

panies use the Collabra Server as a central knowledge base for project information and discussion groups; users can create and manage their own discussions, define custom views, and track discussions across multiple forums. The Netscape Collabra component of the Netscape Communicator is a seamless work environment that integrates with the other SuiteSpot servers.

Administrators can take advantage of the Collabra Server's native replication features of NNTP, security via client-side certificates, SSL, granular access control at the discussion level, and moderation of discussions for content control. Developers can make use of the Collabra Server's APIs to create site-specific customizations to meet the custom requirements within the company.

Directory Server

Netscape Directory Server is a native Lightweight Directory Access Protocol (LDAP) directory service that is the central user name and password repository for all Netscape SuiteSpot servers. LDAP is defined by the RFC-1777 specification and is a subset of the x.500 directory specification, which is an international standard global directory structure. While the Directory Server provides replication capabilities to distribute and synchronize directory information, LDAP is designed primarily as a client-to-server communication architecture as compared to the heavy server-to-server communication built into x.500 and its Directory Access Protocol (DAP). By limiting the overhead of heavy server-to-server communication, the Netscape Directory Server improves performance and scalability to support hundreds of thousands of users efficiently. Microsoft, Lotus, and many database vendors have announced future support of LDAP.

In the past, each server in Netscape SuiteSpot, like most applications, stored its own user directory for identifying users and managing access control. This meant that for every server or application in the company, a separate directory had to be maintained and synchronized with all other application directories within the company. This required a major system administration function for adding, deleting, or changing user entries in the multiple directories. This process was rather unruly, and consequently, the deletion of invalid user accounts often became a security hole in many of these systems. And users objected to the necessary multiple logins and passwords, which caused another security risk at the desktop level: insecure passwords. Users often chose easy-to-guess passwords, wrote them where others could see them, or changed them too infrequently.

In this generation of SuiteSpot, the Directory Server moves to center stage as the source of user information, including user certificates, e-mail addresses, and access control. It identifies a central point of directory information for users and resources within the intranet. This is an important piece of architecture for those companies trying to reach the goal of a single-user login and single point of user management. Many existing systems contain proprietary user databases in which users are required to have and manage multiple passwords to gain access to applications and information needed to perform their jobs. Administrators, too, will benefit from the reduction in the number of user directories to synchronize, secure, and manage.

Certificate Server

The Netscape Certificate Server has much of the underlying security infrastructure of a corporate intranet. Specifically, it is used for creating, signing, revoking, and managing digital certificates, electronic identification issued to users and invoked to authenticate the identity of those users on the intranet. Like a digital passport or badge, certificates protect against impersonation of users or so-called identity spoofing. Digital certificates enable applications such as Netscape Navigator, Netscape SuiteSpot, and custom-developed applications to communicate privately using Secure Sockets Layer (SSL) and Secure Multipurpose Internet Mail Extensions (S/MIME). Digital certificates are stored on physical devices such as hard disks, floppy disks, or smart cards. The combination of a physical file and knowledge of a password is what is meant by

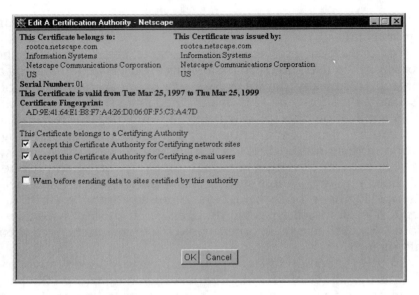

Figure 3.18 Client-side certificate.

the term *strong authentication*. Similar to an ATM card, digital certificates increase security by requiring "something you have and something you know."

Digital certificates are also issued to servers so that users can be confident of a server operator's identity (see Figure 3.18). For example, a user who connects to http://human_resources.acme.com can be sure that the server is actually operated by the human resources department at ACME Corporation. The server proves its identity by presenting a digital certificate and performing a cryptographic operation that demonstrates it is the legitimate owner of that certificate.

Likewise, certificates enable servers to confirm the end-user's identity. When John Doe connects to http://human_resources.acme.com, the human resources department can verify John Doe's identity by the certificate John's Navigator presents to the server (as well as the cryptographic operation John's Navigator performs to demonstrate that John is the legitimate owner of his certificate). The security provided using the certificate server is based on industry standards such as SSL, X.509v3, HTML, HTTP, PKCS, and LDAP.

The Netscape Certificate Server interfaces with the Directory Server to form a single point of authentication credentials to the entire intranet.

For users, this means that only a single userid/password combination is required for access to the intranet. Similarly, because of this integration and the built-in support of LDAP in all of the SuiteSpot servers, developers can make use of this central strong authentication for intranet applications. For administrators, the Directory and Certificate Servers combination forms a single point of authentication and access control for all users. In addition, administration tools are provided for managing the server remotely, to issue, age, and revoke user certificates.

Catalog Server

Once an organization makes the decision to use intranet technologies to disseminate information, the amount of information generated by departments and individuals often grows exponentially. Giving each department (and potentially each individual) the capability to publish information opens up a wealth of possibilities for information sharing and collaboration. Quantitative growth, of course, introduces a new problem to the corporate intranet: locating specific information on a timely basis. This problem is solved with the Netscape Catalog Server.

The Netscape Catalog Server (Figure 3.19) acts as a central information repository indexed for a corporate intranet. It acts as a robot or agent that "crawls" various internal and external Web sites collecting and indexing information it finds. Using Internet protocols (HTTP, FTP, and Gopher), the Catalog Server can index any URL-accessible item including HTML, Word, Excel, PowerPoint, and PDF file formats.

Calendar Server

The Netscape Calendar Server is a collaborative scheduling tool designed to support thousands of users within an enterprise for scheduling meetings and coordinating resources and tasks. Users can schedule in real time and, with permission, view and manage other users' calendars. The Calendar also fully supports SMTP mail for notifying users of meetings.

The Calendar Server includes LDAP support integration so that administrators and developers can share the central user account information stored in the Netscape Directory Server. Companies implement the Netscape Calendar Server to help keep users better informed and coordinated. They are able to manage their calendars and schedules in an environment that is fully integrated into the intranet environment.

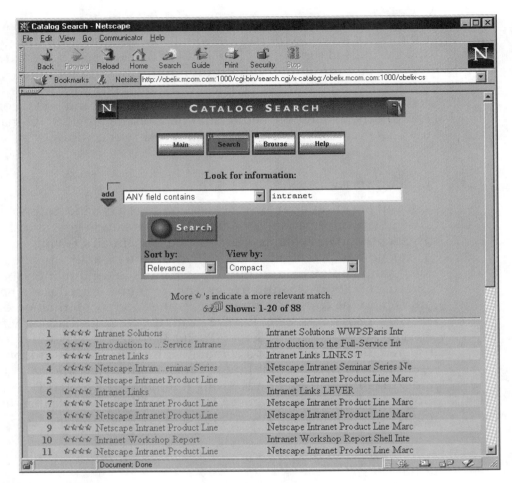

Figure 3.19 Catalog Server user interface.

Application Development Products

Application development is central to strategic intranet deployment. Intranet applications provide centrally managed highly distributed access to, databases, and other enterprise systems.

Netscape ONE

The Netscape Open Network Environment (ONE) is a development platform based on open standards (see Figure 3.20). Netscape ONE is devel-

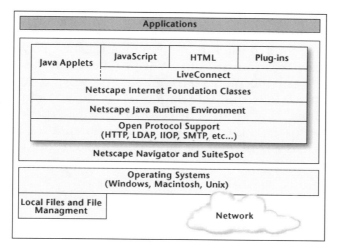

Figure 3.20 Netscape ONE environment.

oper-friendly, supplying the tools necessary for creating robust, platform-independent intranet applications, whose benefits include reduced development time, elimination of software distribution overhead, and increase reusability of applications.

A Netscape ONE application may consist of the following components and protocols:

HyperText Markup Language (HTML)

JavaScript

Java applets

Client plug-ins

LiveConnect

Internet Foundation Classes (IFC)

Internet Foundation Services

HyperText Transmission Protocol (HTTP)

Internet Inter-ORB Protocol (IIOP)

HTML

HyperText Markup Language (HTML) has become the universal portable file format and content container. It makes up the presentation layer of intranet applications and is the container from which objects such as Java applets are executed. In addition, HTML has become more sophisticated through the efforts of the Internet Engineering Task Force (IETF) and the World Wide Web Consortium (W3C) to include richer formatting features. These enhancements have made it possible to develop forms applications solely within HTML. Alone, HTML, the simplest client presentation medium, is often used by companies where the lowest common denominator for users is either very low or undetermined. HTML is, of course, also used as a container for more complicated application code such as JavaScript and Java.

Java

Java is an object-oriented programming language developed by Sun Microsystems, optimized for platform-independence and security in the Internet environment. Java applets can run on any machine that has a Java runtime environment that accepts them and can interpret their code to run on the client machine (called the Java Virtual Machine). Because Java applets can run on any platform and are dynamically downloaded by the client, they drastically reduce application development and distribution time. For this reason, many companies are eager to use Java for their intranets.

To improve performance of Java applets, Netscape has embedded Java compilers in the Netscape Communicator. These *just-in-time* (JIT) compilers accept applets and quickly compile them into native machine code to optimize performance of applications written in Java. To date, Java has been somewhat of a niche player in corporate application development due to the fact that support for Java in 16-bit environments has been limited. Netscape addressed this limitation by including a full 16-bit Java runtime and JIT compiler in the Communicator for Windows 3.1. In the future, Java will play a major role both on the client and server sides of intranet applications; so far, Java has been used more frequently for server-side processing within corporate intranets.

As already noted, in addition to support of 16-bit environments, Netscape has enabled use of digitally signed applets to maintain security and increase functionality to Java programmers (see Figure 3.21). Central to Java is its security architecture, which protects the hosting machine from harm by applets. Although this makes for a great security model for the Internet, it has limited companies somewhat from implementing mission-critical applications using Java. Still, digitally signing objects (including HTML, JavaScript, and Java applets) using certificates means

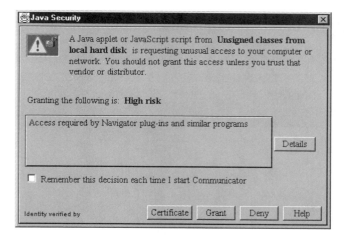

Figure 3.21 Signed Java applet.

users can be absolutely sure of the source of Java applets and can comfortably grant access to local machine resources to enable more complex processing and more robust applications. Users can control the granularity of the access grants and be asked to confirm operations performed by the applet.

JavaScript

JavaScript is a programming language developed by Netscape Communications Corporation that is based on Java, but is much simpler to use. JavaScript is contained directly within an HTML page to provide client and server application processing. The most simple and common use for JavaScript is to create "smart" HTML forms with built-in field validation and client-side computations (see Figure 3.22). Many companies have implemented JavaScript in this way to improve the efficiency and accuracy of forms-driven applications. By validating the HTML page on the client prior to submitting it as a transaction to the server, unnecessary network traffic and server processing is greatly reduced. Client-side JavaScript is inserted between <SCRIPT> tags within the HTML page and executed on the client within the browser.

Like Java, JavaScript can be used to develop both user interfaces and processing on the client as well as transactional processing on the server. Server-side JavaScript is inserted into HTML via the <SERVER> tags which is interpreted and executed on the Enterprise Server. Used in conjunction

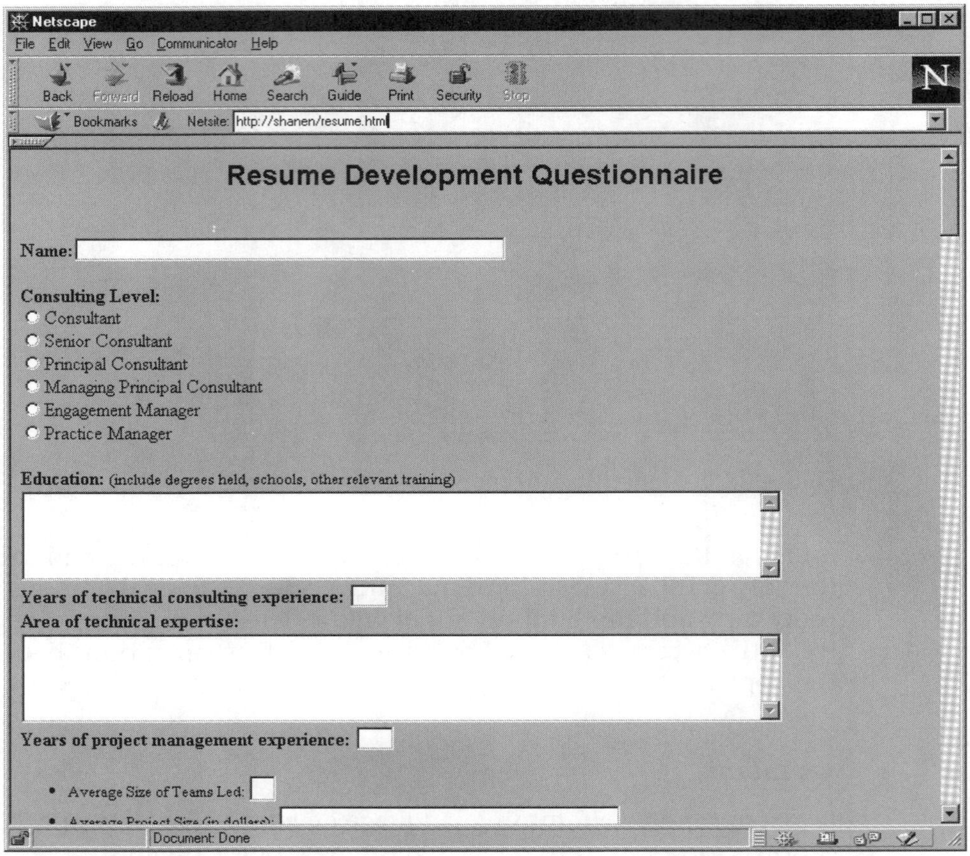

Figure 3.22 JavaScript form.

with the LiveWire segment of the Enterprise Server, server-side JavaScript can interface directly with relational databases, thus enabling embedding of SQL statements directly in HTML pages. In addition, JavaScript is designed to access dynamic objects on the server over the stateless HTTP protocol, enabling applications developers to create robust, transaction-based business processes.

The key gain for companies using JavaScript to develop applications is that it combines the simplicity of an HTML scripting language with state management and client-side processing. This has the effect of drastically shortening development, testing, and deployment time for applications, and reducing long-term maintenance.

Netscape ONE Plug-ins

Plug-ins are programs written and compiled into native code that run either within the client or server. Plug-ins are commonly written in C or C++ and compiled for a specific platform. Both the Communicator client and the SuiteSpot servers provide application programmer interfaces, APIs, so that developers can modify or extend the base functionality of the products. Plug-ins run within the same executable space as the client or server and are used most often to gain access to platform-specific functions. Companies usually use plug-ins to integrate existing C/C++ code into the intranet or to modify the base behavior of the products.

Client Plug-ins   Used extensively by third-party vendors, the client plug-in API gives developers the ability to integrate custom application code into the Netscape Communicator. Many plug-ins make use of platform-specific APIs, such as Win32. Companies use this capability to implement existing applications into the communicator to leverage extant code and to provide a Communicator-centric desktop. Plug-ins are, however, used most often to augment the functionality of the Communicator by adding, for example, an audio player for accepting streaming audio in the Navigator, or as a tool for image map editing in the Composer.

Server Plug-ins   Like the client plug-in API in the Communicator, the SuiteSpot servers also include a plug-in API. Known widely as the Netscape API, or NSAPI, the server plug-in API enables developers to include C/C++ code to extend the functionality of the server. Server plug-ins load as part of the same process as the server executable, and modify the processing of requests made to the server. Two common uses of server plug-ins are: to modify the logging of the server to add either more detailed or company-specific information, and to gain access to platform-specific APIs such as file system security features.

LiveConnect

LiveConnect is a technology that links Java, JavaScript, and plug-ins. By extending the Java object model, LiveConnect enables Java, JavaScript, and plug-ins to share a common object and messaging model, meaning, for example, that Java objects can be addressed from JavaScript. Many companies are using this powerful technology to modularize intranet applications by developing a central library of Java objects specific to their business processes. These objects can then be leveraged by business applications written in JavaScript.

Many companies organize a central Java development group responsible for developing the advanced business process objects and creating a toolchest of objects, which are then distributed to field developers to use in building business applications. In this way, the Java skills of the IT organization are best leveraged across the development organization. The benefit is flexibility in the implementation of the objects, while maintaining common underlying application architectures—an important consideration for enabling communications between these applications.

Until recently, LiveConnect was available only on the client side for linking Java and JavaScript on application pages. Eventually, however, LiveConnect will play a more important role in server-side applications by uniting server-side JavaScript, Java, and plug-ins. Companies should plan to build a central library of Java objects that can then be accessed by server-side JavaScript, as this will prove to be a powerful technology for transaction processing and exchanging information between systems through the use of the Internet Inter-ORB Protocol (IIOP).

Java Runtime Interface

To achieve LiveConnect's purpose to bring plug-ins, Java applets, and JavaScript together, a standard programming interface has been developed called the Java Runtime Interface, or JRI. The JRI provides a way to map these objects to the LiveConnect object model supported under Netscape ONE. The JRI uses a standard set of Java object classes to generate standard ANSI C code to connect a wide variety of objects to Netscape ONE.

Internet Inter-ORB Protocol

Internet Inter-ORB Protocol, or IIOP, is aimed at developing the next level of distributed programming: network object applications. IIOP is part of a larger standard object architecture called the Common Object Request Broker Architecture, CORBA. The goal of CORBA is to establish a standard communications interface between object servers, both on clients and servers. This interface would allow servers to communicate with each other across the Internet or corporate networks. LiveConnect is addressing connectivity of objects on the same Web page, while CORBA and IIOP are addressing object connectivity across networks.

IIOP and the larger CORBA standard are supported by the Object Management Group (OMG) standards body made up of 600 member companies. In addition, many vendors are building CORBA interfaces to existing applications to enable IIOP connectivity by writing wrappers around existing applications to map CORBA standard methods to the modules that make up the existing application. The Netscape Enterprise Server and Communicator client include a fully CORBA-compliant object request broker and support of IIOP to natively network enable Netscape ONE applications.

Eventually, IIOP will play a crucial role in developing network applications, but to date, it has been used most often by companies integrating existing systems with the intranet environment. For example, in order to supply an intranet front end to an extant order entry system, a company could wrap the current system with a server-side Java or JavaScript program that maps ordering routines to CORBA standard methods, which would be called from the Netscape ONE environment. IIOP will become a critical link of corporate intranets, enabling companies to work together over the Internet. In short, CORBA and IIOP will be central in bridging multiple systems within companies.

Netscape Internet Foundation Classes

Netscape ONE includes a suite of platform-independent objects developed to provide the building blocks of Netscape ONE applications called Internet Foundation Classes (IFCs). All of these objects are based on the standards previously discussed and are aimed at addressing business requirements in developing network applications. Netscape IFCs include objects designed to jump-start application development by providing the basis for user interface, applications services, security services, messaging services, and distributed object programming. For example, many companies have used the first release of Netscape IFCs to provide standard user interface components across platforms for a consistent look and feel.

Future releases of the IFCs will include objects to provide standard access to the user and network services of the full-service intranet. Companies will likely use Netscape IFCs as the starting point for application development for intranets and extranets. Netscape has developed a visual IFC Constructor (see Figure 3.23) that developers can use to build application interfaces based on IFC classes. Working with Sun, Netscape has incorporated the IFC functionality into the standard Java Foundation Classes (IFC) library.

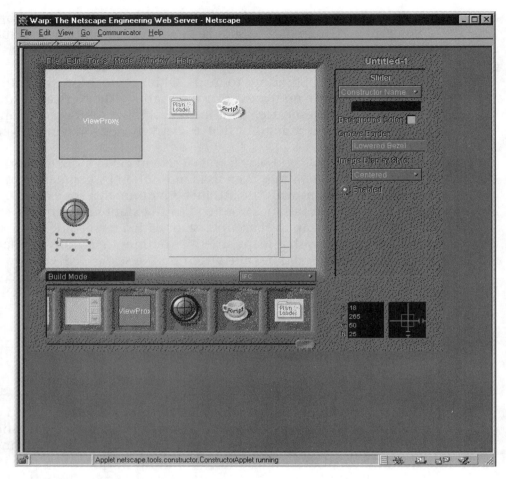

Figure 3.23 Netscape Constructor.

Visual JavaScript

Visual JavaScript is a component-based visual development environment based on the Netscape ONE platform designed for corporate developers to rapidly write cross-platform, standards-based applications. Visual JavaScript includes a page builder that enables developers to dynamically construct and view application pages through use of an extensible component palette that allows drag and drop of page components (form elements, JavaBeans, and widgets) to the Web page (see Figure 3.24). The palette comes with a standard set of components

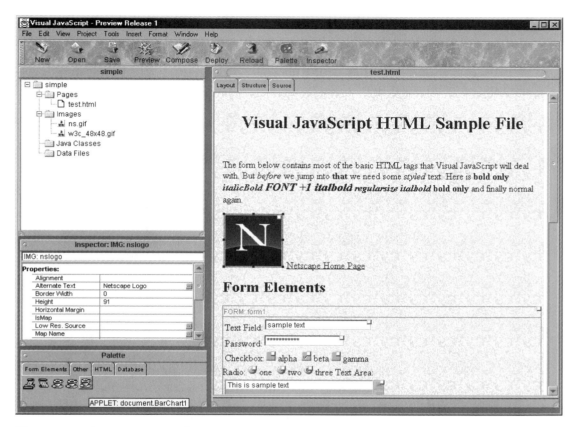

Figure 3.24 Netscape Visual JavaScript.

for building application pages, and allows the developer to import components to extend the palette. These components can be developed using Visual JavaScript to meet specific functional business needs. This is an enabling technology for companies that want to provide a standard toolkit to a distributed development community. Programming resources can be highly leveraged to develop custom JavaBeans and other Netscape ONE components that can be distributed and reused throughout the company.

Visual JavaScript is a full development environment for mission-critical applications that grants source code control and supplies deployment tools using the Enterprise Server content management system- and source-level debugging tools. These tools represent an important step toward a full-featured development environment for corporate developers.

Using Visual JavaScript developers can take advantage of the full service intranet; they are granted access to the LiveWire environment, the Messaging Server, and the Directory Server. Visual JavaScript, then, brings together the components of the Netscape ONE platform in a visual development environment.

SuiteTools

Netscape SuiteTools were designed specifically for intranet application development. Taking a best-of-breed approach, Netscape has selected products from and teamed with Symantec, NetObjects, and NetDynamics to fill a toolchest for companies developing intranet applications in the Netscape ONE environment. Certainly, many tools can be used to develop and manage intranet applications, but Netscape SuiteTools specifically addresses support of open standards, ease of use, and applicability to business needs.

Netscape LiveWire and LiveWire Pro

Netscape LiveWire is a site management tool and application development environment distributed with the Netscape Enterprise Server. LiveWire includes a graphical interface to the contents of the Netscape Enterprise Server and tools that administrators can implement to rearrange documents and maintain link integrity. LiveWire Pro contains the LiveWire technology and includes a copy of the Informix Online Workgroup database. LiveWire grants access to relational databases by bundling native client libraries from Oracle, Sybase, and Informix for optimum performance with these databases. LiveWire also supports ODBC connectivity to the Microsoft SQL Server and all other ODBC-compliant databases. The databases are accessed using SQL statements within server-side JavaScript.

In addition to providing connectivity via database libraries, LiveWire gives the developer predefined LiveWire objects for managing the user state. For example, the client object can be used to maintain the position of a database cursor within the current transaction as the user reads through the results of a query. Traditionally, because HTTP is a stateless protocol, managing this state information required substantial coding effort. For these reasons, many companies use LiveWire to grant intranet access to legacy systems and to create new applications that require structured data storage and retrieval. The benefits of Netscape LiveWire include the state management features of the predefined LiveWire objects and access to databases using nothing but server-side JavaScript.

Symantec Visual Café

Symantec Visual Café Pro is a Java visual development tool. Similar in presentation to visual development tools from Microsoft and Delphi, Symantec Café Pro generates pure Java for completely platform-independent intranet applications. Symantec includes all of the widgets needed to create full-feature graphical user-interface applications. In addition, Café Pro includes more than 100 prebuilt JavaBeans or Java components that can be used for rapid application development. Symantec Café Pro also enables real-time code generation and two-way programming, which means the user can see the Java code being generated when using the graphical programming interface, or can modify the code and instantly see the effects on the graphical interface. Consequently, Café Pro is a powerful teaching tool for developers. Along with these coding features, Café Pro includes advanced debugging and layout management tools to speed the Java development process.

Like LiveWire, Symantec Café includes database access to Oracle, Sybase, and Informix through a form wizard. Symantec's dbANYWHERE Workgroup Server, included with Café Pro, provides database access from Java applets. The introduction of 16-bit Java support in the Netscape Communicator, coupled with widespread interest in using it in intranets, means that tools like Symantec's Visual Café Pro will play an important part in application development.

NetObjects Fusion

NetObjects Fusion is a visual Web site management tool designed to speed development and maintenance. It contains a site structure editor for drag-and-drop reorganization of a site, link maintenance, and site staging. Fusion also provides style management tools for maintaining the visual consistency of a site. These tools use style sheets for central control of sitewide navigation tools, borders/frames, and graphical look and feel. Other NetObjects Fusion tools can be used to create singular pages, control page layout, and insert objects (code, plug-ins, etc.) into pages.

Administrators and designers together can create and release a unique site style, or use one of the many styles included with Fusion that let companies jump-start the development of intranet Web sites. NetObjects

Fusion is often used in combination with the Netscape ONE tools described earlier to design and build intranet applications. The first step is to create and maintain the high-level structure and style of the site, then insert Java or JavaScript logic into the shell. Thereafter, Fusion can be used to globally change the look and feel of the site or to reorganize it. This is important to keep in mind when selecting tools: There is no be-all-end-all tool for the development of intranet sites and applications. A long list of tools make up Netscape ONE and SuiteTools because there are so many ways to create intranets. Be aware that the creation and maintenance of an intranet requires multiple tools and skill sets.

NetDynamics

NetDynamics is a visual, Java-based enterprise database application tool. Whereas Symantec Café creates purely client or client/server applications, NetDynamics is more focused on the server-side architecture, and implements a three-tier Web architecture by introducing an application server to the picture. This application server sits between the Web server and the client to handle complex transactional processing for database applications. NetDynamics generates HTML and JavaScript on the client side and pure Java on the server side to create these three-tiered applications.

NetDynamics includes support of Informix, Sybase, Oracle, and ODBC databases, and can include APIs for SAP and PeopleSoft for intranet integration. NetDynamics is meant to take advantage of the platform independence and performance of Java on the server side while not requiring Java-enabled clients. This strategy coexists comfortably with many heterogeneous corporate environments. By far the most complex of the SuiteTools, NetDynamics has been used by companies to address difficult integration issues in intranet environments. However, the three-tiered architecture on the intranet side adds a level of complexity to applications and should be used specifically for applications with heavy and complex transactional volumes, such as PeopleSoft and SAP applications, rather than for more simplistic search, query, and reporting database applications.

Conclusion

This chapter has presented the individual product offerings from Netscape. While modular by design, the products are fully integrated to deliver the full-service intranet solution.

Part II

PLANNING AND DEPLOYING THE INTRANET

CHAPTER

INTRANET BUSINESS REQUIREMENTS

Deployment Goals

Prior to deploying the intranet, it is important to identify the criteria for success of the system. Each company will, of course, have its own detailed set of requirements for the full-service intranet, but there are some common high-level goals that most companies seek in deploying Netscape technology. This section identifies those goals and itemizes the steps to take to achieve them. Note, however, that these goals are only the starting point for many companies. It is important to understand and include the detailed goals and requirements of the intranet specific to your organization in addition to recognizing these high-level goals.

Provide User and Network Services

The central goal of any system is providing its users with utility; or services, in the case of the full-service intranet. The primary decision in the deployment process is the determination of which services will be provided to users and what the nature or extent of those services will be. Once determined, the architecture of the system and the administrators that support it are responsible for establishing and maintaining the promised level of service to the user community.

63

Leverage Existing Infrastructure

By supporting multiple platforms and operating systems, Netscape technology is uniquely positioned to leverage companies forecasting investments in hardware.

Hardware

As part of garnering a large return on investment, many companies have chosen to implement intranets using existing hardware and networking infrastructure. As discussed earlier, the roots of intranet technology lie in Internet technology, and therefore the underlying protocols are engineered to support a minimalist computing infrastructure. This is one of the first technologies that actually live up to the promises of leveraging "old iron" within the company. This model minimizes the amount of hardware required by the system, thus also reducing the resources required to support it.

Support Resources

By leveraging the existing investment in hardware and operating systems, many companies have found that their support resources can also be leveraged to support the intranet. Because the intranet often does not require the introduction of new and different hardware platforms and operating systems, the administration of the new system requires only application-specific training/learning. This means that all existing procedures for backup and restore and disaster recovery can remain unchanged with the introduction of the intranet. In addition, the integrated and standardized system administration tools provided by the Netscape SuiteSpot level the short learning curve for system administrators.

Network

Given the existing network infrastructure of an organization, it is important to determine the appropriate number of servers and locations to deploy them. An inefficient use of bandwidth results in poor performance and higher overall system costs to transport information. Often, deploying replication services in strategic locations on a WAN is more efficient than running one central server that responds to all of the requests from the organization. There is a trade-off between hardware and bandwidth costs to reach an acceptable level of performance to users. Using redundancy in a system results in efficient use of bandwidth and provides alternative sources or fail-over tolerance to keep the system available to users.

Leveraging the existing network infrastructure requires that the introduction of the intranet not impact negatively on existing network applications. Taking advantage of the replication tools in SuiteSpot will make the most efficient use of the existing network topology within the organization.

Standardization

The bottom line in minimizing administrative costs of business systems is standardization. Standardization is nothing new in corporate computing. Unfortunately in the past, there were so many standards to choose from, and choosing one meant locking into a single vendor. Now, however, the new widely adopted open standards from the Internet technology translate to administrative cost-savings in many areas: no more multiple user directories to manage, e-mail gateways, conversion utilities; and only one version of application code to maintain. Standards minimize administration, and Netscape's commitment to approved, open standards ensures that this improvement will continue with the product line.

Planning Steps

This section outlines the planning steps to take to achieve the intranet goals just listed. Following these planning steps is essential to the successful deployment of the intranet, and thus should not be overlooked. The output of these steps will serve as the high-level requirements for the intranet and will ultimately determine the hardware and software required for implementation.

Identify the Intranet Users

The first and most important questions to answer in the deployment process are:

Who are the users of the intranet?

Where are they located?

What do the users need?

Answering them involves identifying different functional groups within the user community, where these different groups exist, and how many people make up each of these groups. These groups of users include system administrators and developers, as well as end users. This may seem like an academic exercise, but it is essential in succeeding with an accurate and efficient deployment of the intranet. The best way to approach this task is to use the user and network services outlined earlier and map them to the geographic and functional organization of the company. And don't forget that the needs of users may change over time.

Given the choice, every user would request all of the user services. Probably this is the case in the long term, but in the short term, those users may require only a subset of the services in the full-service intranet. In this case, a phased deployment can prove to be a useful solution. For example, some user groups may require only messaging, navigation, and viewing of information during the initial launch of the intranet. Over time, however, these same users may need to create and distribute their own information. At this time, the initial deployment of the intranet would require only the Communicator to be distributed to these users, and possibly a Proxy Server. Later, however, users might require an Enterprise Server to create and host content. Similarly, in the area of network services, this same group of users may not have system administration resources on-site, which would preclude certain of the network services being distributed to that site and require them to be hosted centrally.

Identify User Services

Again, the central goal of the intranet and all systems is to meet the needs of the user community. It follows then that it is important to determine the specific needs and priorities for the user services to be provided by the intranet. The full-service intranet model is a good starting point for mapping the needs of the user community to the functionality available in Netscape products. *Information sharing and management, communication and collaboration, navigation,* and *application access* are the broad categories used to begin this process. Each must be explored further to expose the detailed requirements of the organization. The next step is to determine the extent to which these user services are needed within the organization and plan for their future use.

Information Sharing and Management

In the area of information sharing and management, it is important to identify the publishing needs of the user community. For some companies, the intranet is viewed solely as the information delivery mechanism rather than part of the document creation/authoring process. In this scenario, users create documents using a variety of tools and convert or post the information to the Web after it is completed.

What is the current publishing environment? What types of documents are published—formats, and so on? What is the distribution of those documents? What is the volume of the documents? What specialized publishing needs exist within groups in the company? What is the relationship of paper and electronic documents within the company? All of these questions are important to answer when determining the role of the intranet in information sharing and management.

Communication and Collaboration

Communication and collaboration is frequently either a very simple or very difficult area of decision for an organization. Messaging is normally a clear-cut choice; it is either time to upgrade e-mail systems or it is not. Complicating this decision is that many Netscape users interested in deploying intranets are unaware of the rich messaging environment provided in SuiteSpot and that it is fully integrated into the universal Communicator client. This means that there is nothing more to buy to gain the advantages of open e-mail that is fully integrated into the intranet environment.

The Netscape messaging solution, which provides e-mail as rich as the Web, augments the very compelling aspects of platform-independent, fully integrated, open communication platform of the Netscape intranet. The use of standard protocols and storage formats eliminates the need for e-mail gateways and the administrative headaches caused by them. The result? There are no message translations required and all attachments are unharmed. Questions to ask regarding messaging include: How many e-mail users are there? Where are the users located? What existing mail systems are there and what are the conversion issues? Will users require Internet e-mail access?

The groupware aspects of the full-service intranet provided by the Collabra Server complement the information sharing and management aspects of the full-service intranet. The standard NNTP protocol and HTML content provide a seamless information-sharing and knowledge base for the organization. Questions to ask here are: What is the current groupware/collaborative environment? Are there conversion issues? Will external Usenet access be required? Are discussion groups indicative of the corporate culture—that is, will they be used?

Navigation

Navigation is a must-have to deal with the torrent of information that comes from an intranet. In fact, the question regarding navigation is not whether or not there is navigation, but what is the configuration of the navigation. The configuration is more part of the network services side of the intranet. It is important to understand how users will usually search for information on the intranet. Will they come to the intranet cold and want to search the entire contents for topics of interest? Or will they probably search only portions of the intranet germane to their job tasks? Based on the document types stored on the intranet, what will be common ways to access information: by date, by author, by title, by content? All of these questions help determine the configuration of the network services behind navigation.

Application Access

Application access is an area of great interest and import to the user community. Here, it is important to understand the existing information needs of the user; that is, which systems they currently use and what applications are needed. All companies have existing information systems in the form of mainframe CICS application, client/server database applications, and so on. The platform independence, consistent look and feel, and ease of application distribution using the universal client makes application development a very compelling prospect. For this reason, many companies consider moving the existing applications base to the intranet and building a future applications intranet platform. When evaluating application development, the question is not if, but when, and what first? The upcoming section on enterprise applications details trends in intranet application development. As part of the intranet planning phase, it is important to develop a list of applications and assign priorities to them based on the needs of the user community.

Prioritize User Services

Once the services required by the organization have been identified, the next step is to assign priorities to the services. Determine which of the services is needed first and to what extent? These priorities will become important in arranging the sequence of deployment steps. In addition to the order of need, it is important to identify the mission-critical nature of each service. What level of support is expected of the system? Is any downtime acceptable? What level of system performance is expected? What level of security is required for the information held by the system? All of these questions map directly to the system and personnel infrastructure required for building the intranet. The more secure, higher performance, and over-all more bulletproof the system has to be, the more hardware, software, and support personnel are required, all of which make the system more expensive. These are important decisions that must be weighed in deploying any system, including the full-service intranet.

When discussing the options with users, and asking the questions regarding the need for failover protection and redundancy, security, and support infrastructure, usually they'll answer all of the questions "yes." Later though, when it becomes apparent that these requirements increase the expense of the system, somehow they become more malleable. The point here is to first consider the needs and requirements of the system *independent* of the capabilities of the technology in order to arrive at a less biased, more realistic list of priorities based on the business needs of the company. This is why it is important to have functional user and manager representation on the intranet task force; these people understand the business reasons behind the requirements and can make judgments after weighing options like performance versus security and failover versus costs.

Map SuiteSpot Servers to User and Network Services

After the user services and priorities have been identified and assigned, the next step is to map them to the infrastructure or network services needed to supply the functional aspects of the intranet. As the underlying platform upon which the user services run, the network services are precursors to the user services. The network services of the full-service intranet, include directory services, replication, security, and management.

The SuiteSpot servers map to the user and network services as follows:

❑ Information sharing and management requires the Enterprise Server to enable the creation, publishing, and distribution of information.

❑ Communication and collaboration requires the Netscape Messaging Server and the Netscape Collabra servers respectively to enable electronic messaging and collaborative discussions. Communication and Collaboration can also include the Netscape Calendar Server to provide group scheduling.

❑ Navigation requires the Netscape Catalog Server to index and bridge multiple information servers.

❑ Application access requires the application development tools provided by Netscape ONE and SuiteTools.

These tools enable the integration and development of applications that communicate with existing systems. These applications often make use of a combination of the SuiteSpot servers, including the Enterprise Server for distributing and presenting information and the Directory Server for accessing user and resource information as well as user access information.

Directory services require the Netscape Directory Server to provide centralized user and resource management via the LDAP protocol. Replication requires the Netscape Proxy Server which automatically distributes information on an as-needed basis to users and creates a local cached copy of the information to increase performance and ease network load. Security requires the cooperation of all of the SuiteSpot servers. The Netscape Certificate Server is used to issue client and server identification certificates, providing strong authentication for access to the system. The Netscape directory holds user and resource information, including the public key side of the certificates. Management requires the Administration Server, which ships as part of each of the SuiteSpot servers. Management also requires the Administration Kit, which allows for the centralized customization and distribution of the Netscape Communicator client.

All of the services require the universal Netscape Communicator as the client. The components of the Communicator map directly to the services they provide. The Netscape Navigator is used as the browser for displaying HTML, Java, and JavaScript. The Netscape Messenger is the messaging client that can support either IMAP4 or POP3 connectivity. The Netscape Composer, formerly known as Netscape Gold, is the HTML editor used for the creation of rich HTML documents. Netscape Collabra is the NNTP client that is tightly integrated with Netscape Messenger to provide feature-rich discussion functionality. Netscape Calendar is the user interface for the Netscape Calendar Server, supporting CAP connectivity. Finally, Netscape AutoAdmin works with the Administration Kit to deliver standard configuration and updates to the Communicator. Table 4.1 shows the mapping of the services to the SuiteSpot servers.

Prioritize Network Services

As for user services, it is important for companies to define the requirements and importance of network services within the company, but here, the question is not whether a network service will be implemented, but to what extent.

Directory Services

Often, the first network services required by the intranet are directory and security. The directory supplies information about people and elements that make up and use the system. In the past, each of the Netscape SuiteSpot servers held directory information specific to each server; for example, the Enterprise Server had its own user database, the Mail Server had a separate MTA (Message Transfer Agent) database. In the 3.0 release of SuiteSpot, directory services provided by the Netscape Directory Server have become separated and centralized. The Enterprise Server can now use the centralized Directory Server, as can the Messaging Server. For this reason, establishing directory services becomes the first step in implementing the full-service intranet.

With directory services in place, the user services of communication and collaboration, for example, are simply applications that need to be installed on top of the directory, whereas in the past they required extensive configuration of the internal user database within the products. Further, information sharing and management rely heavily on directory services to assign access control to information stored in the Enterprise Server. The implementation of directory services first enables much simpler mapping of access control rather than having to again create and configure a separate user database. Companies choose whether to add the intranet directory to the existing directory infrastructure, thus introducing another username/password combination to the user; to integrate it with existing directories; or to convert existing directories to open standard LDAP directory services to provide single-user login to all systems.

Security Services

All companies are security conscious when implementing intranets. Netscape intranet technology addresses this concern by raising the bar for secure corporate computing by supporting strong authentication via client and server certificates, encrypted transmission of information over Secure Sockets Layer (SSL) protocol, and signed-encrypted messaging with secure MIME (S/MIME). But even with all of these tools and choices, it is most important to focus on the nature of the information, because all systems are penetrable in some way. Therefore, the goal of system security is to make the effort required to break into a system greater than the value of the information (i.e., decide how tall and how wide to build the walls around the information).

Because security tools are implemented on top of the standard intranet infrastructure, they do introduce a level of complexity for system users and have implications for system performance. Consequently, companies must establish security service requirements carefully. The amount of security required for information often varies widely across any organization, and the security implementations should follow those requirements.

Replication Services

Replication services vary based on the need to distribute information in the face of infrastructure issues such as limited network bandwidth, failover/redundancy, and load balancing. Companies most often introduce replication services in conjunction with the information sharing and management user service. The extent to which replication services are needed within the company depends on the existing system infrastructure and the required levels of system performance and uptime. A company that requires full mission-critical $24 \times 7 \times 365$ operation of a global intranet, including transparent access to information from all points on the network, will require far more replication services than more lenient situations such as remote locations with slow connections that are expected to have lower levels of system performance. In determining the extent to which replication services are required, then, companies need to understand their existing network infrastructures and define performance levels for all parts of the intranet.

Management Services

Like replication services, management services are defined by the resources within a company. For management services, the location, responsibilities, and skill sets of systems administrators will dictate primarily the way management services will be distributed. For some companies, system management is a centralized function; for others, each location takes care of its own. Either model can be implemented to support the intranet. Tools for remote management are built in to all Netscape products. Management tools are implemented as part of the products; companies need to develop and implement with the system the policies, procedures, and responsibilities of management.

Table 4.1 Mapping of the Services to the SuiteSpot Servers

	Information Sharing & Management	Communication & Collaboration	Navigation	Application Access	Directory Services	Replication	Security	Management
Enterprise Server	✖			✖				
Messaging Server		✖						
Collabra Server		✖						
Proxy Server						✖		
Calendar Server		✖						
Certificate Server							✖	
Directory Server					✖	✖	✖	
Catalog Server			✖					
Netscape ONE & SuiteTools				✖				
Admin Server & Kit								✖

Security

The topic of intranet security alone could fill several books. As discussed earlier, the most important decision regarding the intranet is one of company policy. Where some companies view the intranet as analogous to their phone and fax services, others see it as a mission-critical system for transporting strategic information vital to competitive advantage. The good news is that the products now available provide a new and higher level of information security than ever before. As with all aspects of intranet technology, security's sordid past in the Internet realm has focused attention on the possible breaches of intranets. To reiterate, companies must understand and decide the level of security that is required for the intranet, because this decision will impact the architecture and use of the overall system. This section discusses the goals of intranet security and gives brief descriptions to the tools available to meet those goals.

The three basic goals of intranet information security are privacy, integrity, and authentication. Together, they ensure that information is exchanged in the form it was intended between the parties involved.

The goal of information privacy is to prevent outsiders from intercepting or "eavesdropping" on the transmission of data across a network. Encryption, the security tool used to ensure privacy, makes it extremely difficult for intruders to interpret data not intended for outside access. SSL uses encryption keys to encode information; only the client and server can decode such data using the keys. These keys are regenerated and negotiated between the client and server every 90 seconds to make it more difficult to intercept information. For intruders, the effort required to intercept information handled this way is greater than the potential reward.

The goal of integrity is to ensure that information is received by the client in exactly the same form as it was sent by the server. Information integrity aims to prevent outsiders from tampering with information in transmission. SSL achieves this goal by computing a binary hash of the information, prior to it being sent. This hash algorithm is then applied to the information after it reaches the client, and the two are compared. If the file has been modified in any way, the result of the hash computation will be different and will identify the information as being invalid. If the file has not been altered in the transmission process, the hash computations will have the same result and the integrity of the information will be confirmed.

The goal of authentication is to confirm the identities of the parties exchanging information. This may be the server proving that it is, for example, www.acme.com (server authentication), the client proving that she is Sally Smith of ACME corporation (client authentication), or both confirmation of the client and server identities (mutual authentication). Authentication protects against outsiders impersonating authorized clients or servers to gain access to information. In the past, authentication was based on a basic username/password entry passed across the network in the clear. Today, x.509 certificates provide strong authentication by adding a binary piece of identification to a password to prove the identity of the holder. As noted earlier, that is similar to an ATM card or PIN number, requiring "something you have and something you know" to ensure identity. An identity is then mapped to the access control list of the SuiteSpot servers to allow or deny access to information.

Security Models

Companies request two general models of information access control in intranet systems: *proactive* and *reactive*. Traditional Web technology uses the reactive model, which is sometimes called the "try and deny" method of access control. In this model, as the user surfs through different links on the intranet and controlled areas of the server are requested, the user's access control permissions are checked, and he or she is allowed or prohibited access the documents. For some companies, this security model is not sufficient because knowledge of the existence of documents (from the URL) is too much information.

Showing users only the URLs that they are allowed to access requires the proactive security model. To implement this model, modifications can be made to the Enterprise Server to redirect its built-in access control processing using the Netscape Server API (NSAPI). In addition, the proactive model requires logic for creating a dynamic session based on user profile. This can be accomplished in two ways. Several different sites can be created for different user access levels; for example, different sites could be created for common users, management level users, and executive level users. From the home page login, each level of users could be directed to their respective sites. The alternative is to generate pages dynamically per user requests by storing component parts of documents separately and assembling them on-the-fly based on user profile. In this scenario, lists of URLs, graphics, text, and code objects are stored for each user level, plugged into the page template, and displayed to the user.

Many companies requiring proactive security have integrated relational databases with the Enterprise Server using NSAPI to capture user requests, query the database for access control information, and redirect user requests or dynamically construct documents based on user profiles.

Because additional processing is required to respond to client requests, there is often a performance hit associated with the proactive security model. The redirection of users to different sites based on their profiles is less processor-intensive than the dynamic construction of pages and, therefore, enables a higher level of performance. On the other hand, proactive security also requires a large amount of content duplication because fully functional sites are maintained for multiple user profiles. The dynamic content model, however, provides a high degree of flexibility to update information and maintain a single content store.

A hybrid of these solutions is to employ the security and filtering capabilities of the Netscape Proxy Server, which can be configured to redirect or deny URL requests from users. For example, a user request from the manager group of http://acme.com/reports/projections.html could be redirected to http://acme.com/manager/reports/projections.html; similarly, the CEO's request of the same URL could be redirected to http://acme.com/executive/reports/projections.html. Although, placing the Proxy Servers between clients and the Enterprise Server is done to balance load, many companies have found the filtering and security features to be useful tools for managing access to Enterprise Server resources. The automatic Proxy configuration available in the Communicator adds a point of dynamic administration that is transparent to the user. It places a URL in the Proxy Server Preferences box in the Communicator's user preferences, rather than a hard-coded Proxy Server name. This URL can be resolved on the server based on the profile of the user to a Proxy Server configured for that user's access level. This means that administrators can change the Proxy Server assigned to users as profiles change or as the system grows. In addition to providing security and filtering features, the Proxy Server, will, by default, replicate content and distribute load within the system.

In general, sites using proactive security are far more complex to develop and administer than those using the reactive security model. NSAPI requires additional development and often modification when upgrading to newer versions of the Enterprise Server. For this reason, whenever possible, the simpler traditional reactive security model or the hybrid proxy model should be used to provide access control within the intranet. Companies should carefully evaluate the nature of the information that will be hosted on the intranet and explore the true security implications of that information under both the proactive and reactive security models.

Access control is first and foremost about mapping users to content. Because content must be distributed to provide scalability and performance, so must access control. For this reason, to implement an effective access control model within an intranet, it is important to understand the nature of the content that it will hold. All companies have concerns about access control of information and have guidelines for mapping employees to information. Mapping users to the content of an intranet is at the core of effective access control; time and resources should be devoted to identifying buckets of information based on its sensitivity. These buckets of information should then be placed on separate Enterprise Servers within the intranet, each of which maintains the access control information for the resources it stores. This proved particularly important in designing intranets using the 2.0 version of the Enterprise Server. Why? Because the user database was stored within the server itself since not all content and users could be stored and replicated throughout a large company. The Enterprise Servers had to be distributed to provide performance and scalability.

The strategy is to identify content that is viewable by everyone, store that content on a server without access control, then link it to lower-level content on multiple servers with access control and the appropriate mappings for the resources it holds. The Directory server will enable centralization of the user account information (i.e., user titles, groups, etc.), but it will not contain the access control mappings to resources stored in other servers. Most companies set the default access control to prohibit access to resources; the servers allow only those groups and users for which it has access control mapping to access its resources. Administration of these access levels can be a tedious task if they are at a granular level—mapping one user to one document at a time. For this reason, it is important to identify functional groups of users that can map access control to the buckets of information identified within the company. Remember, intranets are intended to be distributed. The most efficient use of access control is to map functional groups of users to functional buckets of information. In this way, users can be added to the system; and by virtue of their groups in the Directory Server, access control will be enforced on the servers that make up the intranet, thereby abstracting access control and easing system administration.

Authentication

Authentication is the process of confirming the identity of the user by answering the question, "How do I know you are who you say you are?" The goal of authentication is to prevent "spoofing" of user identity. Traditionally, authentication invoked user ids and passwords to establish the identity of a user, a faulty system that fell prey to stealing or sharing. Today, user certificates and Secure Sockets Layer technologies augment the username/password authentication processes.

Certificates

A certificate can be considered the driver's license for the intranet. A user must "take a test" and prove his or her identity to a certifying authority in order to be issued a certificate that allows him or her to use the intranet and servers. The certificate is actually a software key that can be stored electronically on a hard drive, a diskette, or a smart card device. Similar to the concept of an ATM card, the certificate (something you have), in conjunction with your password (something you know), serves as the means for proving who you are and granting you access to information. Until recently, certificates were distributed only by certificate authorities (CAs) such as VeriSign or RSA, from whom users can request and purchase client-side certificates. As part of the application process, these companies conduct a thorough screening of applicants, complete with background and reference checks. Once the CA is satisfied that a user is who he or she claims to be, the certificate is issued to the user who can then download a copy of that certificate. On the server side, companies go through a similar process to gain a server-side certificate, which is used to enable encrypted transmissions between the server and clients.

Because these certification processes are time-consuming and expensive for large companies, Netscape developed the Certificate Server to enable companies to create and issue their own certificates, in effect becoming their own certifying authorities. Using the Certificate Server, a company can determine the requirements for user proof of identity and eliminate the time and maintenance of dealing with an external CA. Once servers and users are equipped with certificates, Secure Socket Layer transport encryption and S/MIME e-mail encryption can be invoked to protect information.

Encryption

Encryption encodes information to render it extremely difficult to translate, thereby making data unusable to hackers who might intercept it. In Internet technology, there are two forms of encryption: *data* and *transmission* encryption.

```
Message-ID: <33807380.B56046B2@netscape.com>
Date: Mon, 19 May 1997 08:36:32 -0700
From: reece@netscape.com (Reece Markowsky)
Organization: Netscape Communications Corp.
X-Mailer: Mozilla 4.0b5 [en] (Win95; I)
MIME-Version: 1.0
To: shanen@netscape.com, sijacic@netscape.com
Subject: [Fwd: Gateway]
X-Priority: 3 (Normal)
Content-Type: application/x-pkcs7-mime; name="smime.p7m"
Content-Transfer-Encoding: base64
Content-Disposition: attachment; filename="smime.p7m"
Content-Description: S/MIME Encrypted Message
X-Mozilla-Status: c009
```

```
MIAGCSqGSIb3DQEHA6CAMIACAQAxggJtMIHMAgEAMHYwYjERMA8GA1UEBxMISW5OZXJuZXQx
FzAVBgNVBAoTD1Z1cm1TaWduLCBJbmMuMTQwMgYDVQQLEytWZXJpU21nbiBDbGFzcyAxIENB
ICOgSW5kaXZpZHVhbCBTdWJzY3JpYmVyAhBFEshcc5OheW6WiIgDqtWJMAOGCSqGSIb3DQEB
AQUABEC5BqdQReNKDPSNdFssulkv43U5zUate9GhuhNbldAxQMhHRFxQodd3EwUvau4iJztn
Ood4kT4OqEAsNHytAC9ZMIHMAgEAMHYwYjERMA8GA1UEBxMISW5OZXJuZXQxFzAVBgNVBAoT
D1Z1cm1TaWduLCBJbmMuMTQwMgYDVQQLEytWZXJpU21nbiBDbGFzcyAxIENBICOgSW5kaXZp
ZHVhbCBTdWJzY3JpYmVyAhAN3+A1O1KnU/fgpAISCevPMAOGCSqGSIb3DQEBAQUABECYkBbX
HfieoVwKHesfsHXa/sOA76owyEC12Wm+Bz61073x9Z89w6vFZNRtlxnjxpHvMiWF+DYZTTQ/
g6jUcbOIMIHMAgEAMHYwYjERMA8GA1UEBxMISW5OZXJuZXQxFzAVBgNVBAoTD1Z1cm1TaWdu
LCBJbmMuMTQwMgYDVQQLEytWZXJpU21nbiBDbGFzcyAxIENBICOgSW5kaXZpZHVhbCBTdWJz
Y3JpYmVyAhBGjgV1LgAdTzWunQ+4oJaxMAOGCSqGSIb3DQEBAQUABEC3VvD9+gEerxZVGBq+
OutHqFOTZVCOwqZdasMDp654acrpi6f2CqCOJNjs4fZLz8DnII7Q80cGeUUu39BzUnqQMIAG
CSqGSIb3DQEHATAaBggqhkiG9wODAjAOAgIAoAQI7+OQzv7/fu2ggASBsNegz/AoAM3Ueq0Q
Bvsgq2NXyebsaUSHgdaWGz1roqutEf21aSZe6rH2V7bGTbMVnkGSr/XhFXUmzHcyTLmCtGKb
9XYMbfu3ctygOO48A313h5VswmC5zTKTr3gPOXnxDvpeKOGROoIzHgzLB1tu7V7bggC1GOAh
V19195677jRYn+YGLRA9J1QQ/v3+cAz/yJ9MtqKRBQgxGQo4e5hCNpneibF3tx/3LqjOqtPZ
5mnlBFBMpkR8YIJmmSsxF5odQ8mpdaJcFNUoTsBfzHPf2FIFmA8d7bZ7LC2Z77evTu6e1sVr
pgmob4BBkYE47CETDOK32tLqRoJ9gB6WEz7o7IMWowQI6/D+Awso1ssEKEJ9K38akcnW1HQ/
/2UO2fOSOmyAZDZghWDFDxd+/1NqUCWE5jFbrekECOaNK64tvlvTBCAR3M/5Z8f7Ne4I1TpS
OZRhEtKTepbLUsBtZvjaJjOs4QQwMcPtwgCUNrxmWCVYNOz+yAJ+EAVJK4n57bNMDvoNU3Tw
fjXJUXRF/b3Twgwkf3ctBCAdKIqWqZnbZITfCPm6DAnH+GsyWw8azs69rrKz7rc2ggQIUMr4
Hf4iLuOESK9VdnCaEkVPdyoOtqhz0XfxfaO4snKVSJ6sXjEAJUAbjfhlAOaVrUxBsxRAX7/n
NgfuwvDd55x6KViVjRemqDsf5VHHjU+M7ARQvZQx9TjOz34U12YXgQx1+xI2sZu5IfZZCik/
```

Figure 4.1 Encrypted e-mail message.

Data Encryption   Data encryption is the process of encoding information *before* it is sent over the wire to make it uninterpretable to unauthorized users (see Figure 4.1). This type of encryption requires the establishment of an agreed-upon code between sender and receiver. The most common use of encryption in intranet systems is for messaging where the sender encrypts a message prior to sending it. A public key is made available via a directory system; then prior to releasing a message, the sender looks up the recipient's address and uses his or her public key to encode the message. Only the user with the matching private key can decode and read the message. Because mail is an asynchronous communication, encryption is often used to protect that information as it is stored on a server during the routing process. The S/MIME standard is a good example of data encryption of e-mail messages. Since e-mail messages are stored on network or local hard disks, it is often important that this data be encrypted.

Transmission Encryption: Secure Sockets Layer   Transmission encryption addresses a real-time communications environment by encrypting information in a dynamic process as it is being passed between the client and the server. Secure Sockets Layer encryption, or SSL, is the standard for this process and is available in Netscape servers. SSL masks the data as it passes through the network from the client to the server. Running on top of the TCP/IP protocol, but below application-level protocols like HTTP, SSL ensures that any information is secure.

Secure Sockets Layer encryption works by generating dynamic keys, which are agreed upon between the client and the server. These keys are dynamic in the sense that a new one is generated every 90 seconds during a session between client and server. In this way, even if a hacker can break the code between the client and server, he or she will only be able to understand the data for the remainder of the 90-second interval, an unfruitful hack as it were; therefore, SSL is a very successful tool in protecting transmissions. The SSL connection and encrypted communication is initiated by a three-part SSL handshake. First, the client and server exchange x.509 certificates, which are checked for validity based on expiration date and signature of a trusted issuing body (certificate authority). Next, the client dynamically creates encryption keys that are encoded using the server's public key and sends them to the server. Finally, the server uses its private key to decrypt the keys sent by the client and selects the strongest encryption algorithm available from those presented by the client. The client and server then use the encryption keys and algorithm to begin encrypted communications over an SSL connection.

Kerberos

Developed at MIT, Kerberos is a network authentication system based on a dynamic key distribution model. Its purpose is to enable users communicating over networks to prove their identity to each other, and thus prevent eavesdropping or replay attacks. Kerberos aims to provide data stream integrity (detection of modification) and secrecy (prevention of unauthorized reading) using third-party cryptography systems.

Kerberos works by assigning users with tickets, which they can use to identify themselves to other principals, and secret cryptographic keys for secure communication with other users. These tickets are then embedded in network protocols on which applications are developed. Kerberos is most often used in application-level protocols such as Telnet or FTP to provide user-to-host security. Less frequently, it is used as the implicit authentication system of a data stream (such as SOCK_STREAM) or RPC mechanisms. Many companies and government agencies are adopting Kerberos as the standard communications security mechanism for authentication and secure transmission. Kerberos can and is being used with HTTP, and will probably be implemented in the future by companies using IIOP.

In the Kerberos architecture, a Kerberos server sits between the client and the server to which both must connect; the dynamic keys are mitigated by the Kerberos server. This has several implications for intranet users. First, the Kerberos server must be up and running for the user to connect. Second, the Kerberos server must be relatively close to the user to allow acceptable connect speeds. This has obvious system architecture ramifications for highly distributed intranets. Kerberos will likely be a supported authentication mechanism in future releases of Netscape's intranet products.

Network Infrastructure

With intranet technology, the network is indeed the computer. Connectivity plays a central role in providing the user and network services of the full-service intranet. Consequently, when planning for the intranet, many questions arise regarding network infrastructure. This section aims to point out key considerations and establish high-level guidelines for planning a network infrastructure. Detailed analysis and tuning is always required for the specific needs of any intranet.

As for deployment, there are several approaches to network and hardware sizing. Following the classic chaotic deployment model, network and server hardware is loaded until a problem arises—that is, performance degradation occurs. This model works for some companies, but the result often is an unpredictable system that performs well one day and poorly the next. The alternative deployment model, which is more predictable, involves analyzing the current networking environment and anticipating growth to sustain a high level of performance over time.

Analyze Current Networking Environment

The first step in planning the architecture of the intranet is to understand the networking infrastructure upon which it will be implemented.

This is the role of the system/network administrator on the intranet task force. The two essential network factors are its *topology* and *capacity*. Topology refers to the placement of nodes or subnets within the overall network. Often, regional and local offices have their own local area networks (LAN) connected to the company's wide area network (WAN). Frequently, LANs have a higher bandwidth or data throughput than WAN connections, which are far more expensive. This very common network architecture banks on the fact that most network traffic in intraoffice in nature.

Bandwidth is a familiar infrastructure constraint for distributed systems, particularly for networks distributed to remote parts of the world. For this reason, when designing the intranet, it is important to know the current network's capacity and load. The requirements of the intranet are directly dependent on the volume of information and number of transactions a system will support.

A company system or network administrator should be able to supply the metrics of the current networking infrastructure (the raw bandwidth) and estimate current usage to arrive at a net bandwidth available for the intranet. It is then important to account for the exchange of bandwidth that may occur for systems that the intranet will be replacing: for example, if the intranet will be replacing Lotus Notes for messaging and groupware, the current resources used by Notes becomes available for the intranet.

The general rule for determining whether network upgrades are required is to look at the current utilization; if current network use is greater than 60 percent, network upgrades will likely be needed with the introduction of the intranet. Although, this is a rather broad generalization, it is based on experience in the field, and is given as a guideline for it is a frequently asked question. There are architectural strategies involving replication that can provide acceptable performance with minimal bandwidth utilization.

Internet technology was designed to leverage low-bandwidth networking resources, but the features and rich information required for corporate systems has raised the bar considerably in terms of bandwidth and network infrastructure required. The key to estimating bandwidth needs is to understand the nature of the documents on the system; specifically, the overall size and the number of hits per page are the drivers of bandwidth.

When analyzing the current networking environment, you'll find it helpful to consider these questions:

1. *What is the current bandwidth/capacity of the existing network?* The answer to this question drives decisions on centralizing information and services. For some companies, all points on the network have virtually the same bandwidth across the LAN/WAN, in which case, the location of the servers is unimportant and can be centralized, in other cases, bandwidth on a LAN may be much higher than the WAN and placing servers closer to the users provides better performance and leverages infrastructure.

2. *How many nodes or subnets does the network have?* The number and distribution of nodes and subnets that make up the network help determine how many and where intranet servers should be located. Often, network subnets or nodes are created to isolate traffic within a small groups of users. These subnets are used to map the intranet servers to supply user services at the point of need.

3. *How many and where are the remote locations on the network, and what is their connectivity?* As with the location of subnets and nodes, it is important to understand the connectivity of the remote locations of organization. These two topologies might map one-for-one in a company with one subnet for each remote location. But some companies have remote offices with one or just a few employees who rely on dial-up connections to the nearest office on the WAN, and these users are the toughest to support from a systems perspective. It is important to understand the current usage patterns of these remote users, the security issues related to remote usage, and the method of connectivity. For this purpose, many companies consider using the Internet as the virtual WAN, thus allowing remote users to subscribe to a local ISP and enter the corporate intranet via the Internet. This is a viable solution for those companies with remote locations for which buying WAN connectivity or even direct dial-up connections is difficult or impossible. As stated earlier, this raises the bar in terms of the security requirements of the intranet, now gone extranet. Strong authentication and encrypted transmission becomes requisite when offering connections from outside the firewall.

4. *How many and where are there connections to the Internet?* If the choice is made to connect users to the Internet, it is important to take a close look at the placement of that connectivity. As with bringing information closer to the people who use it most, it is important to distribute Internet connectivity similarly. Following

the geographical division of the company, Internet access points are usually installed at each regional location. If users at the local office level require extensive access to the Internet, it may be appropriate to install an Internet connection locally to alleviate network usage from the local offices across the WAN to the regional offices and then to the Internet. In the end, usage patterns will dictate the number of regional and local Internet connections required.

5. *How many users per location need access?* The number of users per location is a metric used to determine the number and location of intranet servers by estimating the volume of intraoffice network traffic. Ten or more users in an office normally generate enough traffic to warrant placement of local intranet servers. The logic here is that, for example, users sending intraoffice mail should not be wasting precious WAN bandwidth back and forth to centralized servers. These numbers are driven by the usage patterns within the offices. Publishers of great quantities of complex documents, for example, benefit from local servers, which decrease network impact. The point is, the number and the nature of the users within an office determine the placement of intranet servers to meet their needs.

6. *Where are there support administrators and what skills do they have?* Important to deployment decisions is the location of system administration resources within the organization. Many companies are interested in distributing the system administration functions across the organization. In order to do this, it is important to survey the location, number, and skill sets of administrators within the company, and to consider the roles and responsibilities of these resources. For example, determine which administrators will be responsible for the creation and maintenance of user accounts. The distribution of these responsibilities is a key component to placement of servers that provide the network services of the full-service intranet.

7. *What are known bottlenecks and peak periods; and which applications drive the network traffic?* The intranet will definitely impact the existing network infrastructure. For this reason, it is important to be aware of the network bottlenecks as they relate to the current application environment, so that it is possible to schedule network-intensive operations of the intranet, such as replication or indexing, around peak usage times. A good understanding of the

current network utilization will also help determine the need for network upgrades with the introduction and growth of the intranet.

Conclusion

Clearly identifying the goals and objectives of the intranet is an important input into the design and development of the system. Companies should spend time identifying those areas for the intranet to target to improve communication and efficiency before implementation. These goals will define the implementation and shape the future success of the intranet.

5

INTRODUCING THE INTRANET

Task Force

Whether starting from scratch or redeploying an existing system, the formal introduction of the intranet to the enterprise is an important step in implementing the full-service intranet within the organization. First and foremost, any system must have a clear owner and champion. Specifically, there must be one group or individual who is the chief contact and proponent of the intranet. This is an important distinction between the preexisting grassroots intranet and the full-service intranet. Many companies have created intranet task forces to champion the intranet within the company. The following is an example list of profiles for members of such a task force:

Project Sponsor. Executive-level supporter of the project. Responsible for management-level buyin for the intranet.

IT Manager. Intranet project manager. Responsible for assembling resources and day-to-day management of the project team.

Functional Manager. Manager from the functional business area for the initial intranet rollout. Has a vision for the utility of the intranet in his or her department and its effects on the users.

Development Team Lead. Application/technical development team lead. Responsible for system architecture and application design for the intranet.

System Administrator/Web Master. Responsible for installation and ongoing maintenance of the intranet. Able to address the existing system architecture and personnel infrastructure as it relates to introducing a new system.

Not to be confused with the entire team required to deploy and support an intranet, these five individuals are representatives from the constituent user, management, and system administration communities. These are the profiles that are commonly used in planning sessions with Netscape Professional Services to make decisions and create policies and procedures for intranets within large companies. This is the group that will be responsible for carrying the intranet forward within the organization. For this reason, it is important that this group understand the functional aspects of the industry, the cultural aspects of the company, and the technical infrastructure upon which the system exists.

Phased Approach

Most companies prefer to approach the formal deployment of the intranet in phases. This allows both users and administrators to learn and improve the intranet in the deployment process. It is also consistent with the fast moving, iterative state of Internet technology which allows companies to better mold the intranet to their business.

By phasing intranet deployment, companies are able to decrease the negative impacts of change by giving users and administrators the opportunity to gain experience and develop procedures for using and maintaining the system. The intranet becomes less of a threat to the status quo of information sharing and, in the long run, is better accepted. This is especially important for system administrators since the intranet often challenges the existing technology paradigm within the company.

An interesting point here is that users often feel threatened by the fact that information will be readily accessible across the company. Users can feel a loss of power or control when information of which they are the owners and keepers is made readily available to everyone via the intranet.

For system administrators, change is often viewed as a threat. This was very clear in the transition to client server systems in the last decade. The old pro "mainframers" where certainly threatened and very resistant to the introduction of this new paradigm of computing. The same is sometimes true of the intranet. It has been and will continue to be challenged by proponents of the existing mainframe and client server experts within corporations. There are indeed areas where the intranet is not the appropriate platform for computing and there are applications which are much better suited for client/server or mainframe system architecture.

Identifying Phases

Functional Phases

There are two ways that companies commonly slice the intranet into deployment phases; functional deployment and geographical deployment. Functional phases are most often identified by the user and network services as outlined in the full-service intranet: information sharing and management, communication and collaboration, navigation and application access. Noteworthy is that most companies view the intranet as a form of communication that cuts across the entire organization, rather than it being specific to any internal functional area such as marketing or human resources. Traditionally, systems have used the organizational structure of the company to roll out systems, but it is assumed that all areas of the company will require the intranet similarly to computer operating systems or, more generally, a telephone system. Functional organizations do, however, play a major part, as they always have, in the area of application development, for this is where the specific needs of each department are identified and addressed with tools to build applications on top of the intranet platform. Application development on the intranet platform is discussed in detail later in this chapter.

Geographic Phases

The second method of breaking up the intranet rollout is by geography. Deployment by geographical region is a natural way for most companies to create phases for the intranet because the component pieces of the intranet are easily identifiable based on the locations within an organization. Splitting the intranet deployment into geographic phases is often useful in separating the challenges of the various network topologies that make up an intranet's infrastructure. Frequently, companies will have vastly different network and personnel resources at their headquarters, regional locations, and local offices. These divisions also have various user and network service needs.

The geographic and functional components of the intranet can be combined to produce an overall deployment strategy. By identifying these components, an organization can accurately map technology to the deployment plan. The following subsections use a fictional company, ACME Corporation, as a case study for intranet deployment. This example is based on a wide range of experience in planning intranets for Fortune 1000 companies.

Functional Rollout

Quick Wins

It is important to focus first on the so-called quick wins of the intranet, to develop and distribute the information and functions that are most widely used by the organization and will be easiest to implement. As stated earlier, the core competency of intranet technology is to distribute information in a one-to-many relationship; that is, people create and post information on the intranet for use by others in the company—a true internal web. This accomplishes two important goals of deployment: It distributes the product to the user community and demonstrates immediate value. It gives both users and administrators time to acclimate to the technology, and answers the what and why questions regarding intranet technology. Information sharing and management, followed by communication and collaboration, navigation and application access, has proven to be a successful model for phase functional deployment for corporate intranets.

Communication and Collaboration

Many companies choose to implement communication and collaboration as the first services in the intranet because e-mail and groupware need to be ubiquitous if users are to communicate effectively. Most companies view e-mail as a utility; simply, it must work all the time. Communication, messaging specifically, is often the first service provided to users. Messaging is a good place to start because it grants the user community with instant e-mail functionality. Information management and sharing services are also popular as intranet starters, but those services require some time for a critical mass of information to be developed to provide utility.

Netscape's messaging solution is based on open standards, amplified by HTML content and SMTP transport. The interrelationship of e-mail and the Web is a powerful combination, which many companies are exploiting through Netscape technology. This relationship redefines workflow and groupware processes. Workflow processes are no longer self-contained systems with limited functionality, but seamlessly integrated with the application environment. The Netscape Messenger displays messages in HTML 3.0 to provide rich-text composition and application functionality through JavaScript. This puts live forms directly in the user's inbox. With active HTML in the inbox, the user can be taken directly to the application needed to complete a task. Further, this application can change in content or location without interrupting the user. The marriage of messaging and application environments gives developers a great deal of flexibility in designing and maintaining collaborative application.

Like the Netscape messaging tools, the discussion/news products are also based on HTML and give users the same capability to seamlessly invoke applications from within discussion forums, which are used as an organized ad hoc communications forum for various topics within the organization from new product ideas to commuter groups. Over time, these groups become important knowledge bases, supplying an invaluable history of decision making and related information. With all of these great ways to create and share information, the next step is providing tools to locate valuable information in an intuitive, efficient manner.

Information Sharing and Management

Another logical place to start functionally is with what is considered to be the core competency of Internet technology: the one-to-many distribution of information. Although this seems obvious as an application for the intranet, it is often forgone in the race to build applications on top of the base intranet technology. Often, the most used intranet application is that which enables surfing for information. For this reason, it is important to give equal planning time and consideration to deployment in this area. Users require procedures and technology to enable the publishing of information on the intranet. They need to know the what, the where, and the how of putting information up on the intranet. This involves distributing tools and training for document creation or conversion to HTML. One of the most frequently asked user questions in the publishing area is, "How do I put my Microsoft Office documents on the Web?" Users must have the tools to convert and create documents at their fingertips. This requires not only the technology, but an understanding of what it can and cannot do. Users must understand when a document should be authored in HTML (most of the time) and when specialized tools are required. They also should understand the effects that conversion of their documents to HTML means to the end format of that document, when it is necessary to include attachments to the original documents, and when HTML is all that is necessary. They also must know where to put all of this information on the system.

Currently, many IT departments have taken on the role of document publishers for the enterprise; accepting documents in various formats, taking responsibility for converting them to HTML, and cleaning them up for distribution on the intranet. It is clear after the first month and the exponential growth in many intranets that this process is one that will collapse under its own weight. Frequently, the reason given for using this model is that the IT department wants to review and approve information prior to releasing it for public consumption on the intranet. This model is a carryover from more traditional forms of publishing information inside the organization, such as newsletters or bulletin boards, that required approval prior to printing or posting. Unfortunately, this is a very demanding and inefficient way to publish on the intranet, and thus is an area that can benefit greatly from a decentralized model. The solution is to give the power and responsibility of document publishing to the users. From a higher-level perspective, the goal of the IT department should be to create a knowledge base for the enterprise; information should be stored in a logical order so that it can be easily tapped today and in the future.

Navigation

After giving users the capability to generate and distribute information using document creation and distribution tools, leveraging that information in the future is the next step. Again, the single most important goal of any intranet is to share information across the enterprise. There is nothing more frustrating than knowing that certain information exists and not being able to find it. Sadly, often the authors of information have difficulty locating their own documents. Intranets can quickly turn into a confusing maze of information, where users only know where they have been before. Navigation tools are the answer for finding the way through that maze. These must be sophisticated search tools that help users navigate large volumes of information quickly to find relevant information. These tools must make the intranet, which can be made up of numerous servers and hundreds of gigabytes of information, appear as one cohesive, intuitive knowledge base.

Application Access

After making it possible to create and find information of the intranet, accessing existing information is a crucial aspect of any new technology. Intranet technology brings the universal client to the game. By enabling access to legacy information systems through the open standard of the intranet, users are no longer limited by hardware or operating systems. Furthermore, application developers only have to design, write, and test one version of application code for all users. Tools provided by Netscape ONE make this possible; with development tools for Java, JavaScript, HTML, and NSAPI, Netscape ONE bridges the gap between the old and the new.

Geographic Roll-out

Following the physical distribution of the company, a geographic rollout can provide a useful model for deployment clearly understood by the employees.

Model Organizational Structure

Another strategy that many companies use to organize intranet information is to model the organizational structure of the existing organization. Starting with the companies' organizational charts and storing information by department as listed therein, IT departments can ensure that users will understand the organization of the site so that it appears intuitive. Certainly, some companies choose to use technology to reengineer the organization, but the intranet is most often implemented to reflect the existing informational structure rather than to redefine it. This section, therefore, describes a phased implementation plan based on an existing geographic organizational structure of a company.

After working with several Fortune 1000 companies, certain patterns have become apparent in designing a geographic rollout. Since the focus here is on deploying a communications system, it is important to look at the different types of information within an organization. Most large companies can be broken down geographically into global, regional, and local categories. The headquarters of any company is responsible for publishing information that communicates the state of the company to the regional and local offices. This information is needed by all locations within the company. Similarly, regional hubs are responsible for publishing and distributing information germane to their respective regions. This information is typically used by employees within a region at the local office level. The local offices also produce information specific to their location, information used primarily by employees there. This intraoffice communication, of course, also exists at both the regional and headquarters levels. This high-level structure provides a three-tiered structure of information based on geography.

Using this structure, a natural way for a company to phase its intranet deployment is to implement information sharing and management services starting at the headquarters level followed by the regional hubs and the local office locations. This lets the headquarters location develop policies and procedures, standards, and system support skills that can be subsequently presented to the regional and local offices upon deployment of the intranet in those locations. The following case study uses a combination of functional and geographic deployment phases to exemplify this model.

Case Study: ACME Corporation

The purpose of this deployment case study using a large international company is to demonstrate a phased approach to intranet deployment using the services model provided by the full-service intranet described earlier. Based on real-world experience, this section implements the guidelines just given. Certainly this example will not apply directly to all companies, but the best practices and concepts used in designing this solution can be considered universally.

Overview

ACME is embarking on a strategy to move to an open, standards-based, scalable communications platform based on Netscape technology. This platform will provide the user services of communication and collaboration, information sharing and management, navigation and application access, as well as the network services of directory, security, replication, and management for a full-service solution.

ACME is a worldwide producer of widgets. Headquartered in Chicago, Illinois, the company is divided into three geographic regions: the Americas, Asia, and Europe, each of which has an information technology (IT) office responsible for supporting users in its respective re-

Table 5.1 Location and Anticipated Number of Intranet Users

User Location	Region	Total Users
Chicago, IL	Americas	1,000
New York, NY	Americas	500
Los Angles, CA	Americas	500
Paris, France	Europe	500
London, England	Europe	200
Frankfurt, Germany	Europe	100
Hong Kong, China	Asia	500
Tokyo, Japan	Asia	200
Singapore	Asia	100

gion. Table 5.1 outlines the location and anticipated numbers of users for the ACME intranet.

IDENTIFY GEOGRAPHIC ORGANIZATION OF THE COMPANY

It is essential to identify the geographic and functional organization of the company in order to successfully architect and deploy an intranet.

Goals

The first step in planning an intranet is to understand the goals of the company. Identifying these goals and developing a clear vision for the intranet is essential for designing a successful system. For ACME, the following goals have been identified as the guiding principles driving design and deployment decisions.

- ❏ Provide access to the intranet from anywhere with full functionality.
- ❏ Build a thinner, simpler browser-centric desktop environment.
- ❏ Distribute management of content and access.
- ❏ Architect the intranet with built-in resilience and failover.
- ❏ Establish a global network to support international growth.

❑ Centralize data storage while providing transparent distributed access.

❑ Implement an open application development platform.

ACME, like many companies today, has an immediate need to replace its current messaging system. ACME would like to eliminate the technical and functional issues associated with the existing proprietary mail system, including difficulty of administration, user confusion due to differences in configuration for local and remote usage, gateway translation problems, and lack of broad-based message security. In addition to providing the user service of communication, messaging will demonstrate the advantages of open standards and platform independence to all ACME employees. Immediately, users will see the advantages of open standards, because they won't have to worry about attachment formats and gateway translations. Along with these benefits, messaging will require much of the underlying intranet infrastructure and thus build the foundation for additional user services and applications.

The deployment of a messaging solution requires the infrastructure component or network service of directory services. Directory services take center stage with the introduction of SuiteSpot 3.0. The directory is the reference point for information about resources; people and things, access control, and security. As such, a solid directory is essential to the success of the messaging implementation and the intranet as a whole.

The network security service is also required for messaging. To meet this requirement, the Certificate Server is an infrastructure component with the Directory Server as part of the messaging infrastructure. The Certificate Server is the creation tool for client and server certificates, which are then managed by the Directory Server in conjunction with the Certificate Server. Messaging, of course, also involves the distribution of a client component Netscape Messenger part or the Netscape Communicator.

Second to messaging, ACME would like to provide information sharing and management services to its users to leverage the directory infrastructure for user profiles and access control. This service requires the installation and configuration of the Netscape Enterprise and Proxy Servers to enable publishing and distribution of information. Hand in hand with the creation and distribution of information is the navigation user service. This will introduce the Netscape Catalog Server to the intranet. All of the information sharing and management functions are involved through the Netscape Navigator component of the Communicator client.

Once users have information sharing and management services, the next logical service area to address is collaboration, which enables users to share information and work together. As described previously, Netscape Collabra Server provides enterprisewide discussion and news services, and Netscape Calendar Server provides enterprisewide calendaring and scheduling. Both servers also work with the directory services for referencing user information and providing access control. The last service on which ACME would like to concentrate is application access. Once the infrastructure of the intranet has been deployed, it will provide an excellent platform for application development. The following outline details ACME's intranet deployment sequence in terms of services and products.

IDENTIFY AND PRIORITIZE GOALS

It is important to identify and document the goals of the intranet for reference as the system grows in technology and scope.

Communication
Directory
Security
Messaging
Management
    Netscape Messenger (Communicator)
    Netscape Certificate Server
    Netscape Directory Server
    Netscape Messaging Server
Information Sharing and Management
Publishing
Navigation
Management
    Netscape Navigator/Composer (Communicator)
    Netscape Proxy Server
    Netscape Enterprise Server

Collaboration

Discussions

Calendaring

Management

Netscape Calendar/Conference/Collabra (Communicator)

Netscape Calendar Server

Netscape Collabra Server

Application Development

Custom Applications

Management

Netscape ONE

Netscape SuiteTools

MAP USER SERVICES TO INFRASTRUCTURE

Once user services and priorities have been established, it is important to identify the network services and products needed to supply those services. Doing so will help to determine the series of implementation tasks.

Communication

To provide the communication user services, ACME must first deploy directory services as part of its intranet.

Directory Services

Directory services will make information available on users and resources within ACME based on standard formats and protocols, enabling better communication throughout the company. In addition to a central user and resource repository of user information, ACME will be able to use a central directory service to store preference and access control information that can be downloaded to mobile users wherever they choose to work. As the central repository of public keys, directory services also play a vital role in the implementation of secure e-mail.

Current Environment

ACME currently has a global network infrastructure and has implemented proprietary directory services in all parts of the company. The network, e-mail system, databases, and custom applications all store separate proprietary directories requiring multiple user logins and multiple points of administration. ACME would like to make use of the open standards supported by the Netscape Directory Server to move to a singular directory service, provide single user login, and reduce system administration requirements.

Implementation and Architecture

Implementation of a directory service architecture requires designing a directory schema; determining distinguished naming standards; and for ACME, identifying the administration responsibilities of the directory, designing a security model, and finally initiating the migration of existing directory data. The Netscape Directory Server is at the center of the login process for all Netscape servers. As such, it must be a readily available system, one that is implemented with redundancy and failover in mind.

Directory Schema An important step in designing the architecture of directory services is to identify the administrative ownership responsibilities of user accounts and resources in the intranet; that is, deciding who will be responsible for creating and maintaining users and resources. Because ACME is a growing multinational company, it must enable access to user and resources information on a global scale (see Figure 5.1). For this reason, it is recommended that directory services be designed for redundancy and the distribution of administration.

The main IT offices of each region—Chicago, Paris, and Hong Kong—will be the supplier/owner of user and resource information for their respective regions. Each region will maintain a complete copy of the ACME directory, although each will be responsible for maintaining only its regional subtree. This schema can be carried further to distribute administration by assigning smaller offices to their respective subtrees.

The directory schema can be based on standard x.500 distinguished name attributes (DN) or may be modified to more closely represent the ACME organizational structure. For example, the standard x.500 DN does not contain a region attribute, which could be added to the schema. Adhering to the standard x.500 DN will ensure smooth interoperability with external systems, but it is likely that ACME will elect to introduce

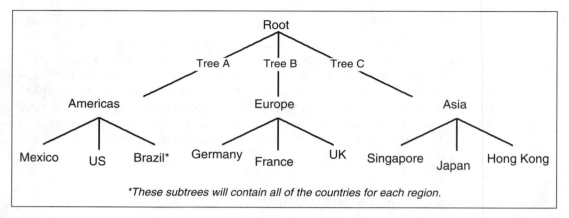

Figure 5.1 Data hierarchy tree structure.

custom attributes that more closely match its organizational structure and to create access control rules to be followed with other servers and applications within the intranet.

Distinguished Name   The first task in the implementation of directory services is the accurate definition of a directory schema and assignment of a root distinguished name (DN). This involves mapping the organization to a data hierarchy that represents the company. Using the standard x.500 distinguished naming standards, the following are examples for ACME that can serve as the starting point for the Directory Server implementations. In the future, ACME may introduce additional attributes to enable more granular security and access control for information and applications within the intranet.

c=US, cn=Jane Doe, l=Chicago, o=ACME, ou=Sales, reg=Americas

c=France, cn=Jaque Louis, l=Paris, o=ACME, ou=Accounting, reg=Europe

c=Japan, cn=Dave Nguyen, l=Tokyo, o=ACME, ou=Information Technology, reg=Asia

Attributes

e-mail address

phone number

title

skills

DETAILED DESIGN SESSION

A detailed design session is required prior to implementation of the Directory Server architecture. This session should focus on identifying directory system administration responsibilities and future security needs for the intranet.

Netscape Directory Server Architecture

Initially, ACME should install and configure a Netscape Directory Server in its headquarters—the Americas regional hub in Chicago. This server will contain all ACME user and resource entries, and be configured as the supplier for all users and resources based in the Americas region. Similarly, a "full-copy" of the Netscape Directory Servers should be deployed at each regional hub office—Paris and Hong Kong (see Figure 5.2). These

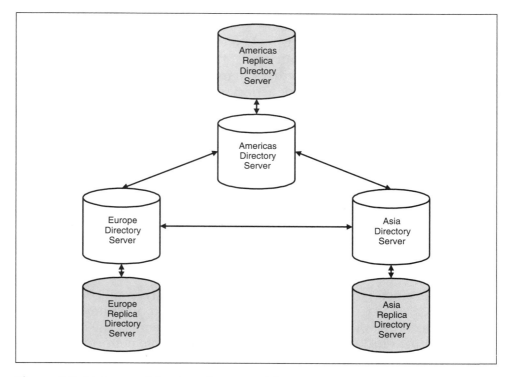

Figure 5.2 Netscape Directory Server architecture.

servers will own/supply the entries for their respective regions. Each of these Directory Servers will contain a complete set of the user and resource entries for built-in redundancy and failover for the intranet. In addition to the full-copy replicas in each of the regions, ACME could also deploy full replica copies in each of the regional hub offices for an even greater and higher performance redundancy and failover architecture. This architecture will play well in the intranet with the enhanced replication features of the Directory Server 2.0, which will allow for dynamic assignment of consumer/supplier status of Directory Server branches. For the smaller, remote ACME locations, replica/consumer Netscape Directory Servers could also be configured to provide a high level of performance and reliability. Depending on the needs of the users in these remote locations, these replicas could contain only the subtree for its region or an entire replica of the global directory.

Netscape Directory Server Failover

Maintaining full replicas of the directory in each region enables a first line of failover for directory services. The DNS server on each of these servers will implement the DNS rename function to provide transparent failover to users, in which case, the first DNS rename occurs in each of the regional offices so that the replica Directory Server can respond to requests made to the production server (see Figure 5.3). As a second line of failover, DNS could be further configured to rename one of the other regional Directory Servers should the local replica server go down.

Deployment Locations

The initial deployment calls for 12 machines in the locations shown in Table 5.2.

Sizing

A Directory Server machine can be relatively small because disk and CPU usage are not particularly intensive; instead, the number of network connections is the primary limiting factor. The machine configurations shown in Table 5.3 would provide acceptable performance for the ACME intranet. If possible, it is best for each Directory Server instance to have a dedicated machine.

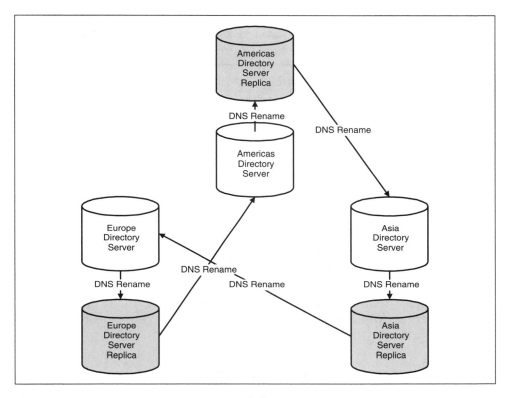

Figure 5.3 Netscape Directory Server failover.

Table 5.2 Netscape Directory Server Locations

User Location	Total Users	Directory Servers
Chicago, IL	1,000	2
New York, NY	500	1
Los Angles, CA	500	1
Paris, France	500	2
London, England	200	1
Frankfurt, Germany	100	1
Hong Kong	500	2
Tokyo, Japan	200	1
Singapore	100	1

Table 5.3 Netscape Directory Server Hardware Requirements

Hardware	Directory Server
Sun	Sparc 2/20
Intel	Pentium 200mhz
HP	D-Class
SGI	Challenge S 200MHz
RAM	128 MB
Disk	2+ GB

Security

ACME will make use of both the internal and external security aspects of Netscape Directory Server. Internal security refers to access control and rights to administer the server and to create or modify entries in the directory. External security refers to the use of the directory by other servers and applications to provide access control to resources or information within the intranet.

Internal/Administrative Security   Netscape Directory Server can be administered securely via SSL connections from an HTML browser. Access to individual subtrees of the data hierarchy can be assigned to system administrators. This distributes the task of creating and maintaining users and resources. For example, system administrators in Tokyo can be granted access to create or modify entries in the Asia subtree, while prohibited from administering the Europe subtree. This is accomplished by storing access control information in Netscape Directory Server.

If custom attributes are assigned as the DN of the ACME directory, custom administration tools may be necessary to assist in the task of distributed administration. This may involve command-line or HTML-based utilities for adding, deleting, or updating the custom attributes.

External/Application Security   Because Netscape Directory Server holds the entire company's user and resource information and grants high-performance access to that information, it is a logical place for applications to reference for access to information and system resources. Future Netscape SuiteSpot servers will rely heavily on the information contained in Netscape Directory Server for access control mapping. For this reason, the data hierarchy in Netscape Directory Server should be planned to expose all of the attributes—such as groups, levels, and positions—that can be used to map access control.

Directory Conversion   The final task for ACME's implementation will be to convert the entries from existing directories within the company. This data can be loaded via LDAP inserts to the Directory Server or preferably, by using the LDAP Data Interchange Format (LDIF) file format. Although there are conversion tools for Microsoft and Lotus directories, currently there is no migration tool from ACME's current proprietary directory to LDAP. ACME developers will have to make use of the Directory Server LDAP Software Developers Kit (SDK) and Netscape ONE to build conversion utilities to migrate legacy directory data to the intranet directory service.

Messaging

With directory services in place, ACME can quickly implement messaging to provide communication services to its users. This will demonstrate the utility of the intranet to all ACME users and address the issues of the existing e-mail environment.

Current Environment

ACME's current e-mail environment is built on a proprietary mail system running across multiple servers. Internet access to the mail system is provided through a gateway system. ACME currently maintains about 2,500 users in its existing system, but would like to expand the number to include all ACME employees, totaling around 3,600. User migration will have to be made to a LDAP server; a centralized LDAP server gives one location for additions and deletions of users from the mail server.

As indicated earlier, ACME would like to eliminate the functional and technical issues of the existing proprietary mail system. These issues include difficulty of administration, functionality, connectivity, and security.

Administration

One administrative problem is the management of separate proprietary user directory services. Solving this problem requires the centralized management of another corporate directory of users, because management of multiple copies of the same information inevitably leads to out-of-date and unsynchronized information.

Functionality

Currently, users access their e-mail based on location; for instance, when a user accesses his or her e-mail on the corporate LAN, the e-mail is received differently from the user who accessed his or her e-mail from a remote dial-in connection. A universal access method is critical to establishing an easy-to-use and maintainable e-mail system.

Connectivity

With ACME's current mail solution, messages must go through a mail gateway conversion process in order to be delivered outside the company. Any type of message conversion can introduce errors, particularly during the conversion of message attachments and binary program files. Furthermore, a gateway institutes an unnecessary bottleneck for the entire system, an important factor as more corporate electronic mail is sent outside the company.

Security

Finally, ACME's proprietary mail systems contain propriety security mechanisms. Because these security methods are not transportable to other mail systems, any communications outside of the proprietary mail system (i.e., outside the company) are insecure. As communications between corporations increase, security of these communications becomes imperative.

Implementation and Architecture

The Netscape Messaging Server architecture shown in Figure 5.4 details only the locations at which mail servers are allowed through the corporate firewall. All other necessary mail servers will receive and send messages through the primary sending and receiving servers. Starting from the top of the diagram, the two Messaging Servers receive messages from the Internet from outside the firewall. These servers then forward the messages to one of two machines inside the firewall. This configuration

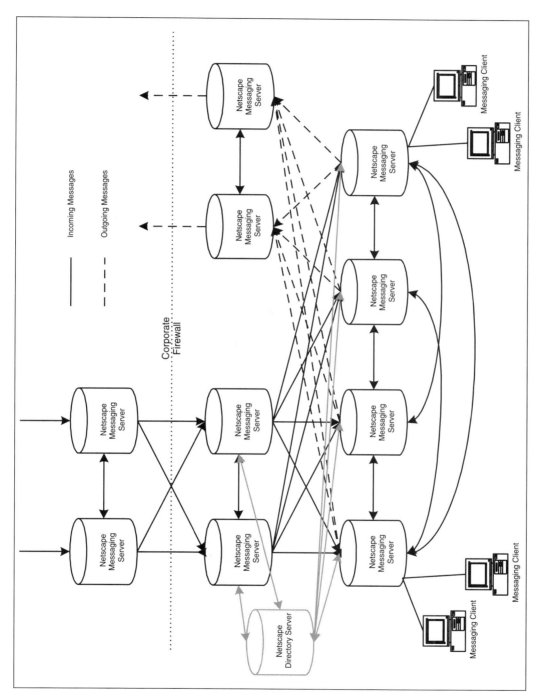

Figure 5.4 Netscape Messaging Server architecture.

is specified for both security (only these machines can cross the firewall on port 25 to go to one of two IP addresses using the SMTP protocol) and redundancy (optimally, the company should have redundant ISPs to provide failover contingency).

The two receiving machines immediately inside the firewall are used as message routers. Their main purpose is to forward messages to the specific machine in which the user's messages physically reside. These servers use ACME's central Netscape Directory Server to determine users' addresses and their primary messaging server for delivery information. Other Messaging Servers could be anywhere within the ACME intranet, including overseas branches. Two servers are used for redundancy.

The messaging servers depicted in the figure show a simple Messaging Server configuration. These servers handle all the messages for users. For additional reliability, these servers should be configured with RAID storage devices. Clients use their assigned messaging server to access their messages through the IMAP or POP.

Messages that are sent to other users within the ACME domain will be routed among the user-level messaging servers themselves using Directory Server queries. This means that internal messages never go through the messaging machines that are connected to the firewall.

External messages go through the external sending servers, which are the only messaging machines that are allowed to communicate outward through the firewall. Two servers are used for redundancy. For additional security, the user-level Messaging Servers are not allowed to send messages outside the firewall.

Deployment Locations

Anticipated Messaging Server locations are outlined in Tables 5.4 through 5.6 which use a conservative estimate of 700 users per mail server. The actual location of the mail servers is dependent on available network bandwidth. The exact number of users deployed on a single mail server will be determined during pilot testing. These numbers assume that all users will link via the connection-oriented IMAP protocol.

Sizing

Netscape Messaging Server machines must be fairly robust in configuration. Disk requirements are determined by the caching of messages for the messaging routers and external message receivers and senders. Disk usage on the servers that hold user message (user servers) stores is based

Table 5.4 Netscape Messaging Server Locations: Americas

User Location	Server	Server Location	Total Users	Logged-On (75%)	Active Users (25%)
Chicago	ns1.acme.com	Chicago	700	525	175
Chicago	ns2.acme.com	Chicago	200	150	50
New York	ns3.acme.com	New York	500	375	125
Los Angeles	ns4.acme.com	New York	500	375	125

Table 5.5 Netscape Messaging Server Locations: Asia

User Location	Server	Server Location	Total Users	Logged-On (75%)	Active Users (25%)
Hong Kong	ns5.acme.com	Hong Kong	500	375	125
Tokyo	ns6.acme.com	Tokyo	200	150	50
Singapore	ns7.acme.com	Singapore	100	75	25

Table 5.6 Netscape Messaging Server Locations: Europe

User Location	Server	Server Location	Total Users	Logged-On (75%)	Active Users (25%)
Paris	ns8.acme.com	Paris	500	375	125
London	ns9.acme.com	London	200	150	50
Frankfurt	ns10.acme.com	Frankfurt	100	75	25

Table 5.7 Netscape Messaging Server Hardware Guidelines

Hardware	External Mail Receivers	Message Routers	Internal User Mail Servers	External Mail Senders
Sun	Sparc 2/20	Sparc 2/20	Sparc 2/20	Sparc 2/20
Intel	Pentium 200MHz	Pentium 200MHz	Pentium 200MHz	Pentium 200MHz
HP	D-Class	D-Class	D-Class	D-Class
SGI	Challenge S 200MHz	Challenge S 200MHz	Challenge S 200MHz	Challenge S 200MHz
RAM	128 MB	256 MB	256 MB	128MB
Disk	2GB	2GB	1 GB + User Space Mirrored/RAID	2GB

on the quotas enforced by ACME. Messaging servers are normally light-bandwidth users and therefore often have little effect on existing network volumes, particularly when replacing an existing messaging system. Each end-user messaging server configured as detailed in Table 5.7 should be able to handle between 600 to 800 users. Information regarding exact number of users for IMAP support will have to be tested during a pilot phase of Netscape Messaging Server deployment.

Messaging Security

Security is a concern in messaging due to communication across the firewall. Internal messaging servers inside the firewall accept connections only from the two registered receiving servers or from themselves. No external connections are made, and these machines deal only with SMTP traffic, with no other services running. And, after ACME distributes client-side certificates, users can sign and/or encrypt messages using the Internet S/MIME standard for secure communication.

Users sending messages from Netscape Communicator follow these steps to send secure messages:

1. The message is written normally.
2. The message is addressed to the selected recipients.
3. The message is encrypted using each recipient's public key, then sent, and signed with the sender's private key.

At the receiving end, the following steps are used to decrypt:

1. The user retrieves the message from the Messaging Server.
2. Invoking the user's private key, the message is decrypted, and the signature is examined.
3. The signature is used to determine if the sender was the original author, or if the message has been tampered with.
4. If everything checks out, the message is displayed to the user.

Finally, users can also use client certificates to provide authentication for themselves to the Messaging Servers. This eliminates the need for usernames and passwords to retrieve messages.

Security Services

ACME would like to institute stronger security of information, but in a way that does not interfere with easy access to mission-critical information, messaging, and applications. Technology, as well as policies and procedure must be carefully implemented to ensure that employees can access data both securely and quickly. The decision to use strong authentication via certificate-based security offers a robust, yet transparent secure application and communications environment.

Netscape Certificate Server

To achieve a secure intranet, ACME must deploy access control faculties by registering users of the corporate intranet. This process involves issuing a public key to each employee empowered to access the corporate intranet. Public keys, also known as digital certificates, digital IDs, or digital passports are defined by an international standard called X.509, and are the digital equivalent of an employee badge, passport, or driver's license.

Using Netscape Certificate Server, ACME can build a secure infrastructure using X.509 certificates. Netscape Certificate Server allows a corporation to act as its own signing authority, whereby clients and servers can authenticate each other through the use of certificates. Using strong authentication, clients can present certificates instead of passwords to servers. Using these certificates means there are no passwords to compromise and no passwords to send over the network; furthermore, certificates contain public key information to allow encrypted communications. Authentication using server-side certificates assures the user of a secure server.

Current Environment

ACME's current network environment uses traditional security features; that is, username/password combinations are required throughout the corporation for information access. There is no data or transmission encryption in the current system. ACME is concerned about protecting its internal information as the company connects to the Internet, but it also wants to make security transparent to the user.

Implementation and Architecture

The public-key is stored in Netscape Directory Server. As such, a Netscape Certificate Server is recommended for each administration point (where users are created or removed) and one global Netscape Certificate Server for all regional certificate servers.

　　The high-level Netscape Certificate Server will be used to issue certificates to all subordinate certificate servers within ACME, and be at the top of ACME's certificate hierarchy (see Figure 5.5). This Certificate Server will certify the lower servers to issue certificates for ACME. This will al-

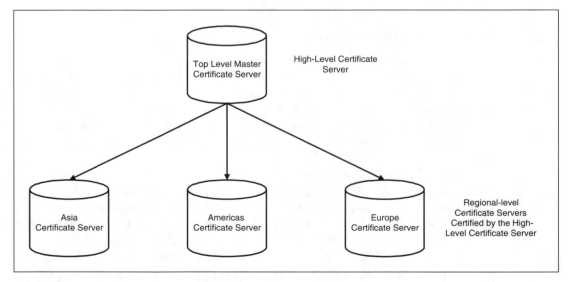

Figure 5.5 Netscape Certificate Server architecture.

Table 5.8 Netscape Certificate Server Locations

User Location	Server	Server Location	Potential Users
All Servers	cert1	Chicago	10,000
Americas	cert2	Chicago	10,000
Europe	cert3	Paris	10,000
Asia	cert4	Hong Kong	10,000

low regional administrators to issue user and server certificates that will be recognized and accepted throughout ACME's intranet.

CERTIFICATE SERVERS MAP TO DIRECTORY SERVERS

Typical Certificate Server architecture mirrors that of the Directory Server. Certificate Servers, like Directory Servers, are recommended for each location where users are administered.

Deployment Locations

Table 5.8 lists ACME Certificate Server locations.

Sizing

A Certificate Server can have a relatively low-end configuration, because disk and CPU usage are not particularly intensive. It is primarily the frequency and volume of certificate issuance and maintenance that determine higher configurations or multiple machines. Table 5.9 lists specifications for the servers recommended for standalone Certificate Servers. Certificate issuance is normally a scheduled event and has relatively low day-to-day use, so ACME may choose to install these servers on the same machine that holds the replica Directory Servers in each region. The initial deployment will call for four machines with this configuration.

Security

Security with Netscape Certificate Server is primarily procedural. The following rules of thumb should be observed.

Table 5.9 Netscape Certificate Server Hardware Requirements

Hardware	Certificate Server
Sun	Sparc 2/20
Intel	Pentium 200MHz
HP	D-Class
SGI	Challenge S 200MHz
RAM	64 MB
Disk	2+ GB

Netscape Certificate Server's private key is used to sign the certificates issued by the server. If this private key is compromised, all certificates that have been signed with this key will be compromised. Security of this key is vital for the security of the network.

Care must be used in the issuance of certificates. A valid certificate issued to an invalid person can be dangerous. Certificates should be issued through formal steps to confirm the identity of the users requesting certificates.

Certificate Attributes

An X.509 certificate is typically a small file containing several fields. Table 5.10 presents the minimum contents of an X.509 certificate.

In addition to the minimum fields shown, certificates may contain special data (in the form of X.509v3 extensions) that can be used to customize a site for a particular user. For example, the certificate might contain attributes such as Native language=English or Account Number= 1238X018 or Clearance=Top Secret. These attributes may control in which language the Web server presents its documents, which parts of the site a user may see (i.e., user privileges), or some other unique customization to meet ACME's needs. X.509 version 3 certificate extensions are powerful mechanisms by which to grant end users privileges (e.g., Read=ResearchPapers); however, certificate extensions should not completely replace a server-based access control model describing to which resources particular users have access. If a user's privileges are changed, certificates must be reissued and old certificate privileges must be revoked. In dynamic systems where information and user accesses change frequently, a server-based access control model may be much easier to

Table 5.10 X.509 Certificate Fields

Field	Description	Example
Subject's distinguished name (DN)	A name uniquely identifying the owner of the certificate.	C=US, O=ACME, OU= Accounting, CN=John Doe
Issuer's distinguished name (DN)	A name uniquely identifying the certificate authority that signed the certificate.	C=US, O=ACME, CN= Accounting Root
Subject's public key	The owner's public key.	512-bit RSA key
Issuer's signature	The certificate authority's digital signature from which the certificate derives its authenticity.	RSA encryption with MD5 hash (signature itself is not human readable)
Validity period	Dates between which the certificate is valid.	Not before Wed, Nov 9, 1995, 15:54:17 Not after Fri, Dec 31, 1997, 15:54:17
Serial number	A unique number generated by the certificate authority for administrative purposes.	02:41:00:00:01

administer. For ACME, a combination of X.509 attribute certificates and a server-based access control model offers the most flexible framework to support ACME requirements.

CERTIFICATE ATTRIBUTES

Although certificate attributes can be used to customize or tailor applications, changes to these attributes require regeneration and reissuance of these certificates. This attribute information is better stored in the Directory Server in intranet implementations.

Certificate Distribution

Employee X.509 certificates must be distributed between various servers and clients within the ACME intranet. For example, if an employee wishes to send a secure e-mail message to another employee, the message originator requires the recipient's X.509 certificate. The Netscape Directory Server provides the facilities to distribute certificates and employee information throughout the ACME intranet. As employee X.509 certificates are generated from the Certificate Server, it posts each certificate to a Directory Server for distribution throughout the intranet. The directory information tree held in the Directory Server reflects the distinguished naming hierarchy of the employee certificates.

A user's distinguished name embedded within the certificate locates the user within the directory tree. Alongside X.509 certificates, the Directory Server can store other information about ACME employees, such as e-mail address, phone number, and office location. In this way, the Directory Server can play dual roles; it can serve certificates to clients and servers requiring them to perform security-related operations, and it can serve as an online phone book/locator for internal ACME employee information.

After creating certificates, the Certificate Server uses the LDAP protocol to post them to a local Directory Server. Figure 5.6 shows the X.509 certificate creation and distribution architecture. Although the Directory Server can maintain up to 200,000 users in a database and service up to 100,000 queries per hour, ACME should deploy Directory Servers at its primary sites to limit risk in case of failure and to ensure high performance at remote sites.

Information Sharing and Management

As stated throughout the book, the core competency of intranet technology is the distribution of information in a one-to-many paradigm. It is no surprise, then, that information sharing and management is a central goal of the ACME intranet. The architecture recommended in this section is intended to build a publishing and distribution environment for ACME. Information sharing and management functionality will leverage the directory and security architectures implemented to provide communication services.

Current Environment

ACME's current publishing environment is largely document-centric, based on Microsoft Office formats. Distribution is accomplished through ad hoc e-mail attachments of these documents. As a result, e-mail is of-

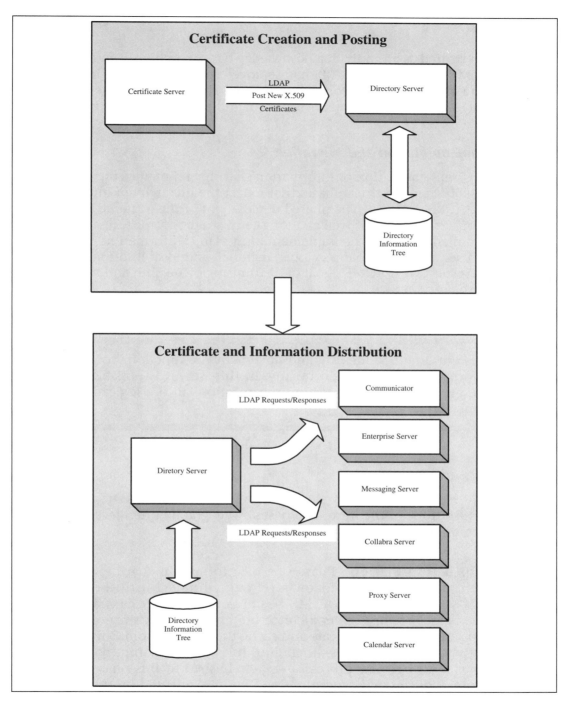

Figure 5.6 Certificate posting and distribution.

ten treated as an individual knowledge base or archive of information for ACME users; further ACME has deployed some Web servers internally. To date, the publishing process has required IT intervention for converting Microsoft Office documents to HTML and posting these to the intranet.

Implementation and Migration

The implementation of information sharing and management services will be staged in three phases that reflect the hierarchy of information in the ACME intranet. The phased deployment of the intranet will yield short-term results, as well as a long-term strategy for information sharing and management. The implementation plan is information-driven and focuses on the company's global, regional, and local information needs, consistent with ACME's goal of distributing ownership and management of the intranet.

IDENTIFY FUNCTIONAL ORGANIZATION

It is important to identify and document the functional organization of information within the company. In this way, it is possible to combine the geographic and functional organizations into a logically phased intranet deployment.

Phased Deployment

A phased deployment strategy prepares both the users and system administrators for the intranet. Phases by geography often leverage HQ information and move to lock information.

Global Information   Phase one of information sharing and management deployment will follow a centralized model with the master content server residing at ACME headquarters in Chicago. Similar to the Netscape Directory Server architecture, the company's regional hubs, Europe and Asia, will replicate and cache the content from Chicago. It is important that procedures—including rules of ownership, posting/staging policies, and review processes—be established in this phase. These publishing policies and procedures will be implemented by the entire company as the publishing process becomes more distributed.

ESTABLISH PUBLISHING POLICIES

By focusing on global information first, ACME will provide the company with useful information and be able to develop policies and procedures for publishing, system administration, and user access in the early stages of implementing the intranet. These policies will be important as the intranet is distributed.

Regional Information   Phase two of information sharing and management strategy will follow an information model similar to that of Phase one. Content sources will be maintained at the regional hub locations and distributed via proxy; in this case, the regional hubs will be able to create and publish regional content.

In this phase, Netscape Enterprise Servers will be deployed to the regional hub sites, and Netscape Proxy Servers to the local offices and at headquarters to provide enterprisewide access to regional information to all employees. This implementation strategy, too, is directed toward distributed ownership and management of information similar to the implementation of the ACME directory service. This enables each of the regional locations to create and manage its own content and share it with the rest of ACME through Netscape Proxy Server replication. The publishing procedures developed in phase one will be implemented as the standard for the regional locations.

Local Information   Phase three will focus on the creation and distribution of local content. Local offices will be provided with Netscape Enterprise Servers to enable the creation and publication of local information. This additional information could be replicated to Chicago and the regional hubs via Netscape Proxy Servers. The publishing procedures developed in phase one will be used as the standard for the local sites.

Content

Over time, the content of ACME's current communications systems will be migrated to the intranet. In the beginning stages, content creation is likely to remain an IT-intensive function, because conversion of Microsoft Office and other document-based information to HTML is required. As the system matures and the publishing function is distributed to the regional and local levels, the use of HTTP upload via Netscape Composer and Microsoft Internet Assistants will place the publishing function at the user level. In addition, the advanced authoring features of Netscape Composer and the Netscape Enterprise Server capability to store Microsoft Office documents natively will limit the need for conversions.

Netscape Enterprise Server also supplies document management tools to assist authors with the creation and publishing of information. Library services such as check-in and check-out which locks files so only one user can edit at a time, preserves document integrity in collaborative editing environments. Built-in version control automatically generates new versions of documents as they are updated, resulting in revision history that enables workgroups to coordinate their work and authors to easily reference old versions when necessary. Phase one will produce publishing procedures and site designs, including creating user directories and guidelines, to streamline the publishing process for users.

Load Balancing and Replication   ACME's central site in Chicago will require multiple servers to attain an acceptable level of performance and failover. Round-robin DNS will be used to achieve the load balancing against these servers. When a client asks for the IP address (for example http://acme.com) the DNS server will return one of several IP addresses, each of which corresponds to a different Web server and all of which have the same HTML content.

There are various tools with which to replicate information between the servers. Currently, these tools are custom-built applications that *push* or *pull* content between servers. ACME will use a custom-built HTTPut utility to synchronize the content of its Enterprise Servers (see Chapter 8 on replication for a description of HTTPut).

Replication of published documents will be provided through the standard Netscape Proxy Server replication functionality. This will enable access to global information almost immediately, while allowing time for application development in Chicago. Information flow in the phase one architecture consists of a strict pull of centralized global information from the company's headquarters.

Remote Access   Remote access will be achieved through existing network connections or dial-up from remote office locations. The remote offices would connect to the regional hubs for intranet connectivity. Since

ACME is distributing certificates to its users, the Internet could be used for secure remote connectivity using SSL and strong authentication.

Architecture Phase One: Global Information

The most leverageable information within the company, global information, refers to that which is germane to the whole company often centralized (see Figure 5.7).

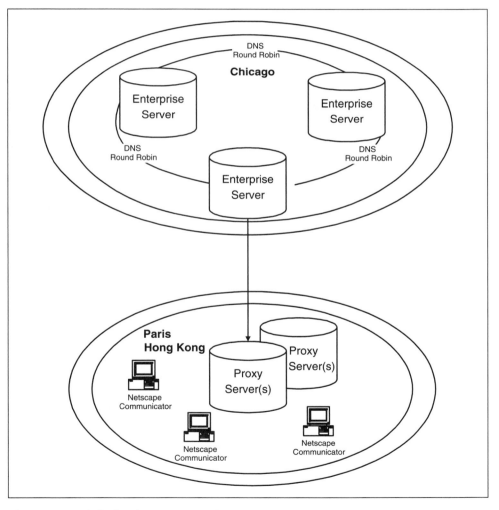

Figure 5.7 Global Information architecture.

Table 5.11 Netscape Enterprise and Proxy Server Locations: Phase One

User Location	Total Users	Enterprise Servers	Proxy Servers
Chicago	1,000	3	0
Paris	500	0	1
Hong Kong	500	0	1

Deployment Locations

Table 5.11 lists ACME Phase one server locations.

Sizing

Tables 5.12 and 5.13 provide hardware/software sizing guidelines for planning a corporate intranet.

Table 5.12 Netscape Enterprise Server Hardware Requirements

Hardware	Enterprise Server
Sun	Sparc 2/20
Intel	Pentium 200MHz
HP	D-Class
SGI	Challenge S 200MHz
RAM	128 MB
Disk	2+ GB

Table 5.13 Netscape Proxy Server Hardware Requirements

Hardware	Proxy Server
Sun	Sparc 2/20
Intel	Pentium 200MHz
HP	D-Class
SGI	Challenge S 200MHz
RAM	200+MB
Disk	2+ GB

Phase Two: Regional Information

After information hierarchy, regional information, that which is provided by the large regional offices, is the next to be addressed by the intranet (see Figure 5.8).

Locations

Table 5.14 lists ACME Phase Two server locations.

Phase Three: Local Information

After global and local information, there is an information lock to smaller offices within the company. Often this information is contained within a single office and shared along the employees there (see Figure 5.9).

Locations

Table 5.15 lists ACME Phase Three server locations.

Sizing

To generate precise hardware specifications for Netscape Enterprise and Proxy Servers, it is necessary to understand the nature of the data being generated and its volume. This will be an iterative process in establishing information sharing and management services on the ACME intranet. Sizing estimates identify a solid starting point based on experience with companies similar to ACME.

Netscape Enterprise Server Web server hardware requirements for intranets are strictly dependent on the application and information being served. A single CPU server with 128MB of RAM handles about one million hits per day. The configuration of three of these servers load-balanced using DNS round-robin will establish a strong starting point for ACME's central site. Each of the regional and local offices should start with a single server of this configuration. Of course, as the amount of information grows, more servers will be required at all sites, and can be added into the DNS round-robin configurations as needed. Later, additional Netscape Enterprise Servers should be deployed to handle each major intranet application. Dedicating a server per application enables it to

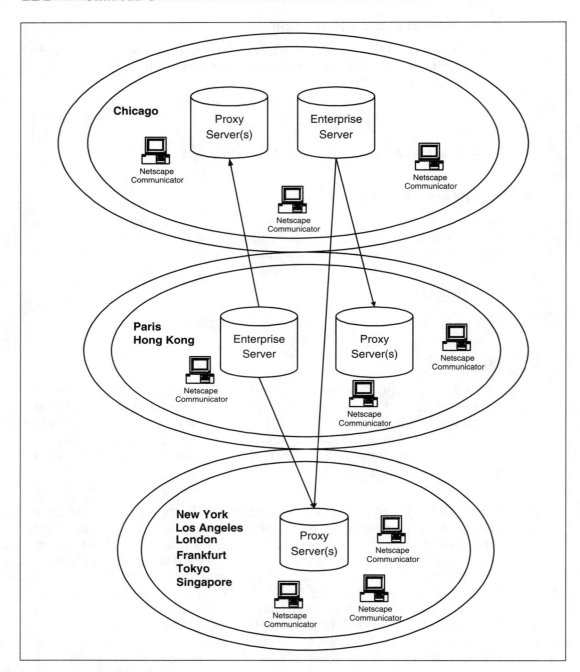

Figure 5.8 Regional architecture.

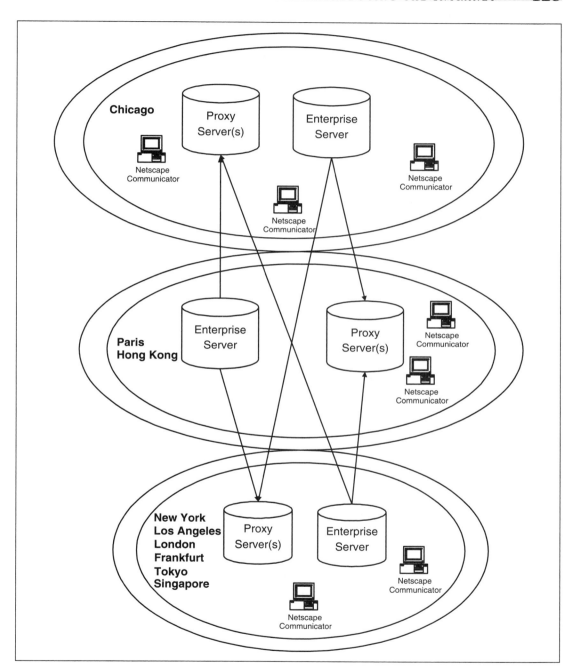

Figure 5.9 Local information architecture.

Table 5.14 Netscape Enterprise & Proxy Server Locations: Phase Two

User Location	Total Users	Enterprise Servers	Proxy Servers
Chicago	1,000	3	5
New York	500	1	1
Los Angeles	500	1	1
Paris	500	1	1
London	200	0	1
Frankfurt	100	0	1
Hong Kong	500	1	1
Tokyo	200	0	1
Singapore	100	0	1

Table 5.15 Netscape Enterprise and Proxy Server Requirements: Phase Three

User Location	Total Users	Enterprise Servers	Proxy Servers
Chicago	1,000	3	5
New York	500	1	1
Los Angeles	500	1	1
Paris	500	1	1
London	200	1	1
Frankfurt	100	1	1
Hong Kong	500	1	1
Tokyo	200	1	1
Singapore	100	1	1

be tuned precisely for the application and allows for better isolation of problems. Sizing application Web servers will be dependent on the needs of the application; such as database access or connections with a legacy system. Table 5.16 summarizes Enterprise Server configurations suitable for ACME.

Netscape Proxy Server   Netscape Proxy Servers should be implemented for each group of 300 to 1,000 users, which necessitates a dedicated single

Table 5.16 Netscape Enterprise Server Hardware Guidelines

Hardware	Enterprise Server
Sun	Sparc 2/20
Intel	Pentium 200MHz
HP	D-Class
SGI	Challenge S 200MHz
RAM	128 MB
Disk	2+ GB

CPU machine for each Netscape Proxy Server. Each Proxy Server runs approximately 32 processes, which require at least 64MB of RAM with a minimum of 128MB swap space. The size of the local cache on each server depends on the amount of data stored on the supplying servers. A 1 to 2GB hard drive is recommended for caching capabilities, considering the targeted organization.

If ACME decides to consolidate proxy servers, larger, multiple-CPU machines may be used in place of several smaller machines. A 512MB RAM dual-CPU machine could support 2,000 fairly active users. Both the proxy server and multiple-CPU machines are feasible alternatives. An initial process pool of 192 is recommended, and this number should be adjusted after real-world analysis is performed on proxy performance.

For local offices, one Netscape Proxy Server usually is sufficient. The machine running this server does not have to be dedicated to the Netscape Proxy Server, and can run 32 processes. A minimum of 250MB is recommended for disk-caching purposes. Table 5.17 summarizes Proxy Server configurations suitable for ACME.

Table 5.17 Netscape Proxy Server Hardware Guidelines

Hardware	Proxy Server
Sun	Sparc 2/20
Intel	Pentium 200MHz
HP	D-Class
SGI	Challenge S 200MHz
RAM	200+MB
Disk	2+ GB

Security

Intranet security is an important aspect of planning the ACME intranet. ACME would like to protect its internal information from unauthorized access from both outside and inside the company.

Netscape Enterprise Server   Netscape Enterprise Server supports LDAP to enable a centralized directory to track users and groups. Users and groups are implemented by the server to control access and to enable a single logon across all intranet resources. In addition, Netscape Enterprise Server makes use of strong authentication via client-side certificates. Running in secure mode, Netscape Enterprise Server can encrypt the transmission of data using the SSL protocol. As stated earlier, Netscape Enterprise Server can use Netscape Directory Server entries and their attributes to map access control to the resources it contains.

Netscape Enterprise Server supports flexible access controls that can be easily managed by the document's author. Authors can specify who can edit and view documents in the content store, thereby enabling workgroups to manage and share critical information. Flexible access controls grant fine-grained access to resources managed by Netscape Enterprise Server and integrate seamlessly with Netscape SuiteSpot's directory and security services. Internet-ready access controls go beyond user names and passwords, so that user access can be based on client certificates, domain names, and other Internet factors.

Netscape Proxy Server   Using Netscape Proxy Server, the network administrator can invoke a username/password, IP address, host name, or domain name to grant or limit access to network resources, including specific sites and documents. It also maintains access control as configured by the requested document's home server. In addition, the Proxy Server can run as a secure server via SSL, and act as the end point of an HTTP transaction. Until now, the Proxy Server has been able to accept only incoming HTTP. For secure administration, both Netscape Enterprise and Proxy Servers use SSL on the Administrative Server.

Navigation

Once ACME implements information sharing and management services for its users, the amount of information made available from departments and individuals will grow at a rapid rate. Because each department, and potentially each individual, may publish information, the possibilities for information sharing and collaboration multiply. The downside to this growing amount of information is that locating it in a timely fashion becomes more difficult. This dilemma is solved with Netscape Catalog Server.

Current Environment

Currently, ACME has no functional equivalent to these navigation capabilities except for the rudimentary manually maintained table of contents and basic file management functions. ACME recognizes the need for tools and applications that will allow intranet users to more easily find the information for which they are searching. In short, as more content is created in the corporation, an automated search and categorization process becomes more essential.

Implementation and Architecture

Netscape Catalog Server consists of two servers: the Resource Description Server (RDS) and the Catalog Server (see Figure 5.10). The RDS acts as a robot to retrieve content from remote sites or servers that are not running Netscape Enterprise Server. (The Enterprise Server has a built-in RDS server controlled by the autocatalog mechanism). The Catalog Server is a modified HTTP server that accumulates and indexes the resource descriptions generated by the RDS and Netscape Enterprise Servers. Complex queries can be made against the Catalog Server's database, given the structure of the documents. For example, users could search for documents based on subject, author, department name, department number, or document number, using the structure within the document's META tag data; documents could also be full-text searched based on relevancy. Redundancy can be achieved by configuring additional catalog servers that request only the resource description database from the Catalog Server that it is backing up.

DESIGN DOCUMENT META TAG STRUCTURE

A document should be created that details a set of required META tags that must appear in all documents on the intranet.

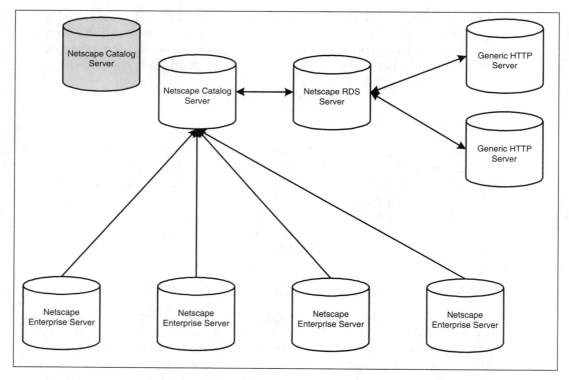

Figure 5.10 Netscape Catalog Server architecture.

Deployment Locations

The Netscape Catalog Server architecture is driven primarily by the availability of network bandwidth. ACME will require full replicas of the catalog in each regional hub location. Table 5.18 describes recommended Catalog Server locations.

Sizing

Catalog and RDS Server machine requirements (see Table 5.19) are similar to those required for an Enterprise Server. Disk usage is based on the amount of content and number of servers cataloged. Messaging between the RDS and Catalog Servers consume very little bandwidth. The RDS server's robots, however, consume a relatively large amount of bandwidth and should, therefore, be configured to crawl sites when

Table 5.18 Netscape Catalog Server Locations

User Location	Server	Server Location
Chicago	cat1a and cat1b	Chicago
Paris	cat2a and cat2b	Paris
Hong Kong	cat3a and cat3b	Hong Kong

bandwidth usage is minimal. Scaling the RDS servers to crawl more sites simply requires that additional RDS servers report back to the central Catalog Server. Scaling the Catalog Server to support greater numbers of users or more user activity requires adding more catalog replica servers.

An RDS server is not required to crawl a Netscape Enterprise Server, because the Netscape Enterprise Server is capable of responding to a Catalog Server directly. RDS servers are required only for external servers or internal servers that are not running the Netscape Enterprise Server.

Security User-level security is available for the Netscape Catalog Server, but all other security is enforced by the servers that house the content indexed by the Netscape Catalog Server. These servers control access to the full document content, and the Catalog Server provides a synopsis of each document in the results lists returned from queries. The extent of the document synopsis can be configured as appropriate for secure information.

Table 5.19 Netscape Catalog Server Hardware Requirements

Hardware	Catalog Server	RDS Server
Sun	Sparc 2/20	Sparc 2/20
Intel	Pentium 200MHz	Pentium 200MHz
HP	D-Class	D-Class
SGI	Challenge S 200MHz	Challenge S 200MHz
RAM	128 MB	64 MB
Disk	5-10 GB	2+ GB

Collaboration

Discussions

ACME would like to implement project and corporate discussion capabilities. Netscape Collabra Server, a high-performance, open standards-based discussion server with integrated encryption makes collaboration and knowledge sharing among teams of people inside and outside ACME easy, effective, and productive. It offers a comprehensive collaborative environment that ACME can use to share knowledge and enhance communication among a virtual community of employees, partners, and customers.

Current Environment

ACME currently does not have a collaborative discussion system, but would like to create a scalable, open solution that integrates with the intranet environment and results in a global collaborative environment.

Architecture

Netscape Collabra Servers can handle thousands of discussion groups and thousands of users, making only a relatively small deployment of servers necessary for ACME. Specifically, ACME's implementation will require two Netscape Collabra Servers for the Americas region, for the Asian region, and for the European region (see Figure 5.11).

Each server will be able to replicate discussion forums to other servers automatically using the Network News Transfer Protocol (NNTP). These would most likely be the corporatewide functions, such as human resources or corporate newsletters. These regional Netscape Collabra Servers could also house discussion groups that are not replicated, but that contain forums of local interest only. The discussion groups will likely fall into the global, regional, and local of information categories identified for information sharing and management services.

Deployment Locations

Table 5.20 lists ACME Collabra Server locations.

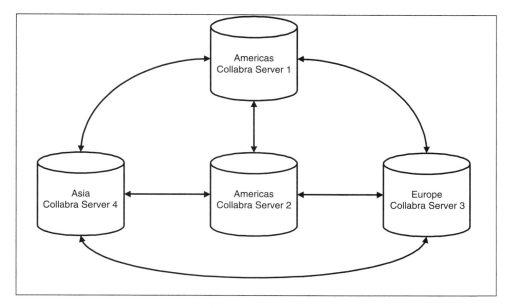

Figure 5.11 Netscape Collabra Server architecture.

Table 5.20 Netscape Collabra Server Locations

User Location	Server	Server Location	Potential Users
Americas	collabra1	Chicago	5,000
Americas	collabra2	Chicago	5,000
Europe	collabra3	Paris	5,000
Asia	collabra4	Hong Kong	5,000

Sizing

A Netscape Collabra Server machine does not have to be highly configured in terms of CPU, but rather make good use of additional memory, with incremental gains in performance with additional RAM. It can always use more disk space as discussion groups grow in number and size. Instead, server machine input/output (I/O) is based primarily on the number of network connections they serve. Table 5.21 lists the system configurations recommended for ACME.

Table 5.21 Netscape Collabra Server Hardware Requirements

Hardware	Collabra Server
Sun	Sparc 2/20
Intel	Pentium 200MHz
HP	D-Class
SGI	Challenge S 200MHz
RAM	128MB
Disk	5-10 GB - RAID

Security

Netscape Collabra Server uses three techniques to keep information secure.

1. **SSL.** Through the use of the snews (secure news) protocol, information exchanged between the client and the server is secured using public and private key encryption. SSL is the same underlying protocol that secures HTTP connections through HTTPS. Communications between two Collabra Servers is also secure.
2. **Client Certificate Authentication.** Through the use of client certificates, the Collabra Server can verify the identity of a user without an easily compromised password.
3. **Centralized Control.** Access control with LDAP integration to the Directory Server provides centralized access control management of private discussion groups.

Calendaring and Scheduling

Calendaring and scheduling are important capabilities to have when working in groups. ACME would like to pursue a collaborative calendaring solution that is tightly integrated with the browser-centric intranet, yet scalable to meet the needs of the growing company, and based on open standards.

Current Environment

ACME currently uses a mixture of proprietary collaborative scheduling tools, but would like to move to a more scalable, open solution that is integrated with the intranet environment and provides global scheduling services.

Architecture and Implementation

The first step in planning the deployment of Netscape Calendar Server is to determine the number of servers needed, based on the demographics of the company. Initially, users should be grouped by location and time zone. Users in the same time zone, but with different holidays, should be separated; for example, users in Toronto and New York City, although in the same time zone, celebrate different national holidays and thus should be treated separately. Users in small field offices should be counted as part of the nearest regional office.

IDENTIFY TIME ZONES AND REGIONS

Calendar Server nodes are assigned based on time zones, regions, and demographics of company locations.

The second step is to estimate the number of logged-on and active users of Netscape Calendar Server per time zone. This number is based on the total number of configured users per time zone, generally between 50 and 75 percent of the number of users. The number of active users is based on the total number of configured users per time zone, generally between 10 and 25 percent of that second number. The third step is to determine the number of servers needed to support these users. It is strongly recommended that servers be physically located near all major user population centers.

DETERMINE NUMBER OF USERS AND ACTIVITY

Calendar Server hardware sizing is connection-oriented and therefore based on numbers of active users.

Each Netscape Calendar Server ships with 10 serial numbers, one or more of which may be applied to a node. A serial number may be used only once, however, so the 10 must be allocated among the nodes within a server. Each serial number allows a node to contain up to 999 users; applying two serial numbers to one node would enable the node to grow to 1,998 users. The result is that a server may have no more than 10 nodes and no more than 9,999 users. However, for performance reasons, it is suggested that no more than 3,000 logged-on users be supported on any one server.

Architecture

One Calendar Server will be required in each of ACME's regions and each will have multiple nodes. The Americas region will host the Calendar Servers at ACME headquarters with a node for Central, Eastern, and Pacific time zones to support Chicago, New York, and Los Angeles, respectively (see Figure 5.12). The Asian region will host a server in Hong Kong with one node for Tokyo and a second node for Singapore and Hong Kong. Similarly, Europe will be served by one calendar server in Paris with two nodes; one for London, and one for Paris and Frankfurt. Table 5.22 shows the breakdown of these servers.

Sizing

After determining the number of nodes and servers required, this information can be factored in with the usage estimates established earlier to arrive at memory and disk requirements.

Memory Requirements   The amount of memory required per server is calculated by multiplying 350KB by the number of logged-on users for the server. If the server will support more than one node, multiply

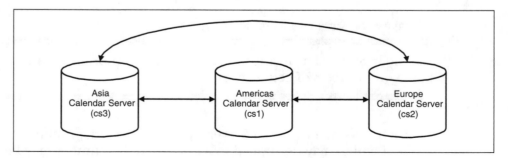

Figure 5.12 Calendar Server architecture.

Table 5.22 Netscape Calendar Server Locations

User Location	Server	Server Location	Node ID	Time Zone	Total Users	Logged-On (75%)	Active Users (25%)
Chicago	cs1	Chicago	1001	UTC-0600	1,000	750	250
New York	cs1	Chicago	1002	UTC-0500	500	375	125
Los Angeles	cs1	Chicago	1003	UTC-0800	500	375	125
Paris	cs2	Paris	1004	UTC+0100	500	375	125
FrankFurt	cs2	Paris	1004	UTC+0100	100	75	25
London	cs2	Paris	1005	UTC+0000	200	150	50
Hong Kong	cs3	Hong Kong	1006	UTC+800	500	375	125
Singapore	cs3	Hong Kong	1006	UTC+800	100	75	25
Tokyo	cs3	Hong Kong	1007	UTC+900	200	375	125

350KB by the number of users for all nodes. Add an additional 32MB for system use.

Disk Requirements   Each configured user requires approximately 2MB of permanent storage. If the server will support more than one node, multiply 2MB by the total number of users for all nodes. Add another 50MB for product files and logs, and add an appropriate amount for other storage not directly related to Netscape Calendar Server (e.g., operating system, system swap area, etc.).

   The amount of temporary storage required per server is calculated by multiplying 350KB by the number of logged-on users for the server. Servers supporting more than one node require a larger amount of temporary storage (400KB per user per node).

Additional Requirements   Each server has additional system-level storage and memory requirements that are not affected by the number of users. For planning purposes, each server will require 32MB of extra memory, and 50MB of disk space for Netscape Calendar Server software, including logs and executables. These numbers do not include operating system requirements, which may vary by vendor. For this implementation, the server configurations given in Table 5.23 are recommended.

Internet Access

ACME would like to provide Internet access to its users. Although ACME has concerns regarding security and employee misuse of the Internet, electronic access to free information and to customers and suppliers outweigh these concerns. The following architecture and implementation guidelines have been developed to provide Internet access in conjunction with strong security of internal information.

Current Environment

ACME currently does not have an Internet connection and would like to enable users to browse the Internet from within the company. A small number of users have contracted ISPs for personal Internet access, but no company standard has been established. ACME would like to establish a high-performance, secure link to the Internet for all users.

Table 5.23 Netscape Calendar Servers Hardware Requirements

Hardware	cs1	cs2	cs3
Sun	Sparc 2/20	Sparc 2/20	Sparc 2/20
Intel	Pentium 200MHz	Pentium 200MHz	Pentium 200MHz
HP	D-Class	D-Class	D-Class
SGI	Challenge S 200MHz	Challenge S 200MHz	Challenge S 200MHz
RAM	512-640MB	256MB	256MB
Disk	5+GB	2+GB	2+GB

Implementation and Architecture

ACME requires a combination of hardware and software products to establish a secure Internet connection to the intranet users: network routers, Netscape Proxy Server(s), and Firewall Servers. Connectivity to the Internet must be contracted from an Internet Service Provider (ISP). (Many local and long-distance carriers serve as ISPs for their regions.) The ISP makes connections at various speeds based on the number of users to be supported by that connection. Often, large companies contract with multiple ISPs as a failover measure to ensure coverage. This is specifically recommended for connectivity used for messaging traffic, to help ensure a 24×7 messaging environment. This will become more important as ACME extends its intranet to communicate with its customers and business partners. Internet connectivity is commonly centralized at the corporate headquarters and distributed throughout the company using the corporate WAN, and this is the recommendation for ACME's initial Internet access architecture (see Figure 5.13).

At the top of the figure, the T1 Internet connection is supplied by the ISP and is connected to a network router at ACME headquarters. The router dedicates the connection from the ISP to the single IP address of the firewall, a server machine within ACME. This firewall, in turn, connects only to the IP address of the server machine running the Netscape Proxy Server. The Netscape Proxy Server Machine can communicate only with the firewall B machine, which accepts connections from ACME users via the internal LAN. Limiting the Proxy Server to communicate with only the IP addresses of the firewall machines puts it inside

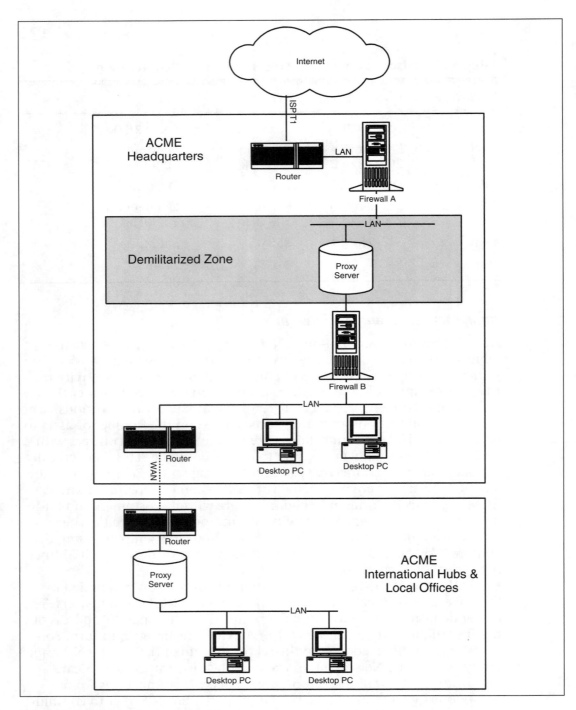

Figure 5.13 Internet access architecture.

what is commonly called the "demilitarized zone" (DMZ). The firewalls can be configured to allow only specified forms of network traffic on specific port numbers. For this implementation, the ports will be limited to those chosen for the Proxy Server and to HTTP traffic. Some router vendors offer software that also enables this type of filtering for double protection. The Netscape Proxy Server caches content from the Internet to save network bandwidth and improve performance. In addition, the Proxy Server can be configured to filter content and/or redirect URLs per ACME's policies to discourage and limit employee misuse of the Internet connection.

Initially, remote ACME sites will access the Internet via the internal WAN to minimize the cost and administration of multiple Internet connections. Netscape Proxy Servers will be deployed in each of the local offices to cache Internet content locally to limit WAN bandwidth utilization and improve performance. Depending on the volume of internal data, the Proxy Servers deployed for information sharing and management services can be used to support this architecture. If, however, over time, Internet usage escalates to a point that lowers the performance of the corporate WAN, ACME may choose to duplicate the headquarters architecture in each international hub location and contract with local ISPs in each region for Internet connectivity.

Deployment Locations

Table 5.24 lists ACME proxy server locations.

Table 5.24 Netscape Proxy Server Locations

User Location	Total Users	Proxy Servers
Chicago	1,000	1
New York	500	1
Los Angeles	500	1
Paris	500	1
London	200	1
Frankfurt	100	1
Hong Kong	500	1
Tokyo	200	1
Singapore	100	1

Sizing

The following section provides sizing information for the Netscape Proxy Server.

Bandwidth   ACME should expect an initial surge in Internet usage upon its introduction to the user community. After a few months, however, usage will likely flatten, then grow in a linear fashion. For this reason, an initial architecture has been suggested with options for growth. For a company of ACME's size, a single T1 connection should provide adequate bandwidth. A second T1 connection from a second ISP may be installed for redundancy, if desired, to provide a failover contingency for Internet access and messaging (see the Messaging section).

Server Hardware   As mentioned earlier, the Netscape Proxy Servers installed to supply information sharing and management services can be leveraged at the local office levels. The headquarters location should implement a separate hardware server for the Proxy Server within the demilitarized zone. These servers should follow the same hardware sizing guidelines given for information sharing and management services and shown again in Table 5.25.

Security

The architecture recommended for ACME is designed to enable access to the Internet while ensuring a high level of security for the company's internal data and systems. Simplicity is key. For this reason, separate server machines are recommended for each of the firewalls and Proxy Servers

Table 5.25 Netscape Proxy Server Hardware Requirements

Hardware	Proxy Server
Sun	Sparc 2/20
Intel	Pentium 200MHz
HP	D-Class
SGI	Challenge S 200MHz
RAM	128MB
Disk	5-10 GB - RAID

listed in the diagram shown in Figure 5.13. Although there are more physical devices, the overall architecture is easier to maintain, and achieves a higher level of security than is possible by combining many functions on one machine. For example, using separate machines for each of the firewalls allows specification of the hard-coded IP address of the Proxy Server in the demilitarized zone. This assures that the Proxy Server machine is the only physical device that may communicate with the firewalls.

Some companies use the restrictions built into routers as firewalls for Internet access, or combine the firewall and Proxy Server machines. However, because this type of architecture combines many functions on one physical device, there are more possibilities for penetration of the system. For example, if the Proxy Server and firewall A were combined on one machine, the IP address of that server machine would have access to the internal network to serve pages to users. Potentially this opens a hole in the security infrastructure of the Internet connection, in that if the IP address of the Proxy Server were spoofed, access to the internal network would be compromised. Of course, the security of any architecture can be compromised with enough effort, so ACME—and all companies—must make informed decisions regarding the nature of the information in the system and the corresponding level of security necessary to protect that information. The architecture outlined in this phase provides a high level of security with a simple architecture.

Conclusion

The ACME example provides a case study in intranet deployment. The concepts demonstrated in this case study are based on experience and can be applied to many companies interested in deploying intranet technology.

CHAPTER 6

INFRASTRUCTURE GUIDELINES

Network Requirements

As noted in the introduction to this book, we assume the decision to implement an intranet has been made and that Netscape has been chosen as the platform. We also assume that the underlying infrastructure for an intranet exists within the organization. Therefore, this section gives only cursory treatment of the underlying infrastructure associated with intranet technology, TCP/IP networks, and associated hardware and software.

TCP/IP

The root of Web technology is in a Transmission Control Protocol and Internet Protocol (TCP/IP) network. Most companies already have TCP/IP networks, are in the process of deploying TCP/IP, or plan to do so in the near future. TCP/IP will serve as the backbone for communication for years to come, and so there is little point in "selling" TCP/IP networking here. Although there are some solutions for bridging between IPX/SPX and TCP/IP, these are seen as transitional for companies making the switch. The bottom line is, TCP/IP must be in place to support intranet communications. This means that all client and server machines must have a TCP/IP stack installed locally and must be identifiable via IP addresses.

In addition to TCP/IP, certain standard services are required for intranet communications such as DNS, FTP, and Telnet. Domain Name Services (DNS) servers are necessary to resolve mapping of IP addresses to common names so that universal resource locators, URLs (home.netscape.com) can be used instead of IP addresses (205.217.237.31) to make connections. A DNS server should be running in each remote location to avoid address resolution over remote connections. File Transfer Protocol (FTP) can be used for copying files between machines, and Telnet enables connections to remote machines over TCP/IP.

Routers

At a very basic level, routers are hardware devices that are responsible for directing network traffic. A router that can support TCP/IP traffic is required for the deployment of an intranet. TCP/IP transmits information in the form of packets, each of which contains address information that determines the recipient of the packet. Routers accept these packets, interpret the address, and determine the best path for the packet across the network. Most existing networks have routers, so the important task here is to determine that the router can support TCP/IP traffic and the increased traffic that the intranet will bring to the network. At this juncture, it is also important to differentiate between routers and firewalls; in short, a router is not a firewall by itself.

Firewalls

To address the security concerns of companies, the firewall has become a requisite piece of the architecture that enables companies to provide secure access to the Internet to its users via the intranet. A firewall is software that works closely with router hardware to limit access to internal networks. Firewalls are used when connecting internal networks to the Internet, and most often are configured to grant access to the Internet for internal users and prevent internal access to external users. One way this is often accomplished is to deploy a Netscape Proxy Server along with the firewall tool, and configure the firewall to accept only TCP/IP connections from the singular IP address of the Proxy Server. In this way, the company can be assured that one, and only one, machine outside the firewall can access the internal network. Incidentally, the Proxy Server was designed for this purpose and therefore provides caching services to store copies of frequently accessed documents to improve performance for internal users. There are many vendors of firewall products, many of which ship with the operating systems.

An interesting point regarding firewalls is the role that they will play in the future of intranet technology. With the introduction of certificate-based authentication combined with data and transmission encryption, the line between the inside and outside of the firewall will blur considerably. Some companies, for example, have started to put intranet servers outside the firewall and leverage the Internet for communications. This movement will be augmented by the demand and utility of extranets enabling companies to communicate more closely with customers, partners, and suppliers. The firewalls will be moved back to protect the legacy systems, and then implemented at the points of integration with the intranet. As more data resides inside intranet technology and security becomes more granular and personalized, firewall lines may become nonexistent.

Bandwidth

Bandwidth is a measurement of the volume of traffic a network can support. How much is needed for the intranet is directly proportionate to the amount of anticipated data and usage patterns. One of the most commonly asked questions in intranet planning sessions is, "How much bandwidth will we need for the intranet?" The answer is, of course, "It depends." It depends first on the average size of the documents on the intranet, and second on the number of hits per document.

Determining an average document size is required before calculating usage metrics, which lead to bandwidth requirements. In general, pages made up of HTML text only should load within five seconds of the request for that page. Requests for pages with inline graphics should take no longer than 15 seconds to load. And pages with external objects with files embedded should take no longer than 30 seconds to load. Using these guidelines, it is possible to calculate the amount of bandwidth to serve a document with acceptable performance.

Hits are an important metric because they map directly to the number of requests made and fulfilled by the Web server, which is the reason Web server performance statistics are often given in number of hits rather than number of documents. The number of hits a document earns is a frequently misunderstood process. A hit represents a request to the Web server. Often, however, a hit is wrongly calculated on a one-to-one basis with the number of documents, when in fact a single document often receives numerous hits. It is true that a request for a document counts as a hit, but requests for each of the component parts of the document—such as frames, images, layers, embedded objects and files—also are hits. In fact, each frame is considered a small meta-document and requests for all of its contents also count as hits. Because of the appearance of increasingly complex Web pages, it is common for a single Web page to have upward of 50 hits.

Table 6.1 shows some simple calculations for the throughput of an intranet for various amounts of bandwidth.

The impact of an intranet on existing network bandwidth varies widely based on the number and size of the documents and the activity level of users. Although it is difficult to estimate numbers at all, it is safe to say that the introduction of intranet technology can add between 10 percent and 25 percent to existing bandwidth utilization when it is placed on top of existing systems. Intranet technology does, however, frequently have the effect of lowering bandwidth utilization when it replaces existing proprietary solutions. Overall, then, the impact of the intranet may net little or nothing to network bandwidth. The bottom line is often additional functionality without impact on the existing bandwidth. In general, analysts recommend that networks run between 10 percent and 60 percent utilization. If utilization is regularly above 60 percent, upgrades are often recommended to handle peak periods and future growth. Therefore, the introduction of the intranet without displacement of other systems will likely require network upgrades if current utilization is in the 30 to 40 percent range. Note that these estimates are very conservative and given only as general guidelines. Detailed network analysis is always encouraged.

For Internet access, Internet Service Providers (ISPs) supply connectivity based on the same bandwidth measurements just shown. Again, the bandwidth required for the intranet is dictated by usage. The standard Internet access connection for companies is a single T1 line. As shown in Table 6.1, a T1 connection can serve tens of thousands of documents per day. A general rule of thumb is to install one T1 connection for every 5,000 to 8,000 users. Many companies use these ISP connections to supply Internet access to their employees; host their external home page on the Web; and exchange e-mail with customers, partners, and suppliers. As a result, the connection to the Internet often becomes an essential part of doing business, and thus requires architectural redundancy to ensure uptime. For this reason, companies often install redundant connections by contracting with more than one ISP to insulate against network hiccups and outages.

Table 6.1 Bandwidth Estimations

Total Throughput of a Web Site

Connection	Max bw (MB/day)	Max bw (bytes/day)	Page Size in bytes	10% load (bytes/day)	50% load (bytes/day)	# hits/day at 10%	# hits/day at 50%
9600bps	79MB	82837504	61440	8283750	41418752	135	674
14.4bps	118MB	1.24E+08	61440	12373197	61865984	201	1007
28.8bps	236MB	2.47E+08	61440	24746394	1.24E+08	403	2014
56K	422MB	4.42E+08	61440	44249907	2.21E+08	720	3601
ISDN	675MB	7.08E+08	61440	70778880	3.54E+08	1152	5760
T1/DS-1	12GB	1.29E+10	61440	1288490189	6.44E+09	20972	104858
T3/DS-3	348GB	3.74E+11	61440	37366215475	1.87E+11	608174	3040870
10mb	108GB	1.16E+11	61440	11596411699	5.8E+10	188744	943718
100mb	1.08TB	1.16E+12	61440	115964116992	5.8E+11	1887437	9437184

Average Page Size in KB: 60

Minimum Bandwidth Needed to Deliver a Single Page

Assumptions: 1. It should take at most 5 seconds to send a page of HTML text.
2. It should take at most 30 seconds to send an external file (images, audio, etc.).

Connection	KB/sec	Size in KB of document 5-second send time (HTML text only)	Size in KB of document 5-second send time (HTML text + inline images)	Size in KB of document 30-second send time (external file)
9600bps	0.96	3.84	2.88	27.84
14.4bps	1.4	5.6	4.2	40.6
28.8bps	2.8	11.2	8.4	81.2
56K	5	25	25	150
ISDN	8	40	40	240
T1/DS-1	150	750	750	4500
T3/DS-3	4350	21750	21750	130500
10mb	1280	6400	6400	38400
100mb	12800	64000	64000	384000

Hardware Guidelines

An important step in planning any system is choosing hardware configuration to provide performance and reliability. While optimizing a system is an intensive process, some guidelines are provided below.

Servers

The capacity guidelines used to determine the sizing for the case study company, ACME, are based on mainstream server computers. For NT installations, the guidelines are based on 133MHz Pentium processor machines with 128MB RAM, and 2GB of hard drive space. The same guidelines apply to single-processor Unix servers with the same memory and hard drive configurations.

Internet/intranet architecture is distributed by nature. As such, recommendations for intranet architecture lean toward numerous servers, each dedicated to a service. To achieve the best performance and greatest reliability, there should be at least one hardware server for each of the SuiteSpot servers implemented. Frequently, multiple hardware and software servers are deployed to provide high performance and reliability to a large number of users. These groups, or clusters, of machines make up the hardware infrastructure of the full-service intranet.

Many companies, however, approach hardware infrastructure from the other direction, and buy highly configured "superservers" to minimize the number of physical machines to support. There are strategies for deploying multiple software servers on a single hardware server, but there is more risk involved with these types of architectures since a server failure translates to multiple unavailable network and user services. The bottom line is that a cluster of single-processor servers dedicated to single functions will outperform and achieve better overall performance than a single multiple-processor server running all of the SuiteSpot servers. In addition, a clustered architecture will provide built-in redundancy and better failover protection.

Clients

Hardware sizing requirements for the Netscape Communicator vary based on platform. The footprint and memory requirements for the Communicator have grown from the Navigator 3.0 with the introduction of new components and additional features. The Standard Edition of the Netscape Communicator requires approximately 16 to 32 MB of disk space and 8 to 16 (Windows/Macintosh) or 32 to 64 (Unix) MB of RAM, depending upon platform, encryption capabilities, and installed components. The Professional Edition requires from 20 to 40 MB of disk space and 10 to 18 or 32 to 64 (Unix) MB of RAM. Note, though, that by using the Administration Kit, it is possible to limit the components distributed to users and thus lower the hardware requirements for the product.

Software Guidelines

After determining the functional order of the intranet deployment, the next step is establishing an overall topology, or placement, of the SuiteSpot servers in order to deliver those functions or user services. Remember, the goal of the intranet, as with any system, is to provide users with functionality at a high level of performance. To achieve this goal, the SuiteSpot servers are deployed based on the number of users, the services provided to those users, and the existing network infrastructure within the company. These three factors drive many of the deployment and configuration decisions for the placement of SuiteSpot servers, all of which are remarkably scalable; in fact, if bandwidth were not an issue, a simple centralized server deployment would be an easy solution. But because network bandwidth and connectivity are expensive, the centralized model, while simple, becomes impractical. To address these bandwidth constraints, servers are often deployed in a distributed fashion to minimize bandwidth utilization.

As discussed previously, two approaches are commonly used to deploy intranets: *reactive* and *proactive*. The reactive approach is often used in conjunction with the chaotic Internet model of deploying the intranet. In this model, grassroots efforts drive the implementation process, and IT departments inherit the maintenance of the eclectic system. To continue this model, servers are deployed one after another on the same machine until performance problems arise; then more hardware is purchased and the servers are distributed. Obviously, this can have negative implications for a system that will inevitably be mission-critical to company operations. This model inevitably leads to retrofitting the existing system in order to achieve an adequate level of service. Furthermore, standards are often difficult to implement in this environment, which eventually necessitates a grand restructuring or redeployment of the intranet.

In contrast, the proactive method of deployment, while somewhat counter to the organic Internet culture, has proven successful for many companies that intend the intranet as the future platform for corporate communications. In this model, the existing infrastructure and the location of users drive the deployment of an intranet that will be easily scalable and maintainable over time. The following subsections list high-level guidelines for proactively planning the intranet, and detail each of the SuiteSpot servers. A case study follows to demonstrate these guidelines in practice.

Enterprise Server

The following section summarizes hardware guidelines for the Netscape Enterprise Server. These guidelines should serve as a starting point for intranet planning. Iteration is always needed to optimize in a given environment.

Information Sharing and Management Guidelines

- ❑ Assign approximately 1,000 users (1,000,000 hits/day) per Enterprise Server.
- ❑ Install Enterprise Servers near authors/publishers.
- ❑ Clustered server architectures are better than one "superserver".
- ❑ Deploy servers in each location with 10 or more users who create content.

As the central information store and application platform, many factors impact the sizing of Enterprise Servers in the intranet: the number of users, the usage patterns of those users, and the nature of the services being provided to those users. Using the standard hardware guidelines, a typical Enterprise Server can handle 1 million hits/connections per day. As a general rule, this will support 1,000 very active users of information sharing and management within an intranet, including the information access and publishing functions. Note that this configuration could support more users depending upon the number and activity of publishers and surfers, but starting with 1,000 users per server leaves room for growth and makes system administration of user and group space more manageable.

There are two ways to increase the intranet's capacity by altering the configuration of the hardware on which the Enterprise Server is installed. The first, increasing the number of CPUs, the RAM, or disk space can address certain capacity constraints by giving the machine greater power. This is used most often to address processing bottlenecks for intranet applications rather than to support greater volumes of information. Input/Output, I/O, the amount of information that a machine can give and receive over a network, is the most common bottleneck for intranet systems. I/O can be increased by adding to the number of machines that perform a given task. The second way, creating groups or clusters of server machines, is the best way to increase both the processing power and I/O of the system. Consequently, using multiple machines, or clustered architecture, is often recommended for intranets. By definition, clustered architectures provide built-in redundancy and failover, and eliminate a single point of failure on both hardware and software.

In addition to capacity considerations, the deployment of the SuiteSpot servers is primarily driven by the functional needs of the users, secondly by the existing network topology/infrastructure, and finally by the capacity those servers can support. For this reason, the topology of the existing network infrastructure, combined with the functional needs of the users, dictate the placement of hardware and software servers. For information management and sharing, there are two constituent groups of users: authors and viewers. These roles obviously overlap, and for some companies, every employee is a potential author. To make authoring available, users need a place to publish to—space on an Enterprise Server. Because authoring and publishing are ongoing and iterative processes, Enterprise Servers are often necessary at each author location to allow local publishing of documents rather than remote publishing via a WAN. This enables authors to create and edit files locally without consuming WAN bandwidth in the highly iterative authoring process. Similarly, multiple Enterprise Servers may also be needed at a location to make publishing to separate functional groups possible, and thus bring the content closer to the author.

Along with delivering the technology required for authoring, policies and procedures are required to guide authors, to identify which areas on the servers are allocated for use, which creation tools are recommended, which conversion tools are available, and who is responsible for releasing/publishing information to the intranet. These policies are often extensions to existing procedures, but for many companies key goals of the intranet are to *distribute* and *delegate* the responsibility for publishing information—to bring the tools to the desktop and empower users to publish and distribute information more efficiently within the company.

Intranet Applications Guidelines

❏ Separate Enterprise Servers should be installed for each application.

❏ SSL, CGI, NSAPI, and parsed HTML require more highly configured machines to serve the same number of users.

❏ Separate Enterprise Servers should be installed for information that requires SSL.

Many applications involve access to information that is stored in legacy systems and/or relational databases. Depending on the architecture and technologies, a database may be 10 to 100 times slower than static HTML. There are different methods for connecting to databases: CGI programs and Netscape's Server Plug-In API or LiveWire.

The Common Gateway Interface (CGI) is the traditional mechanism by which Web servers run server-side programs or scripts to perform processing, communicate with databases, and produce formatted information to the user. CGI programs can be written in many languages—C/C++, Java, Perl, and others. Compiled C code yields high performance for applications, but CGI programs running in compiled C are at least 10 times slower than serving HTML, and CGI programs written in Perl or other interpreted languages are at least 20 times slower than HTML. Decreased performance and processing often require a dedicated Web server (hardware and software) to distribute system load. Applications often involve server-side processing, so these servers can benefit from higher-end configurations (multiple CPUs and increased RAM). CGI programs create, or "fork" a new process on the Web server machine and therefore execute outside of the Web server.

Server plug-ins or programs that make use of the Netscape Applications Programmer Interface (NSAPI) modify the base code of the Web server via C/C++ programs. These programs are executed as part of the server process and most often are used to modify the behavior of the Enterprise Server (something that the server does for every request). For example, NSAPI is often used to modify/augment the logging functions of the Enterprise Server to include more detailed information. NSAPI programs, though high performance, can be difficult to maintain across versions of the Enterprise Server. For this reason, Netscape has released Internet Foundation Services (IFS) as part of Netscape ONE to allow for low-level, portable modifications to the Enterprise Server. Furthermore, NSAPI programs add to the processing requirements of the server and therefore impact performance metrics.

LiveWire is often used for applications that access databases; it executes within the Enterprise Server process and is therefore less taxing on the server machine. The communication and state management require-ments of database applications do, however, increase the processing re-quirements of the Web server.

All applications introduce processing requirements to the Web server. In addition, applications are normally function-specific; that is, they ad-dress a particular user need. For these reasons, it is recommended that ap-plications be kept separate from the basic information sharing and management of the intranet to reduce the risk of single point of failure. This can be achieved by installing an Enterprise Server on the same phys-ical machine as the database or by installing a separate physical server for the application. As for publishing, separating servers provides for better system maintenance.

SSL   Recall that the Secure Sockets Layer (SSL) is a network protocol layer that runs on top of TCP/IP and encrypts the data transmissions be-tween an intranet client and server. A dynamic encryption key with which the data is encrypted is agreed on and generated by the client and server. This key is regenerated every 90 seconds to protect against infiltra-tion. With SSL activated, the server must encrypt the data before it sends responses to client requests. Similarly, the client must decrypt the data upon receipt. Combined with the key generation, this process is signifi-cantly more complex and requires additional processing power on the server and the client. On average, performance decreases between 50 per-cent and 60 percent when using SSL/HTTPS, as opposed to running sim-ple HTTP. This fact often makes companies more selective in terms of the information for which encrypted transmission is "required."

To support SSL/HTTPS, more highly configured machines are often recommended. Multiple CPUs help to speed the encryption and decryp-tion algorithms, as do increases in RAM. The rule of thumb is to double the amount of CPU and RAM from servers that are sized for simple HTTP.

Server-Parsed HTML   HTML documents are normally delivered to the client with the same content that resides in the file located on the Web server. Prior to sending them to the client, the Netscape Enterprise Server can be configured to search, or parse, through documents for specific HTML tags, and insert information at these points in the documents. Server parsing is most often used to insert request-specific information into a document to add dynamic information to otherwise static pages. Though used much less frequently, server-parsed HTML (SHTML) impacts performance in a way similar to SSL. Because SHTML requires the server to parse the entire HTML document and potentially process and insert in-

Table 6.2 Netscape Enterprise Server Hardware Guidelines

Hardware	Enterprise Server
Sun	Sparc 2/20
Intel	Pentium 200MHz
HP	D-Class
SGI	Challenge S 200MHz
RAM	128 MB
Disk	2+ GB

formation before sending it to the client, it is three to four times slower than static HTML.

Unlike SSL, though, SHTML is not a full on-or-off decision for the entire server. Server parsing can be configured to parse a subset of the documents on a server by file extension (.shtml) or by the status of an execute bit on the file. In Table 6.2, you will see hardware requirements for Netscape Enterprise Server.

Messaging Server Guidelines

The following section summarizes hardware guidelines for the Netscape Messaging Server. These guidelines should serve as a starting point for intranet planning. Iteration is always needed to optimize in a given environment.

- A Messaging Server can support 2,000 to 3,000 users with POP3 delivery.
- The same Messaging Server can support 1,000 to 1,500 users with IMAP4 delivery.
- A Messaging Server should be deployed in each location with more than 10 users.

Netscape Messaging Server machines must have fairly robust configurations. Disk usage is based on the message caching for the mail routers, external mail receivers, and external mail senders. Disk usage on the servers that store user mail is based on the quotas enforced by system administrators.

The Netscape Messaging Server can interface with messaging clients using two delivery methods: IMAP4 and POP3. IMAP4 is the next generation of Internet mail; it provides greater flexibility and control of messages. IMAP4 and POP3 differ in the way the client connects to the server to receive messages. For POP3, connectivity is an on-command, all-or-nothing download of messages. Analogous to the stateless connectivity of HTTP, using POP3, a request is made from the client to the server, and the server fulfills that request and waits for the next request. For this reason, the connections and utilization of the server are sporadic and short-lived when a client connects using POP3. IMAP4, on the other hand, connects to the server when a user logs in to the mail account and maintains that connection until the user logs out of the account. By maintaining a session between the client and the server, it is possible to provide richer functionality, such as partial downloads of messages and on- off-line folders. This stateful environment means that connectivity to the server is more constant with fewer smaller downloads of messages (see Figure 6.1).

Assuming that users normally log in to their mail accounts in the morning and keep them up most of the day, the overall impact is that IMAP4 has greater base I/O requirements than POP3. The result is that a

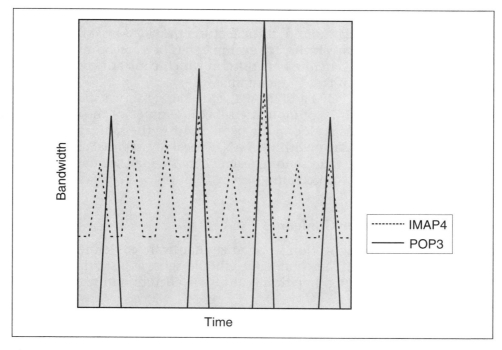

Figure 6.1 Messaging Server connectivity.

Table 6.3 Netscape Messaging Server Hardware Guidelines

Hardware	Messaging Server
Sun	Sparc 2/20
Intel	Pentium 200MHz
HP	D-Class
SGI	Challenge S 200MHz
RAM	128MB
Disk	1 GB + User Space Mirrored/RAID

server responding to IMAP4 connections from the client often supports a fewer number of users than one responding to POP3 client connections. Whereas a single Messaging Server can support as many as 2,000 to 3,000 users with POP3 delivery, it will support approximately 1,000 users connecting via IMAP4 with the configurations listed in Table 6.3. Choosing to use IMAP4 or POP3 is made on the client side via messaging preferences, and can be locked using the Administration Kit. POP3 should be implemented in environments where constant network connections are difficult to maintain or if the features provided by IMAP4 are not needed by the end user. POP3, for example, has been recommended for companies running satellite networks, in which constant connections can be costly and difficult to maintain.

For both POP3 and IMAP4, a Messaging Server should be deployed at each site with 10 or more users, because much of the messaging in office environments is among the people within the same office. By routing intraoffice messages within a LAN, a local Messaging Server is much more cost-effective than sending each client's e-mail separately through the regional WAN connection.

Proxy Server Guidelines

The following section summarizes hardware guidelines for the Netscape Proxy Server. These guidelines should serve as a starting point for intranet planning. Iteration is always needed to optimize in a given environment.

- ❏ A Proxy Server can support 300,000 hits per day (300 to 1,000 users depending on activity).
- ❏ A Proxy Server should be deployed in each location with 10 or more users.

❑ For Internet caching, one Proxy Server for every 500 users should be deployed at the firewall.

❑ Automatic Proxy Configuration, rather than specific Proxy Server assignments, should be used for distributing clients.

❑ Proxy chaining should be used to most efficiently use Proxy Server resources in multiserver configurations.

Proxy Servers should be implemented for each group of 300 to 1,000 users. This requires a dedicated single CPU machine for each Netscape Proxy Server, which runs approximately 32 processes, requiring at least 64MB of RAM with a minimum of 128MB swap space. The size of the local cache on each server depends on the amount of data stored on the supplying servers. A 1 to 2 GB hard drive is recommended for disk-caching space.

Proxy Servers can benefit from higher-end configurations to support a larger user group with fewer physical servers. For example, larger, multiple-CPU machines may be used in place of several smaller machines; a 512MB RAM dual-CPU machine could support 2,000 fairly active users. Depending upon the company's preference, to administer many small machines or to have a few large central machines to administer, both are feasible alternatives for the Proxy Server. An initial process pool of 192 is recommended, but this number should be adjusted after real-world analysis is performed on proxy performance. For smaller offices, a single Netscape Proxy Server is often sufficient. The machine running this server does not have to be dedicated to the Netscape Proxy Server, and can run 32 processes. A minimum of 250MB is recommended for disk-caching purposes.

With the configurations listed in Table 6.4, a Proxy Server can serve approximately 300,000 requests per day. To replicate intranet content, one Proxy Server should be deployed at each site of more than 10 peo-

Table 6.4 Netscape Proxy Server Hardware Guidelines

Hardware	*Proxy Server*
Sun	Sparc 2/20
Intel	Pentium 200MHz
HP	D-Class
SGI	Challenge S 200MHz
RAM	200+MB
Disk	2+ GB

ple. For replication Internet content, one Proxy Server should be installed at the corporate firewall for every 500 users. Each Proxy Server user should be allocated approximately 2 GB of disk space for caching storage.

In the past, each client had to be configured to use a specific Proxy Server, but no more, thanks to a new feature available in the Proxy Server called Automatic Proxy Configuration. Instead of pointing the client at a specific Proxy Server, a URL may be inserted into the proxy configuration that points to an automatic configuration file located on a Proxy Server. This file then dynamically assigns the client to a Proxy Server for that session. This file can be changed periodically by a system administrator in order to provide load balancing across multiple Proxy Servers, and to alter the proxy architecture without modifying client preferences. In this way Proxy Servers can be added to the intranet, which is transparent to the end user. In addition, the automatic configuration files can specify a back-up Proxy Server to provide important failover and redundancy for information sharing services.

When Proxy Servers are added to the intranet, they can be configured to cache specific or distinct areas of content. One server can be set up to cache only marketing content, while another can be earmarked for engineering content. These servers can then be linked, or *chained*, to provide seamless content caching to the end user. Proxy chaining makes the most efficient use of additional Proxy Servers and storage space to provide faster performance and transparent caching to the end user.

Netscape Collabra Server Guidelines

The following section summarizes hardware guidelines for the Netscape Collabra Server. These guidelines should serve as a starting point for intranet planning. Iteration is always needed to optimize in a given environment.

- ❏ One Collabra Server can support approximately 3,000 to 4,000 non-Usenet users.
- ❏ One Collabra Server can support approximately 1,000 Usenet users.
- ❏ Deploy a Collabra Server in each location with 10 or more users.

The Collabra Server is based on tried-and-true Internet News NNTP standards, therefore, it can be used to provide seamless access to Usenet news and discussions via the Internet. These newsgroups, however, tend to be very content-intensive and thus require far more resources than a

Table 6.5 Netscape Collabra Server Hardware Guidelines

Hardware	*Collabra Server*
Sun	Sparc 2/20
Intel	Pentium 200MHz
HP	D-Class
SGI	Challenge S 200MHz
RAM	128MB
Disk	5-10 GB - RAID

typical internal Collabra installation. For this reason, although a single Collabra Server can support 3,000 to 4,000 non-Usenet or internal corporate users, it can support only some 1,000 users when connected to external Usenet newsgroups. When deploying multiple Collabra Servers at a site, each server should be configured to host different newsgroups to distribute the resource load.

As with IMAP4 connections to the Messaging Server, client connections to Collabra Servers remain open while the user is logged in, so whenever possible, the Collabra Server should be deployed locally to limit the network impact of users connecting via a WAN.

A Collabra server machine does not need to be particularly heavy in terms of CPU, because it makes good use of additional memory and will always use more disk space. Primarily, the number of network connections is the limiting factor in server sizing. As in the Messaging Server, Collabra files are stored in standard file system format, so hardware failover security is best provided by RAID. Table 6.5 shows Collabra Server guidelines.

Catalog Server Guidelines

The following section summarizes hardware guidelines for the Netscape Catalog Server. These guidelines should serve as a starting point for intranet planning. Iteration is always needed to optimize in a given environment.

❑ A Catalog Server can index approximately 150,000 documents.

❑ A Catalog Server can typically support 8,000 users.

❑ Deploy one Catalog Server in each location with 500 or more users.

As noted earlier, the Catalog Server consists of two distinct servers: the Resource Description Server (RDS) and the Catalog Server. The RDS acts as a robot to retrieve content from remote sites or servers that are not running the Netscape Enterprise Server. The Catalog Server is a modified HTTP server that accumulates and indexes the resource descriptions from the RDS and Enterprise Servers.

Catalog and RDS Server machine requirements are similar to those for a medium-level HTTP server. Disk usage is based on the amount of content and number of servers cataloged. Messaging between the RDS and Catalog Servers uses very little bandwidth. The RDS Server's robots are usually set to crawl sites when bandwidth usage is minimal. Scaling the RDS Servers to crawl more sites simply requires adding more RDS Servers to report back to the central Catalog Server; scaling the Catalog Server to support more user activity requires additional Catalog Servers.

An RDS Server is not required to crawl a Netscape Enterprise Server, because the Netscape Enterprise Server is capable of responding to a Catalog Server directly. RDS servers are required only for external servers or servers that are not using the Netscape Enterprise Server.

A Catalog Server can itemize approximately 150,000 documents, and serve some 100,000 queries per day, or support 8,000 users depending upon activity. As content grows, additional Catalog Servers can be deployed or hardware can be upgraded on existing servers. A Catalog Server should be deployed at the central or home-page site and at each site with more than 500 users. Because users make occasional requests to the Catalog Server, it is often deployed centrally and accessed by remote locations via the WAN. The break-even point for WAN bandwidth and number of users is approximately 500, when the number and frequency of user requests becomes large enough that performance and bandwidth utilization warrant deployment of a local Catalog Server. Refer to Table 6.6 for Catalog Server hardware guidelines.

Table 6.6 Netscape Catalog Server Hardware Guidelines

Hardware	Catalog Server	RDS Server
Sun	Sparc 2/20	Sparc 2/20
Intel	Pentium 200MHz	Pentium 200MHz
HP	D-Class	D-Class
SGI	Challenge S 200MHz	Challenge S 200MHz
RAM	128 MB	64 MB
Disk	5-10 GB	2+ GB

Directory Server Guidelines

The following section summarizes hardware guidelines for the Netscape Directory Server. These guidelines should serve as a starting point for intranet planning. Iteration is always needed to optimize in a given environment.

❑ One Directory Server can maintain more than 1,000,000 resource entries.

❑ One Directory Server can handle more than 300,000 queries per hour.

❑ A Directory Server should be deployed in any location where user information is maintained.

The first major task for implementation of directory services is to identify where users and resources will be located in the intranet. This involves assigning responsibility to system administrators to create, modify, and delete users and resources from the intranet directory. The second step in Directory Server deployment is to accurately define a directory schema, which necessitates mapping the organization to a data hierarchy that represents the company. The third deployment task is to populate the Directory Server through conversion of an existing directory. The Directory Server uses an import/export file format called Light Data Interchange Format (LDIF), an ASCII text format that maps to the LDAP directory format. The Netscape Directory Server includes tools for conversion from cc:Mail and others, and has a synchronization tool for running Windows NT directory in tandem with the Directory Server. In addition, Lotus, Microsoft, and most vendors have announced or already support an LDAP gateway to their directories, enabling querying by any client or program via the LDAP protocol.

The Directory Server is at the center of the login process for all Netscape Servers. As such, it must be a readily available system, implemented with redundancy and failover in mind. A Directory Server machine can be relatively small, as disk and CPU usage are not particularly intensive. The number of network connections is the primary limiting sizing factor for the Directory Server. Consequently, multiple physical machines distributed throughout a company's WAN are often recommended to provide redundancy and failover resiliency for the intranet. Using the configurations listed in Table 6.7, a single Netscape Directory Server can contain more than 1,000,000 resource entries and handle up to 300,000 or more queries per hour.

Table 6.7 Netscape Directory Server Hardware Guidelines

Hardware	Directory Server
Sun	Sparc 2/20
Intel	Pentium 200MHz
HP	D-Class
SGI	Challenge S 200MHz
RAM	128 MB
Disk	2+ GB

To facilitate the distribution and redundancy requirements of directory services, the Netscape Directory Server has sophisticated replication features. For example, specific branches of a directory tree can be owned or supplied in a distributed fashion; subsequently, those ownership properties can be dynamically switched in failover situations. In addition, because of the inherent efficiency of the LDAP protocol, many companies maintain several full-replica copies of their directory to provide full, instantaneous recovery should one server go down. Similar failover strategies as those used with the Enterprise Server can be employed with the Directory Server, such as DNS rename to automatically redirect users.

Certificate Server Guidelines

The following section summarizes hardware guidelines for the Netscape Certificate Server. These guidelines should serve as a starting point for intranet planning. Iteration is always needed to optimize in a given environment.

❑ One Netscape Certificate Server can maintain 15,000 users in a database.

❑ One Netscape Certificate Server can handle up to 100,000 queries per hour.

❑ Certificate Servers are commonly deployed in the same locations as Directory Servers, wherever user info is generated, maintained, and deleted.

Netscape Certificate Server is used to create, sign, revoke, and manage digital certificates, which enable applications such as Netscape Communicator and Netscape SuiteSpot to communicate privately using Secure Sockets Layer (SSL).

Table 6.8 Netscape Certificate Server Hardware Guidelines

Hardware	Certificate Server
Sun	Sparc 2/20
Intel	Pentium 200MHz
HP	D-Class
SGI	Challenge S 200MHz
RAM	64 MB
Disk	2+ GB

For those companies that want strong authentication of users and servers throughout the intranet, each server and user must be issued a certificate. The public key certificates are stored in the Netscape Directory Server with each user entry, therefore, it is recommend that a Netscape Certificate Server be deployed at each administration point (where user information is generated, maintained, and deleted), along with one central Certificate Server for creation of all the regional certificate servers.

A certificate server machine can be relatively small, as disk and CPU usage are not particularly intensive. It is important, however, to install a Certificate Server on a dedicated machine that can be physically isolated, because it holds the CA key from which all certificates issued are based. If the Certificate Server key is compromised, so are all of the certificates it has issued. The configurations shown in Table 6.8 should be used for Certificate Servers.

Calendar Server Guidelines

The following section summarizes hardware guidelines for the Netscape Calendar Server. These guidelines should serve as a starting point for intranet planning. Iteration is always needed to optimize in a given environment.

- One Calendar Server can support up to 3,000 users.
- Users should be grouped by time zones, and each time zone should be assigned a separate node.
- Hardware sizing is dictated by the number of active and logged-in users for each server.

The first step in planning the deployment of Netscape Calendar Server is to determine the number of servers needed based on the demographics of the company. Initially, users should be grouped by location and time zone. Users in the same time zone, but having different holidays, should be separated; for example, users in Toronto and New York City, although in the same time zone, celebrate different national holidays, and thus should be counted separately. Users in small field offices should be counted as members of the nearest regional office.

The next step is to estimate the number of logged-on and active Netscape Calendar Server users per time zone. The number of logged-on users is based on the total number of configured users per time zone, generally between 50 and 75 percent of that second number. The number of active users is based on the total number of configured users per time zone, and is generally between 10 and 25 percent of that second number. The next step is determining the number of servers needed to support these users. It is strongly recommended that servers be physically located near all major user population centers.

Each Netscape Calendar Server ships with 10 serial numbers, one or more of which may be applied to a node. A serial number may only be used once, however, so the 10 must be allocated among the nodes within a server. For each serial number, a node may contain up to 999 users. Applying two serial numbers to one node would mean the node to grow to 1,998 users. The result is that a server may have no more than 10 nodes and no more than 9,999 users; however, for performance reasons, it is recommended that no more than 3,000 logged-on users be supported on one server.

Guidelines Summary

The following is a summary of the sizing guidelines given in the previous subsections. Again, these guidelines are intended as the starting point for intranet architecture and deployment. Testing, configuration, and fine-tuning are required for every intranet deployment.

ENTERPRISE SERVER

- ❏ One Enterprise Server can service 1,000,000 requests per day (approximately 2,000 users).
- ❏ Deploy one Enterprise Server for every information area—near authors/publishers.
- ❏ Publishing processes may require a staging server for each information area.
- ❏ Clustered server architectures are better than singular "superserver."

❑ Deploy one Enterprise Server for each intranet application.

❑ Deploy an Enterprise Server in each location with 10 or more users who create content.

MESSAGING SERVER

❑ Deploy one Mail Server for every 2,000 to 3,000 POP3 users.

❑ Deploy one Mail Server for every 1,000 to 1,500 IMAP4 users.

❑ Deploy one Mail Server at every site with 10 or more users.

❑ Deploy servers with RAID5 for failover and recovery.

PROXY SERVER

❑ One Proxy Server should be deployed on the firewall for every 500 people at the central site top to replicate Internet content.

❑ One Proxy Server can support 300,000 hits per day (300 to 1,000 users depending on activity).

❑ One Proxy Server should be deployed in each location with 10 or more users.

❑ For Internet caching, one Proxy Server for every 500 users should be deployed at the firewall.

❑ Automatic Proxy Configuration, rather than specific Proxy Server assignments, should be used to distribute clients.

❑ Proxy chaining should be used to make the most of Proxy Server resources in multiserver configurations.

CATALOG SERVER

❑ A Catalog Server can index approximately 150,000 documents.

❑ A Catalog Server can typically support 8,000 users.

❑ Deploy one Catalog Server in each location with 500 or more users.

COLLABRA SERVER

❏ One Collabra Server can support approximately 3,000 to 4,000 non-Usenet users.
❏ One Collabra Server can support approximately 1,000 Usenet users.
❏ Deploy a Collabra Server in each location with 10 or more users.

DIRECTORY SERVER

❏ One Directory Server can hold more than 1,000,000 resource entries.
❏ One Directory Server can handle more than 300,000 queries per hour.
❏ A Directory Server should be deployed in any location where user information is maintained.

CERTIFICATE SERVER

❏ One Netscape Certificate Server can maintain up to 15,000 users in a database.
❏ One Netscape Certificate Server can handle up to 100,000 queries per hour.
❏ Certificate Servers are commonly deployed in the same locations as Directory Servers, wherever user info is generated, maintained, and deleted.

CALENDAR SERVER

❏ One Calendar Server can support up to 3,000 users.
❏ Users should be grouped by time zones, and each time zone should be assigned a separate node.
❏ Hardware sizing is dictated by the number of active and logged-in users for each server.

Client Distribution

Because distribution of the Netscape Navigator is a challenge for most corporations, the following plan of action is recommended to help with this process. First, "piloting" the distribution mechanism is essential for the successful deployment of Netscape within an enterprise. A pilot should consist of a manageable number of users of varying skill levels, to gain an overview of the potential problems that may arise during the full software rollout.

Second, a useful, easy-to-use application should be in place on the intranet so that the pilot users can familiarize themselves with the concepts and terminology of Web-based technologies. A good idea is to start users on the corporate home page that links to departments within the company. A good sample application is a corporate phone directory.

Distributing Netscape Navigator 3.0

The Netscape Navigator 3.0 Administration Kit can be used to configure a customized version of the Navigator, to allow the administrator to enter defaults into common customization areas of the Navigator, such as:

Animated Logo (optional). The animated logo in the upper right-hand corner of the Navigator window is used to show network activity. This can be changed to a customized animation.

Automatic Proxy Configuration URL. This URL is used within the Navigator to configure proxy information.

Default Home Page. Configuration of this default will force the Navigator to display the specified URL as the Navigator's default opening page.

Company Certificate. Inserting the company's public key certificate into the list of certificate authorities that the Navigator accepts as trusted allows users to connect via SSL to servers that present certificates signed by the company.

Once properly configured, the Administration Kit can be used to produce an executable file to install the customized Navigator. This program can be placed on a central server for user installation, distributed through an automatic software distribution mechanism, or e-mailed as an attachment using an existing mail system.

Table 6.9 Mapping Tools to Applications

Tool	Advantages	Disadvantages	Best Implementation
Client-side JavaScript	Portability. Rapid development. Easily maintainable. Available for Win 3.1.	Interpreted, therefore slow by comparison. Source is viewable.	Field validation. Simple client processing. Invoking Java objects via LiveConnect.
Server-side JavaScript	Portability. Rapid Development. Easily maintainable. Executes within server process area.	Interpreted, therefore slow by comparison to complied languages.	Database connectivity via LiveWire. State management.
Client-side Java	Portability. Performance, compiled into bytecodes. Graphics, animation.	Limited support under Win 3.1. Longer development. Process, more complex than JavaScript. Maintainability, more complex than JavaScript.	Complex processing. Graphics and Animation. Extending JavaScript. Writing standalone applications.
Server-side Java	Portability. Performance, compiled into bytecodes.	Longer Development, more complex than JavaScript. Maintainability, more complex than JavaScript. Forks a new server process.	Complex processing. Extending JavaScript. Writing standalone applications.
Perl	String processing. Extensive Web functions libraries available. Leveraging existing code base.	Future support; less popular than Java for development. Forks a new server process.	Complex string processing.
C/C++	Performance. Low-level processing. Flexible programming.	Forks a new server process. Longer development and more complex than Java and JavaScript. Maintainability, more complex than Java and JavaScript.	Complex processing. Leveraging existing code base.

Distribution Using Netscape Communicator

The Netscape Communicator changes a couple of aspects of deploying clients to users. Customizing of the Communicator is much more complex than customizing the Navigator. It is possible to lock certain features to a specified value (for example, the home page can be "locked" to be the company's home page, so that users cannot change it). The Communicator also features the Auto Administration capability, which forces the Communicator to access a specified URL to obtain its configuration information. This configuration information is obtained in a special set of JavaScript commands, and can be highly customized.

Once the initial distribution of the Communicator is complete, which is achieved in a similar fashion as the Navigator 3.0 client, Communicator has a built-in software distribution and update capability, so that it is always up-to-date with the latest releases.

Application Development

Table 6.9 gives some recommendations for choosing application development tools. In general, most any applications can be built with any development tool. These guidelines are based on experience with companies attempting to build applications in the most efficient way possible. The most important factor to keep in mind when selecting development tools is the skills and interest of the development community within the organization. Note that the advantages and disadvantages listed in the table are current as of the time of this writing and will no doubt change over time.

Conclusion

The goal of this chapter is to provide guidelines to the most often asked deployment questions. While none of these guidelines is absolute, they provide solid starting points for intranet deployment. They should be used as planning metrics to amount of hardware, software, and training required to deploy an intranet.

CHAPTER **7**

INTRANET PERSONNEL INFRASTRUCTURE

Like any information system, intranets require support resources to maintain and administer, so it is important for companies to identify and plan for these resources to ensure the continued success of the intranet. Although these resource needs are highly dependent upon the complexity of the information and applications and the overall size of the organization, this chapter presents some general guidelines for arriving at the base requirements for intranet system administration.

System Administration

Webmaster

One of the terms you'll hear often in intranet and Internet system administration is Webmaster. A catch-all title, Webmaster was coined during the early days of the Internet evolution, when one person still could do it all: architect, install, design, develop, and support an external Web site for a company. Today, there are too many products and complexity in the areas of design and functionality in Web systems for any one person to be the "master."

The clearest division of labor in support and development of Web systems is between visual design and development and system maintenance and technical support. Nevertheless, many people still use the term Webmaster to describe those "behind the curtain" of the intranet, but now it refers to a person or group of people who ensure that a Web system maintains a consistent level of service to the user community. Most of what Webmasters do today, then, is what system administrators did in traditional computing environments. They still must be familiar with the applications and design of the systems they support, but they generally do not design or code these applications; they are most concerned with maintaining links, disk space management, backup and restoration of data, and overall performance of the intranet. Though certainly not exhaustive, the following list of tasks describes the modern role of the Webmaster:

- Administer the implementation of the intranet architecture.
- Develop current Web technology expertise.
- Evaluate emergent Web technology.
- Achieve HTML proficiency.
- Ensure hyperlink currency and accuracy.
- Debug basic application errors.
- Tune Web server performance.
- Expand intranet architecture.

Visual Designers

With the maturation of the Web interface, a clear line has been drawn between the Webmaster and the visual designer of a Web system. Visual design and information architecture are jobs unto themselves in today's Web system. Traditionally, in the nascent stages of technology, designing the flow of information and the user experience it defines has been tightly linked to technical development; then as the technology matures, it breaks off into a separate profession. Visual design is nothing new to graphical user interface design, but it is often treated as an afterthought or window dressing for the technology. But because Web systems are based on the graphical presentation of information, visual design dictates the flow of information for communicating an idea or accomplishing a task, hence good visual design is often the difference between an intranet that is used and one that is not.

Recognizing the distinct skill set needed in this area, the Netscape Professional Services employ a group of consultants dedicated to this kind of work. Called Information Architecture and Design (IAD), the group focuses on the presentation of information and applications to convey a message or accomplish a task. This design effort is a central function in the development process of an intranet. In fact, the smoothest intranet implementations are often structured such that the interface design and information flow dictate the technical aspects of the Web system. The back end, technical architecture and application development, is left to a third group, the development resources. A designer's tasks include:

❏ Documenting information flow (and reengineering as needed).
❏ Designing the hierarchy of information.
❏ Designing screen layout.
❏ Developing graphics.
❏ Determining use of graphics (formats, sizes, frequency, etc.).
❏ Developing system identity/theme.
❏ Developing user metaphor.

Database Administrator

A database administrator maintains the back-end database for Web applications that interface with databases. This role is normally filled by a current employee who was responsible for database administration in the past. The intranet is essentially a front-end or client-to-legacy database system, which requires the same level of support as previously required at the database level. If a database is implemented specifically for the intranet environment, someone who can manage and tune the database must fill the role of database administrator.

Development Resources

Application Developers

Application developers are required for building intranet applications. Frequently, these professionals are already on staff in existing information technology departments, and only require training on tools for application development in the Web environment. These developers require all of the traditional skills to identify user requirements, manage project scope and budget, and deliver a product in a given time period. The intranet is not a panacea for development in spite of the fact that the process need only occur one time, can be used on all platforms, and the distribution of the software is considerably more efficient. The intranet development process involves all of the traditional steps in requirements identification and confirmation, as well as user and system testing. The Netscape ONE development environment enables rapid application development, but it does not preclude the design and testing phase. In general, developers must be skilled in HTML, Java, JavaScript, and database query languages. All of this in the context of object-oriented programming is important, as IFC and IIOP are introduced into the development arena.

Many companies structure central development organizations that are tasked with developing a core set of Java objects and HTML/JavaScript templates that will be distributed throughout the company. In this way, functions specific to that company/industry can be developed and maintained centrally. Tools are distributed to developers throughout the organization for use in designing customized applications. This approach is used by many companies to distribute application code tools for developers in field offices, thereby reducing the lower-level coding requirements for functional developers and ensuring standard methods for data access through the intranet. This eases development and reduces the administration resources needed to support the intranet.

Content Development

Content development focuses on presenting information and constructing the path a user follows to arrive at sought-after information. The skills for this task include information organization, layout, and presentation of information in HTML.

ACME Staffing Recommendations

After identifying the resources needed to support the intranet, the next step is to map those resources to locations within the intranet. Picking up where we left off with the ACME case study, this section demonstrates the mapping of system administration and development resources to the intranet. As with mapping hardware and software, different personnel are needed based on the user and network services provided in each intranet location.

Central Site: Headquarters

The headquarters location is the central site of the intranet, therefore more personnel are required there to champion the intranet. This team includes a project manager/architect to promote the high-level technical vision of the intranet, a technical Webmaster to maintain and administer the central site, a visual designer to maintain information architecture, and developers to create and maintain intranet applications. A summary of each team member's duties for central site headquarters follows.

Architect/Project Manager

- ❑ Lead the site architecture design process, as well as review project team milestones and deliverables.
- ❑ Oversee day-to-day project activities.
- ❑ Track project status at management and project team levels and account for issue resolution and escalation process.
- ❑ Develop a detailed, task-level project work plan, assign and schedule resources, and track project progress.

Technical Webmaster

- ❑ Lead the implementation of the site architecture.
- ❑ Develop Web technology expertise.
- ❑ Liaise to content providers.

Visual/User Interface Designer

- ❑ Design presentation layer of intranet project.
- ❑ Develop and enforce use of guidelines, templates, and standards for the site interfaces with content providers.

Developers (One to two developers per application)

- ❑ Build and test applications.
- ❑ Become knowledgeable in HTML, Java, JavaScript, LiveWire.
- ❑ Have relational database experience.

International Hubs

The international hub locations should devote a full-time Webmaster to the installation and maintenance of the regional intranet infrastructure.

Technical Webmaster

- ❑ Lead the implementation of the site architecture.
- ❑ Develop Web technology expertise.
- ❑ Liaise to content providers.

Remote Offices

The remote office locations should devote a full-time Webmaster to the installation and maintenance of the local intranet infrastructure.

Technical Webmaster

- ❑ Lead the implementation of the site architecture.
- ❑ Develop Web technology expertise.
- ❑ Liaise to content providers.

8

INTRANET SITE STRUCTURE AND INFORMATION ARCHITECTURE

The most effective intranets provide access to information across the enterprise. Empowering employees with information from all parts of the company improves efficiency and increases awareness. This leads to the reuse and repurposing of information, which reduces or eliminates repetition. In addition, the awareness of what other groups are currently doing and how they do it are valuable components of teaming and synergy within the organization. Clearly, then, it is important to structure the intranet so that information can be shared among different groups. To achieve this, it must have a logical, easily understood structure for information sharing and management. This chapter addresses important considerations for successful intranet information architecture.

Site Organization

Remember, an important step in implementing information management and sharing services within the intranet is the organization of the internal site. A logical organization bases its content on the current organizational framework diagram. From a user's point of view, the information and content need to be in logical locations to prevent disorientation and confusion in the navigation and publishing processes.

179

Figure 8.1 Top-level intranet site architecture.

Upon completion, the framework will be used to determine the underlying directory structure in the file system. A natural, logical model of the site not only helps the user, but also eases implementation and administration of the intranet. Figure 8.1 shows a typical intranet site, in this case for our case study company, ACME. This organization maps to a traditional hierarchical structure within a corporation.

Information Architecture

The next step in designing the site architecture is to further define each functional area to develop the information architecture or information flow that the user will experience using the site. This process should include readers and publishers from each of the top-level functional areas. The goal here is to identify specific information areas within the site. Figures 8.2a through 8.2h depict the information architecture for the ACME site. Logically grouping content by function is an important part of defining a physical directory structure for the intranet and an access control model that meets the security needs of the company.

Information Task Flows

After defining the high-level information architecture, it is possible to create information task flow diagrams that outline how the user will traverse the site. These diagrams are important in the design phase of the intranet because they clearly communicate the flow of information in the intranet site to the user. It is much more efficient to iterate through task flow diagrams than to create and change actual Web pages. The diagrams in Figure 8.3a through 8.3j show the information task flows of the ACME Widget Corporation intranet. Each of the dots signifies a Web page and its relative position in the information hierarchy of the ACME intranet site.

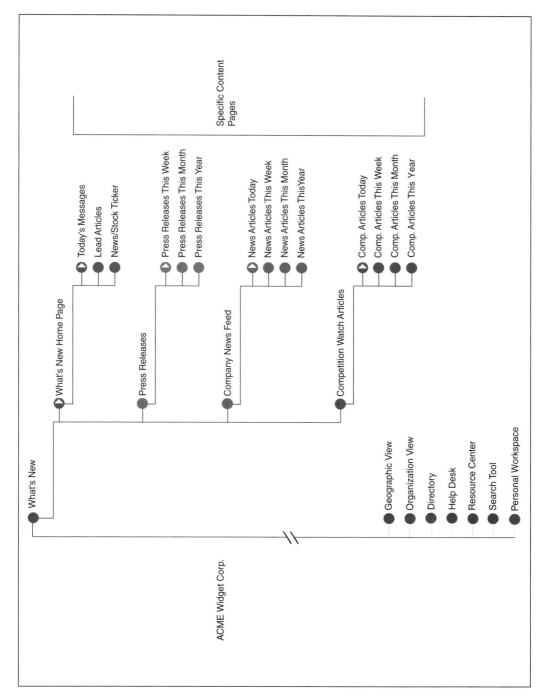

Figure 8.2a ACME what's new information architecture.

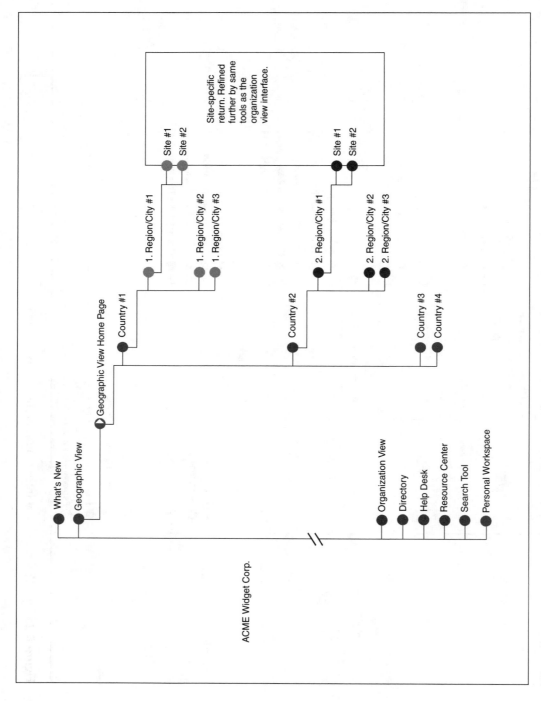

Figure 8.2b ACME geographic view information architecture.

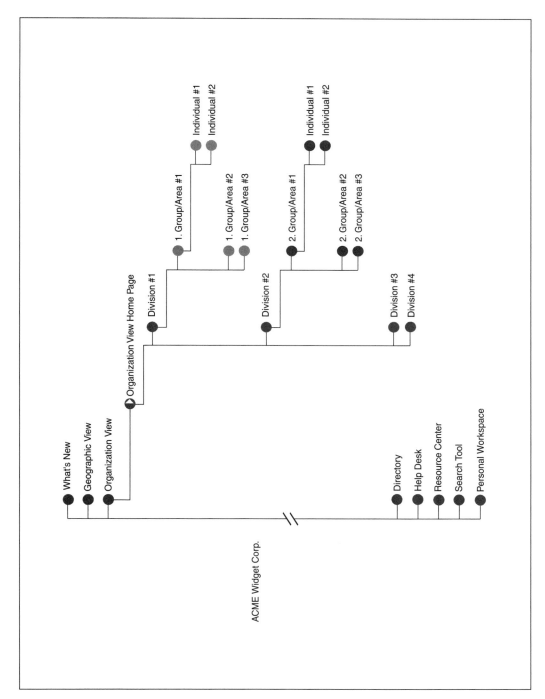

Figure 8.2c ACME organization view information architecture.

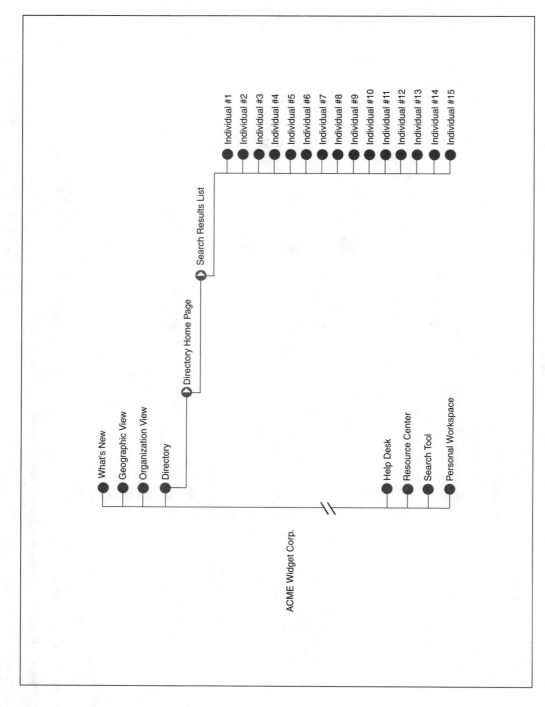

Figure 8.2d ACME employee directory information architecture.

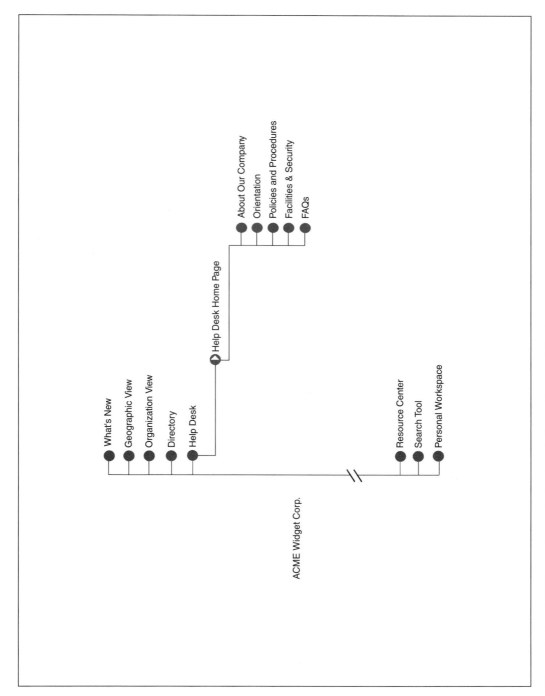

Figure 8.2e ACME employee help desk information architecture.

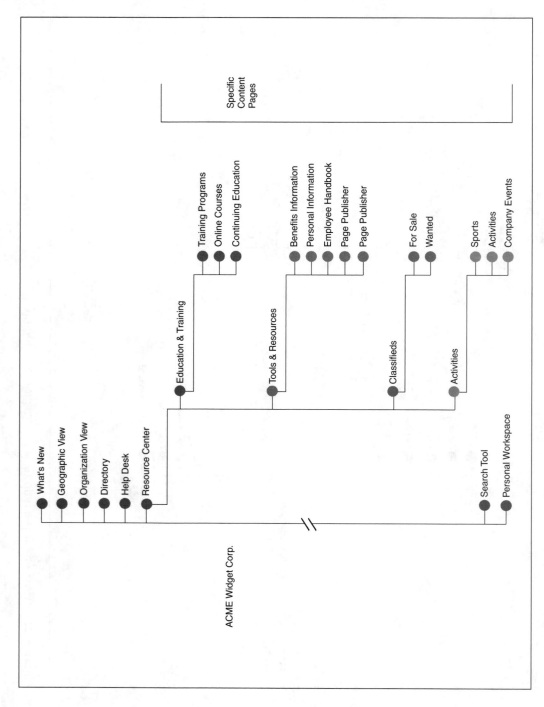

Figure 8.2f ACME employee resource center information architecture.

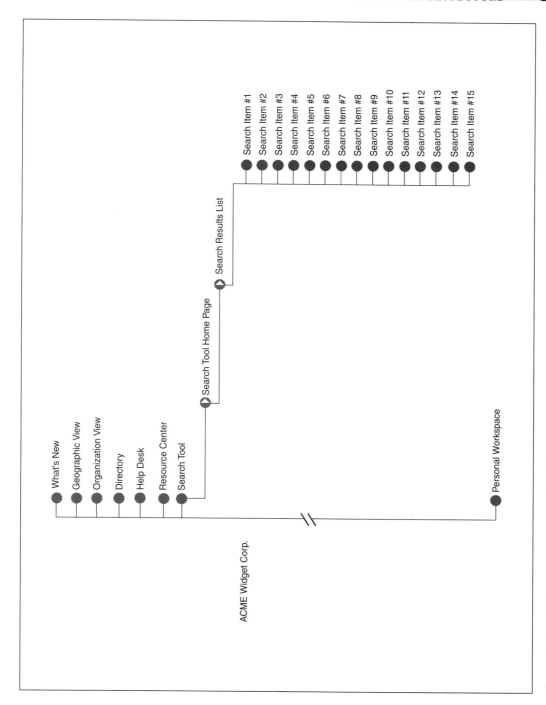

Figure 8.2g ACME intranet search tool information architecture.

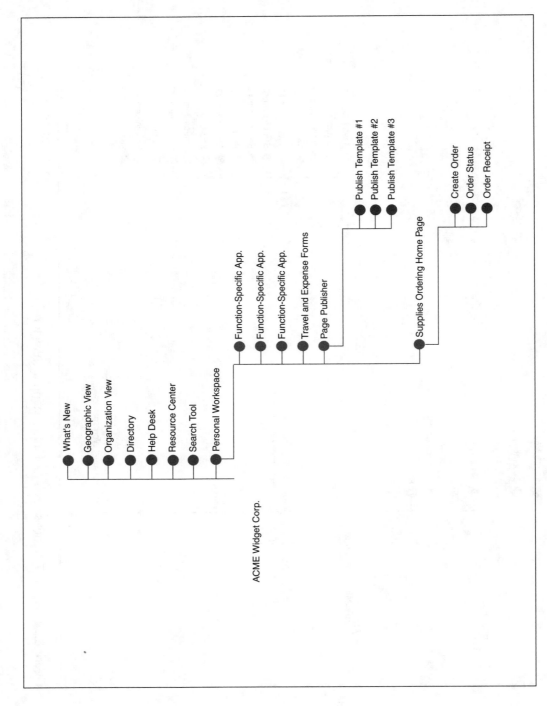

Figure 8.2h ACME personal workspace information architecture.

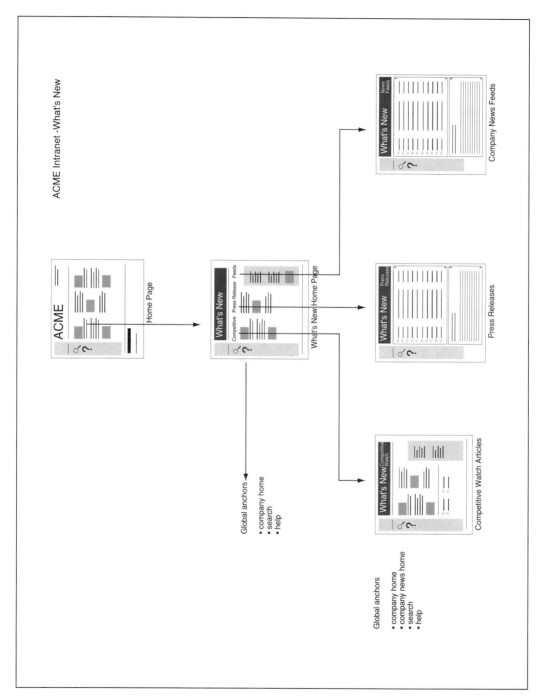

Figure 8.3a ACME what's new information task flow paper prototype.

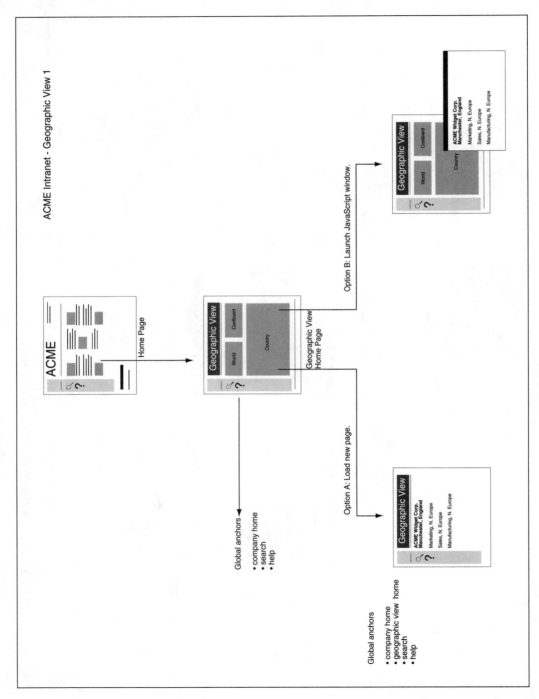

Figure 8.3b ACME geographic view information task flow paper prototype (page 1).

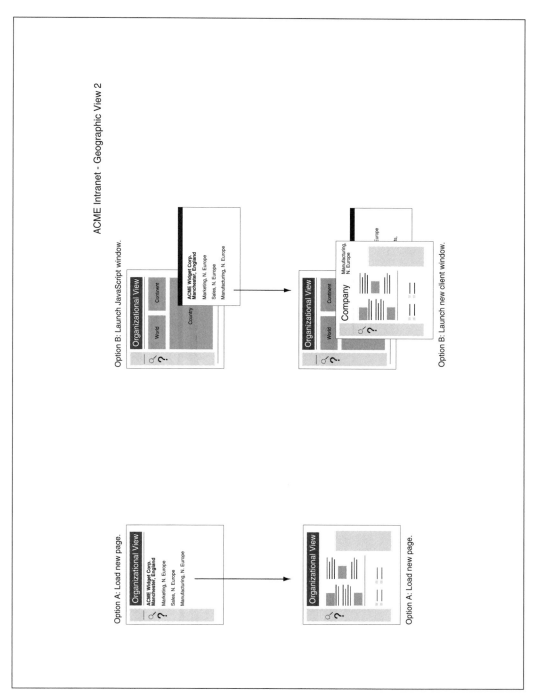

Figure 8.3c ACME geographic view information task flow paper prototype (page 2).

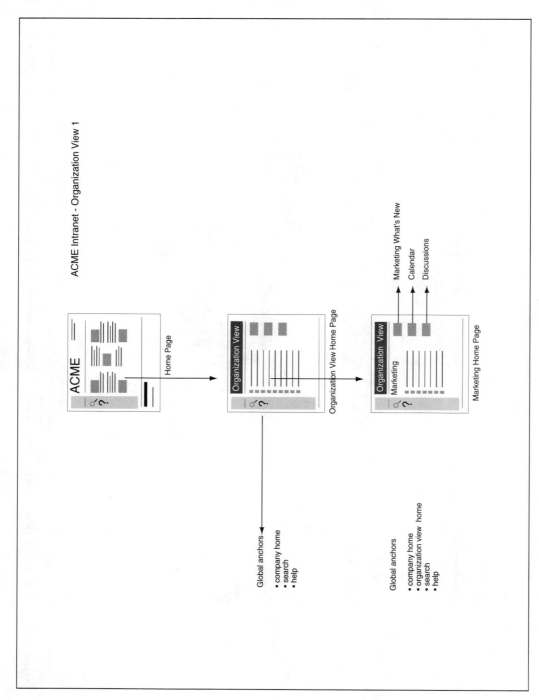

Figure 8.3d ACME organization view information task flow paper prototype (page 1).

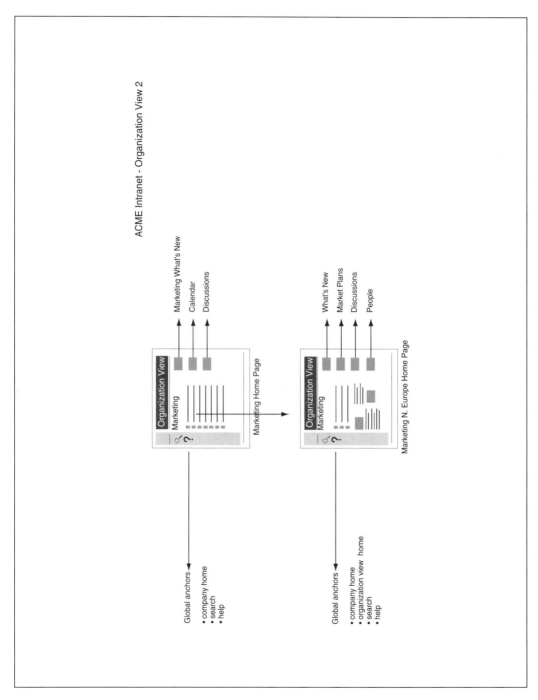

Figure 8.3e ACME organization view information task flow paper prototype (page 2).

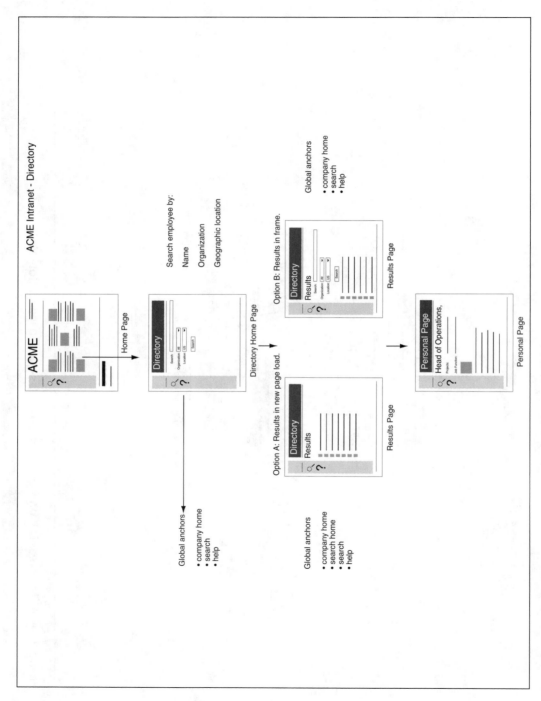

Figure 8.3f ACME employee directory information task flow paper prototype.

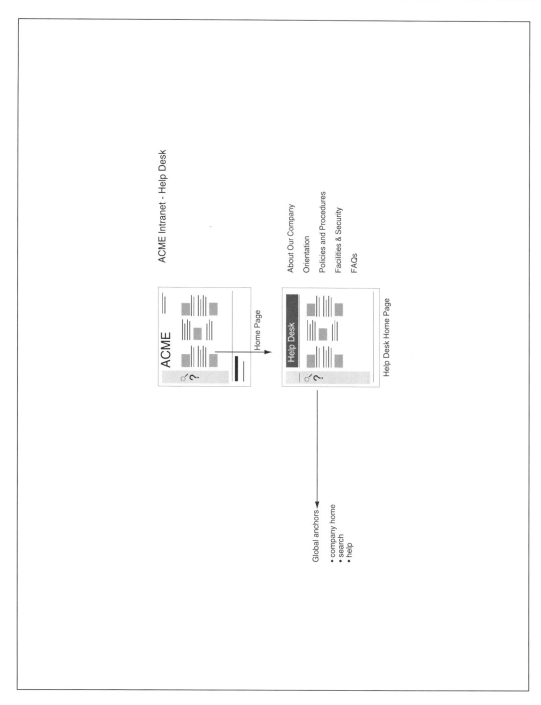

Figure 8.3g ACME employee help desk information task flow paper prototype.

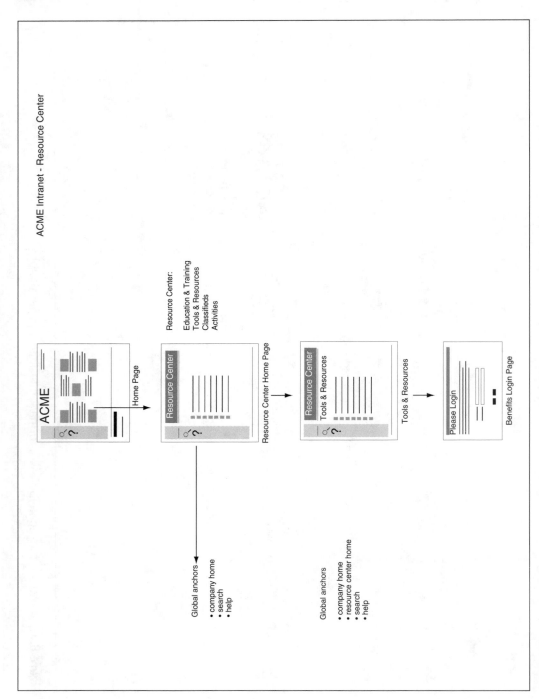

Figure 8.3h ACME employee resource center information task flow paper prototype.

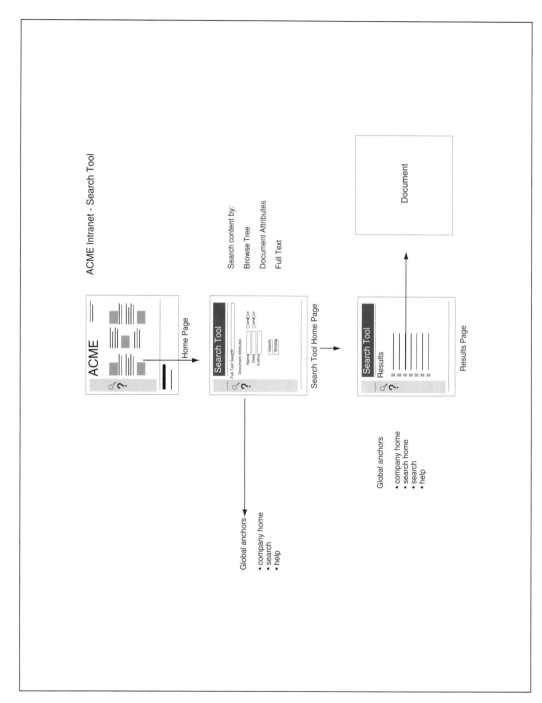

Figure 8.3i ACME intranet search tool information task flow paper prototype.

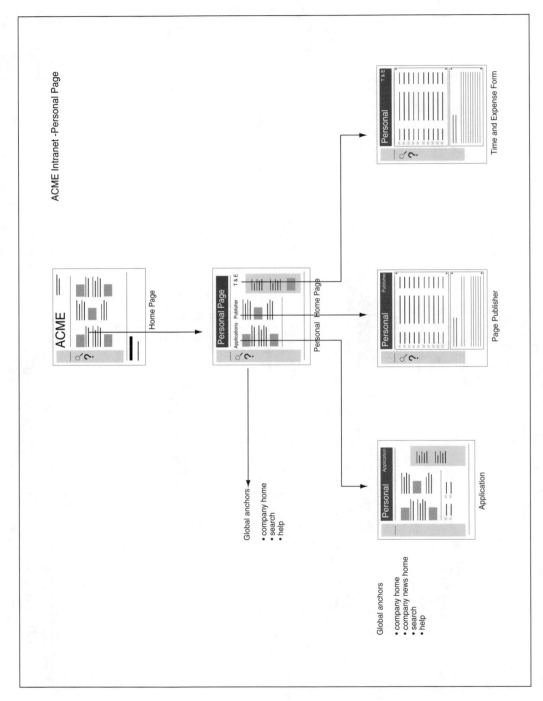

Figure 8.3j   ACME employee personal page information task flow paper prototype.

File System Directory Structure

Figure 8.4 shows a file system directory structure for the ACME site. Each of the folders represents a directory in the file system. Notice the separation of media, graphics, and so on and the HTML that makes up the page content. This directory structure logically groups information by business function, which provides the basis for mapping access con-

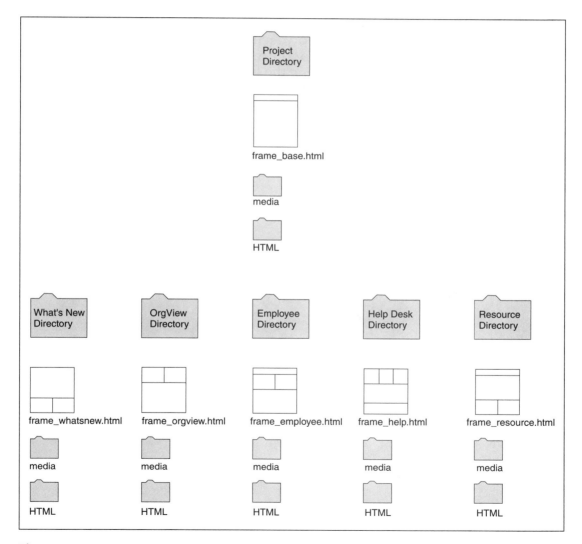

Figure 8.4 Intranet Directory Structure.

trol to the content stored in the intranet. Access control can be assigned on a file-by-file basis, but abstracting content areas to groups of content and physical directories is much more efficient for access control maintenance and system administration in general.

Page Design

Finally, the pages of the intranet site can be designed and built using the information and directory architectures already in place. The first step is to build a home page for the intranet that will serve as the initial access point for users. Following the information architecture defined, this page must establish links to the first tier of functional business areas, which in turn lead to the next, and so on. To launch the intranet, placeholder pages should be developed for all information represented in the information architecture diagrams. Figures 8.5a through 8.5u use ACME Widgets Inc. to demonstrate how the intranet site would look based on the information architecture described.

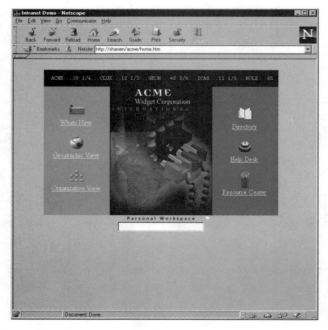

Figure 8.5a ACME top level home page.

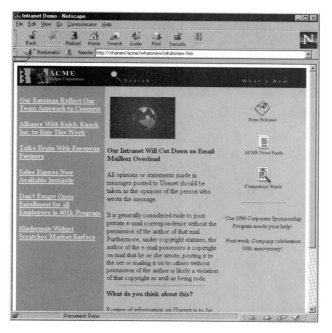

Figure 8.5b ACME what's new (page 1).

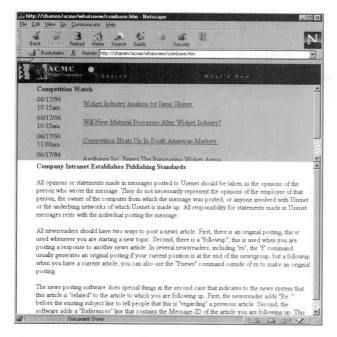

Figure 8.5c ACME what's new (page 2).

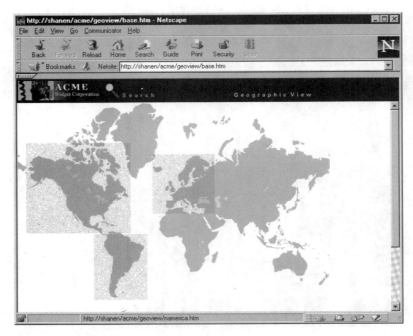

Figure 8.5d ACME geographic view (page 1).

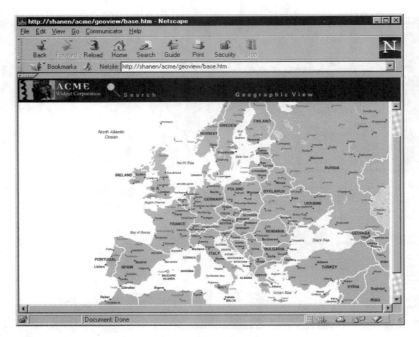

Figure 8.5e ACME geographic view (page 2).

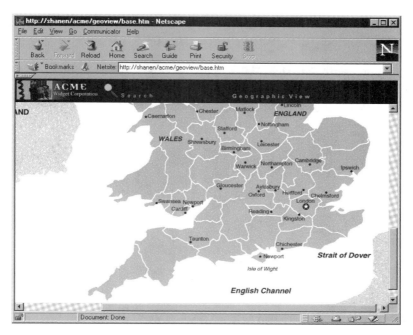

Figure 8.5f ACME geographic view (page 3).

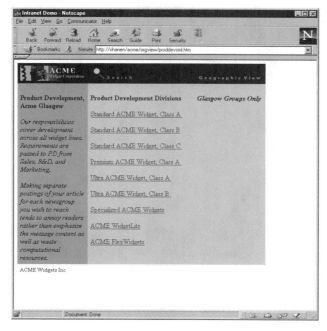

Figure 8.5g ACME geographic view (page 4).

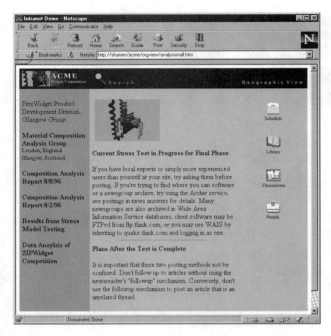

Figure 8.5h ACME geographic view (page 5).

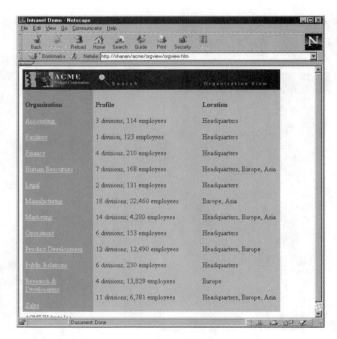

Figure 8.5i ACME organization view (page 1).

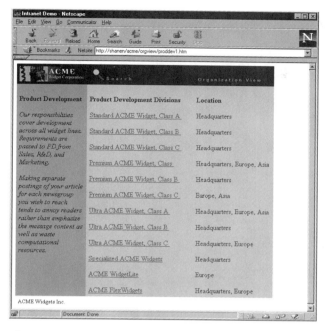

Figure 8.5j ACME organization view (page 2).

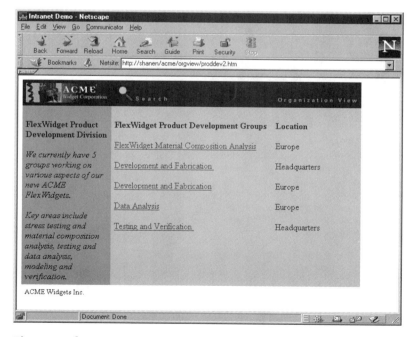

Figure 8.5k ACME organization view (page 3).

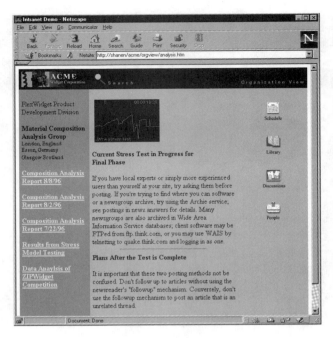

Figure 8.5l ACME organization view (page 4).

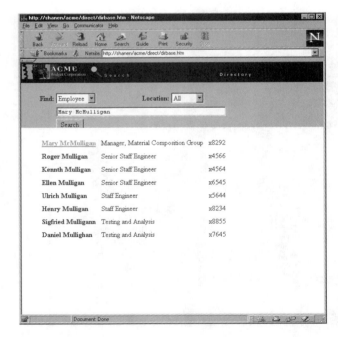

Figure 8.5m ACME employee directory (page 1).

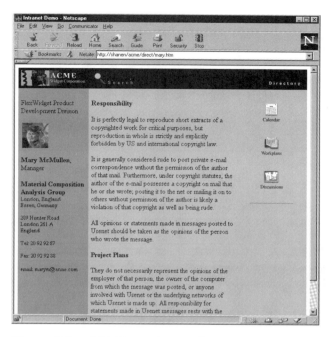

Figure 8.5n ACME employee directory (page 2).

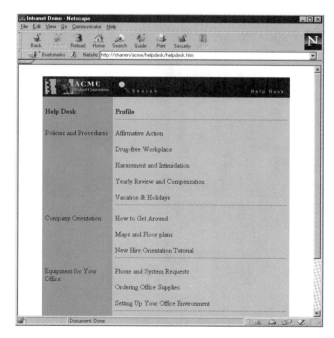

Figure 8.5o ACME employee help desk.

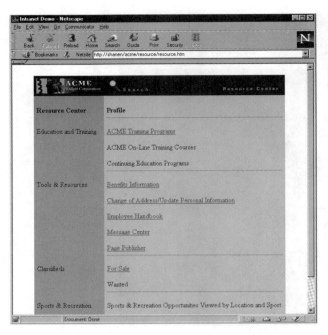

Figure 8.5p ACME employee resource center.

Figure 8.5q ACME employee personal page—executive (page 1).

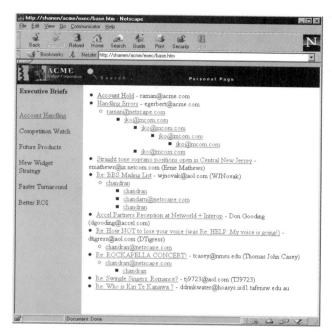

Figure 8.5r ACME employee personal page—executive (page 2).

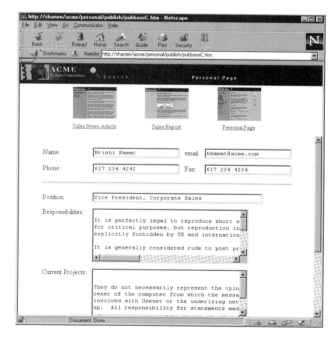

Figure 8.5s ACME employee personal page—executive (page 3).

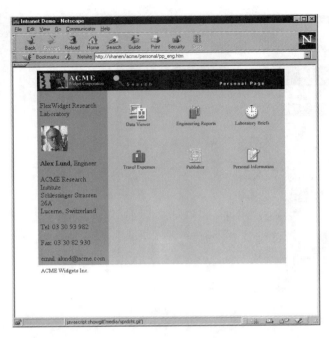

Figure 8.5t ACME employee personal page—engineer.

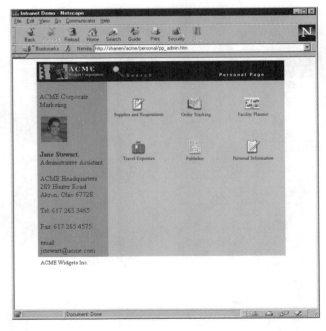

Figure 8.5u ACME employee personal page—administrator.

Content Publishing Architectures

After identifying the information architecture of a site, the logical next step is to develop a publishing architecture to enable users to easily create and distribute content on the intranet. Certainly, the tools for publishing will continue to advance in improving content creation, but a logical structure for the publishing environment is first necessary if the publishing process is to be intuitive and easy for the user. The information architecture defined for the navigation of the site will be based on the logical organization of information that will most efficiently relate that information to the reader. The information architecture is also useful to the *author of the information*, and thus should be leveraged in the design of the publishing architecture. Although some companies use the same site for readers and authors, thereby enabling direct publishing to the intranet from the author's desktop, most prefer to stage and review content prior to its release to the production site. Choosing between a *staged* publishing architecture and a *direct* publishing architecture is a policy issue that must be resolved in the design and planning phase of information sharing and management.

In the direct publishing model, users can publish directly to the production intranet site. This requires that each author have write access to his or her functional area on the site. Although this model reduces system administration by requiring maintenance of only one site, it also reduces control of the publishing process and the content distributed on the intranet.

To support the staging publishing model many companies create a staging intranet server that mirrors the structure of the production site to which authors publish documents. This staging site is then reviewed for content and adherence to corporate policies and released into production. A staging publishing architecture requires appointing reviewing/publishing staff for the publishing process. These reviewers are commonly users within each of the functional areas familiar with the content created by that group and the company's content and presentation standards. Though this is more resource- and system-intensive, many large companies have adopted the staged publishing process so as to more closely monitor the content distributed on the intranet.

In either publishing model, authors must be mapped to directories on the Enterprise Server, to which they are granted write access to publish documents. Using the functional groups defined in the site's information architecture, authors are mapped to their corresponding area on the server. These areas usually parallel departments or workgroups within the company. Once authors are mapped to the directories, they must be directed to the areas in the publishing tools that they will be using. The Netscape Composer, for example, can be prefigured to point to a specific directory on the Enterprise Server for publishing. Users can then use the Composer's one-button publish feature to place documents in their assigned locations on the Enterprise Server.

In addition to defining procedures for the publishing process, policies on content and format must also be established to give authors the tools and guidelines they need to start creating content. This involves creating templates and a standard set of graphics for users (e.g., templates that establish layout and standard company logo graphics). By mirroring the production server directory structures, these templates and graphics can be stored in the standard locations on the staging server that match the directory structures on the production servers (see Figure 8.6). In this way, all graphics and links can be maintained accurately when the document is published to the production site. Note: These procedures and guidelines must be developed prior to the implementation of information sharing and management services.

Content Replication Architectures

Recall that replication is the process of synchronizing content between systems, and is often required in conjunction with the staging model of publishing to move approved content from the staging system to the production environment, or to distribute content within an intranet. Replication architectures also are often implemented to optimize network bandwidth utilization, provide redundancy, and balance server load. For example, companies running a DNS round-robin to distribute load among multiple servers require replication tools to synchronize the servers that make up the round-robin architecture. This is most commonly used in hosting a central site that must scale to support ever more users, as in the case with the Netscape external site.

Currently, Netscape does not supply tools for replicating content from one Enterprise Server to another, although content replication features will be addressed in future releases. Until that time, many companies have developed custom tools for distributing and synchronizing information across multiple Enterprise Servers, and this section details strategies that have been used in the field to accomplish replication.

Replication Methods

There are several models for instituting replication services, which are based on a set of methods and features for synchronizing information.

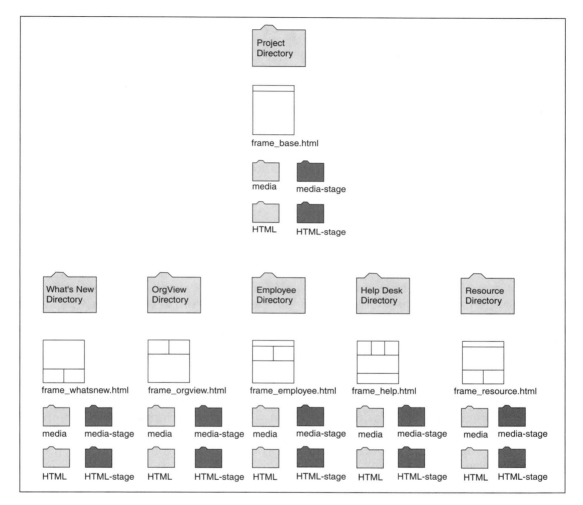

Figure 8.6 Staging directory structure.

Each model has its own positive and negative impacts on system performance, administration, or security, so choosing the right replication model is important to efficiently distribute information on a given intranet. The first step in choosing a replication model is to analyze the nature of the information and its frequency of change.

Pull or Push   Push and pull refer the direction of information flows between servers. The *pull* method is the process whereby the initiator of a connection pulls, retrieves, or downloads the content that is to be replicated. An example is a Web client connecting to a server to GET a page. In contrast, in the *Push* method, the initiator of a connection pushes, deploys, or uploads the content that is to be replicated. An example of a push is a Web client connecting to a server to PUT a page.

The most important difference between the push and pull models of replication has to do with access control to information. Under the pull model, the pulling machine (consumer) requires read access to the supplying machine (supplier); in the push model, the supplier machine requires write access to the consumer machine. Most companies prefer a centralized model of information and access, and thus choose the push model.

Peer-to-Peer or Supplier-Consumer   *Peer-to-peer replication* involves two or more entities synchronizing content that may have been independently changed on some or all of the entities. An example of this is source control systems where many developers alter a source and try to synchronize their changes with a repository. *Supplier-consumer* refers to the process where one or more entities synchronize content with a single source of the information.

Peer-to-peer replication is more flexible and can be more efficient, but it is far more complex to develop and maintain. For example, when a piece of information has been modified by more than one user within the same replication period, a replication conflict results. To resolve this conflict, a decision must be made as to which modification will be accepted and which will be denied. At this point, a human intervention or a programmatic assumption is needed to proceed. In either case, one change must be overridden by another, resulting in lost effort and information.

The supplier-consumer approach simplifies this approach from a programmatic and administrative point of view. The supplier is always the authority of the information, and its changes need to be distributed without human intervention or programmatic assumptions.

On-Command or On-Demand

On-command replication, as described previously, grants system administrators the capability to specify regular intervals for a replication event. The replication tool automatically runs to distribute information at the specified time of day/week/month. This is useful for intranets in which information changes on a predictable basis. By contrast, *on-demand replication* is the execution of a replication request as a result of some external event other than time. On-demand replication is often tied to a user request for a document in the intranet.

Many tools offer a combination of on-command and on-demand replication. In fact, many companies use on-command replication on a nightly basis in conjunction with on-demand replication during working hours to optimize bandwidth utilization and ensure currency of information respectively.

Complete or Partial

Complete replication is the transfer of the entire contents of one server to another; that is, the entire tree of files is copied to the consumer to create an identical replica of the supplier server. Although this model is relatively simple to design and build, it is network-intensive since the entire file tree is moved regardless of whether individual files were changed since the last replication event.

Partial replication transfers only the changes in the file tree to each of the consumer servers. By exchanging only the file deltas, partial replication is often far more efficient than complete replication; however, partial replication is also far more complex to implement successfully, because it requires either logging changes to individual files or "walking the file tree" and comparing time stamps or byte counts to construct a list of files to exchange. An important part of designing a partial replication model is to understand the granularity of changes that will be replicated. For intranet replication architectures, the MIME object that most often translates to individual files frequently represents the smallest piece of information or object, as opposed to replication in database systems that often focuses on field-level information changes.

The decision to use complete or partial replication is driven by the frequency and depth of change of the information within the intranet. If many or most files are revised frequently, complete replication will be quicker to implement and easier to maintain than partial replication. On the other hand, if files change more randomly, and bandwidth resources are scarce, partial replication is often well worth the additional development effort. Most companies choose to implement partial replication models to optimize bandwidth utilization.

Replication Security

When transferring information in distributed environments, precautions must be in place to protect the information. In general, the security tools available within the Netscape ONE application development environment are sufficient to developers building replication tools. Secure Sockets Layer (SSL) protocol, basic or strong authentication, and data encryption are all options for protecting information in the replication process. Here again, the decisions regarding impact on system resources (bandwidth, processor, etc.) need to be weighed against the value of the information being replicated.

Netscape Proxy Server

As discussed in the chapter on Netscape products, the Proxy Server provides replication services by caching information from Web servers via user requests. As a Proxy Server handles requests from a client, it stores these retrieved files in its cache. On subsequent requests, the Proxy Server may serve the document straight from the cache rather than retrieving the file again. The decision that the server makes (serve from cache versus reretrieve) can be controlled by configuration settings. In addition, the Proxy Server can be configured to retrieve a set of documents in batch mode from a given URL at scheduled intervals and place them in its cache. Although this provides a solution for moving content closer to users, it does not synchronize content between Enterprise Servers. Table 8.1 describes proxy replication.

The replication tools in Table 8.1 are examples of custom solutions built to provide replication services between Web servers. Note that these tools are not Netscape products and require custom development effort.

Table 8.1 Netscape Proxy Server Replication Model

Push or Pull	**Pull**
	Using HTTPull, the Proxy Server connects to a remote site to start replication.
Peer-to-Peer or Supplier-Consumer	**Supplier-Consumer**
	The Enterprise Server is always the supplier to the Proxy Server.
On-command or On-demand	**Both**
	Bulk replication can be scheduled. Requested documents are checked for deltas from the supplier.
Complete or Partial	**Both**
	Same as above.
Granularity	MIME object.

(continues)

Table 8.1 Netscape Proxy Server Replication Model (*Continued*)

Security	SSL.
	Basic and strong authentication via certificates.
Pros	Uses standard HTTP protocol.
	Supports connection keep-alive protocol for higher throughput.
	Any markup can be defined as requiring a GET operation (such as img src, an href, area href, etc.).
	No server modifications are needed. This is strictly a client solution based on minimal HTTP protocol requirements.
Cons	Applications cannot be replicated, only the results they produce (i.e., CGI output is saved, not the CGI).
	Only the GET method is used for pulling content.

HTTPull

The HTTPull method is an approach based on downloading a Web site given a starting URL. This is similar to using a search engine robot. The idea is that each page is retrieved and cascades down the links of that page; that is, if a page is made up of text/HTML, then all the links that it contains are retrieved. This process continues until one or all of the "the-end" heuristics tests are met, based on the criteria established by the developer. Table 8.2 describes HTTPull.

Table 8.2 HTTPull Replication Method

Push or Pull	**Pull**
	Connects to a remote site to start replication.
Peer-to-Peer or Consumer-Supplier	**Consumer-Supplier**
	Content is pulled from the remote site to a local disk, one way.
On-command or On-demand	**Both**
	Command-line utility; scheduling can be done from cron or run on-demand.
Complete or Partial	**Complete**
	Crawls entire file tree and links.

(continues)

Table 8.2 HTTPull Replication Method (*Continued*)

Granularity	MIME object.
Security	SSL.
	Basic and strong authentication via certificates.
Pros	Replication is done via HTTP, a standard protocol.
	Supports connection keep-alive protocol for higher throughput.
	Any markup can be defined as requiring a GET operation (such as img src, an href, area href, etc.).
	No server modifications are needed. This is strictly a client solution based on minimal HTTP protocol requirements.
Cons	No cache mechanism exists to support more efficient pulls.
	Applications cannot be replicated, only the results that they produce (i.e., CGI output is saved, not the CGI).
	Only the GET method is used for pulling content.

IndexPull

Like HTTPull, IndexPull is a replication model developed using the pull model to download a URI tree given a starting location URL. Rather than following the links on each page, however, in IndexPull, the initial URL request is retrieved via an INDEX method of the HTTP server, which produces a listing of objects inside a container (in this case, a directory). This allows the client to see the list of objects residing on the server, and subsequently, GET them one by one. As the client runs, it retrieves the MIME-typed objects via a GET request, and container objects via an INDEX request. Table 8.3 describes IndexPull.

Table 8.3 IndexPull Replication Model

Push or Pull	**Pull**
	Connects to a remote site to start replication.
Peer-to-Peer or Supplier-Consumer	**Supplier-Consumer**
	The content is pulled from the remote site to a local disk, one way.

(continues)

Table 8.3 IndexPull Replication Model (*Continued*)

On-command or On-demand	**Both**
	Command-line utility; scheduling can be done from cron or run on demand.
Complete or Partial	**Both**
	Partial content pull is done if files are out of sync with supplier server. A complete pull can be made without references to time stamps and sizes.
Granularity	MIME object.
Security	SSL.
	Basic and strong authorization over HTTP.
Pros	Uses standard HTTP protocol.
	Uses time stamps and file sizes to determine whether an update is needed.
Cons	Content hosted on the master when replicated by Pull operation is not rewritten; care must be taken in designing content.

HTTPut

The HTTPut replication model uses a local list of files and directories to upload the contents of one Web server to another. The file transfer mechanism is based on the standard HTTPut method for uploading files. Files are simply uploaded to the server using the HTTP protocol. The Netscape Site manager LiveWire uses the HTTPut replication model for distributing content, and provides link validation. This method requires the supplier server to have write access to the consumer server. Table 8.4 describes HTTPut replication.

Table 8.4 HTTPut Replication Model

Push or Pull	**Push**
	Connects to remote servers and writes content.
Peer-to-Peer or Supplier-Consumer	**Supplier-Consumer**
	The content is considered master on the local server and is uploaded to the consumer servers.

(continues)

Table 8.4 HTTPut Replication Model (*Continued*)

On-command or On-demand	**Both**
	Command-line utility; scheduling can be done from cron utilities or run on demand.
Complete or Partial	**Both**
	Logs of changed files can be kept and selectively pushed; or all files can be pushed.
Granularity	MIME object.
Security	SSL.
	Basic and strong authorization via certificates.
Pros	Uses HTTP standard protocol.
	Can replicate to several consumers in parallel.
	Can transport file protection information (World, Group, User) with the upload.
Cons	Supplier server needs Write access to the consumer servers.

There are several replication architectures for intranet content. Each architecture has its advantages and disadvantages for distributing data and optimizing performance.

CHAPTER

9

APPLICATION DEVELOPMENT

Continuing the ACME Widgets, Inc. case study, this chapter presents examples of application design and development on the Netscape ONE intranet platform. Once the infrastructure of the ACME intranet has been deployed, it will provide an excellent application development platform, enabling the access of existing databases, data warehouses, and legacy applications from a single interface. New applications can be authored once with JavaScript and Java, and quickly deployed on any platform, across all desktop and server operating environments and hardware platforms; all client-side application logic is downloaded when an application is accessed and the logic is automatically updated. Applications can be interwoven with content and be deployed transparently over the Internet as well as over the internal intranet. Database integration is one of the most common application architectures that companies implement first, and therefore it has been chosen for this example. This application is created using Netscape LiveWire to take advantage of its database connectivity and state management features.

The sample application is deliberately simple, in order to more easily explain the application development process. This same process has been used by many companies to develop a wide range of intranet-enabled business applications.

Current Environment

ACME currently runs a wide variety of custom and off-the-shelf desktop applications to accommodate its many users, some of whom require as many as 20 applications on the desktop, each using custom client applications or terminal emulators to access mission-critical applications and information. ACME sees the intranet as an application platform that will dramatically streamline the development process and simplify the user experience. Netscape ONE and SuiteTools will establish the application development environment in which to achieve these goals.

Development Process

Usually, the intranet application development process is a six to eight week rapid application development cycle made up of three phases: requirements gathering development, prototype and pilot, and deployment and implementation. These phases make for a compact development process and generate fast results for intranet users, while building skills and defining application development within the greater context of the enterprisewide intranet.

The first several weeks of the application development process are aimed at gathering requirements for the application and developing a prototype against those requirements. The online intranet prototype will be utilized by ACME to demonstrate the intranet solution, as well as to educate key executives on its use. The central goals of the prototype are: to promote development skills within the organization, to establish proof of concept to demonstrate the technology, and institute a forum for further requirements definition of the application and the broader intranet. The development of the prototype involves five steps:

1. Architectural review and requirements analysis.
2. Organizational framework design.
3. Detailed design.
4. Coding and testing.
5. Prototype implementation.

Architectural Review and Requirements Analysis

The initial step of any project is to confirm and document project goals and objectives. Therefore, ACME must review, clarify, and document its intranet goals in the context of the planned application. Only after these project goals and objectives are validated can the appropriate content and functionality to support these goals be identified. During this initial planning process ACME users are invited to discussions to define the functional requirements of the prototype application and to eventually produce a functional requirements document. In addition, it is important to establish an understanding of ACME's technical environment, including hardware/software platforms and lowest-common denominators for supporting the application. The following is a breakdown of this process:

Goals

❑ Gain understanding of ACME existing environment.
❑ Define scope of prototype application.
❑ Document requirements and recommendations.

Deliverables

❑ **Functional requirements document.** A functional requirements document is produced to outline the functions provided by the application and high-level task flows users will experience when implementing the application.
❑ **Application architecture diagram.** An application architecture diagram is needed to show the system architecture and interactions for the application. This involves demonstrating the interaction of client and server machines needed for the application.

Organizational Framework and Visual Design

After base requirements are established, the next step is to develop an organizational framework so the user has a clear, obvious structure when traversing the application. A framework is a significant factor in achieving the overall usability, efficiency, and usefulness of the intranet, and thus is an integral part of the design process; it is worked on before any graphics are produced or HTML pages authored.

Designing an effective organizational framework is a two-step process. First, the information space is organized and structured into a networklike diagram, indicating hierarchies of major information groups. Second, the interaction flow of the application for each user task is exposed and isolated through the framework, which is visually represented by individual task-flow diagrams. These diagrams function as early prototypes for testing the structure and architecture of the intranet. Most important, these diagrams communicate functionality and required interaction sequences from the user's point of view.

The next step is to design an interface or visual design for the application to communicate the organizational framework structure to the user. It is at this stage that the look and feel of the application is addressed in conjunction with the incorporation of the ACME identity to accurately and effectively present the organizational structure. Here's the breakdown of this part of the process:

Goals

- Understand the structure of information within ACME.
- Logically position the application within the ACME intranet.
- Design the application information flow.

Deliverables

- **Information architecture diagram.** The information architecture diagram shows the positioning of information within the intranet and the application.
- **Task Flow Diagram.** The task flow diagram outlines the series of pages and interactions the user will encounter in performing business tasks within the application.

Detailed Design

After outlining the flow of information structure within the application, it is possible to design the application in detail. These designs will serve as input to the coding and testing stages of the application code development. Because LiveWire utilizes server-side JavaScript for database connectivity and state management, the application code is contained in each Web page presented to the user. As such, the detailed designs are usually modular by page, specifying the interaction of pages within the application as well as the interfaces to external systems, such as relational databases, following the task flows produced in the information architecture phase. Detailed designs translate the requirements and task flows into application page modules that developers will use as direction for writing the application code. Here's the short version of this step:

Goals

- Produce detailed specifications for application code.

Deliverables

❑ **Application code specifications.** Code specifications are documents that define the functionality and interaction of pages within the application and with external systems.

Coding and Testing

The coding and testing step integrates the detailed designs to create the underlying application code. In this case, server-side JavaScript will be created within HTML documents to produce a LiveWire application. Application developers create a collection of HTML pages embedded with JavaScript to create pages that compose the application. In brief:

Goals

❑ Translate detailed designs into application code.

Deliverables

❑ Functional application.

Prototype Implementation

Implementing the prototype involves introducing the application to a small number of users who pilot its functionality. As the first iteration of the application, the prototype is aimed at delivering a proof of concept on the application and a demonstration of the technology. Further, it focuses on the interaction cycles required to access information or to perform an action and test the navigation pathways through the information space from the user perspective. Functional and technical feedback received from users during this review and evaluation is then documented and incorporated into a second round of functional requirements, which are addressed in the second iteration of development. Here is the wrap-up of this step:

Goals

❑ Implement prototype application within ACME.
❑ Deliver proof of concept of the application and technology.
❑ Generate a second round of technical and functional requirements.

Deliverables

❑ Distributed application.

Application Development Workplan

The schedules in Table 9.1 outline each step of the prototype development phase. In general, the intranet application development process is organic in nature highlighted by continuous changes in technology, and therefore requirements. For this reason, week metrics were chosen for the workplan as presented in the table since tasks often parallel and merge during the development process.

Table 9.1 Prototype Development Workplan

Steps & Deliverables	Week 1	Week 2	Week 3	Week 4	Week 5	Week 6
Step 1: Architectural Review and Requirements Analysis						
Requirements Gathering	▓					
Step 2: Organizational Framework and Visual Design						
Information Architecture Design		▓				
Task Flow Design		▓				
Step 3: Detailed Design						
Application Code Specifications			▓	▓		
Step 4: Prototype Implementation						
JavaScript & LiveWire Development				▓		▓
Application Testing					▓	▓
Error Testing					▓	▓
Performance Testing					▓	▓

Deliverables Examples

This section offers examples of the deliverables described in the prototype development process. These high-level documents are intended to set the stage for the example application and abstract the process to apply to various applications.

Functional Requirements Document

The Supplies Ordering application was identified as the application ACME would use for the prototype stage of this project. The goal of the prototype is to demonstrate the application of intranet technology in the ACME environment. Specifically, the prototype addresses the following:

- ❑ Applicability of intranet technology to the business needs of ACME
- ❑ Performance of intranet technology within the ACME infrastructure
- ❑ System administration of intranet technology
- ❑ Requirements for application development in an intranet environment
- ❑ Viability of intranet technology for a business process
- ❑ Reliability of the intranet system architecture
- ❑ Database connectivity via LiveWire and JavaScript

The Supplies Ordering application encompasses enabling the ACME field offices with the ability to order store supplies in an online environment. Currently, the process of ordering supplies is a traditional paper-based approach; that is, order form to purchase order to receipt. ACME's goal is to streamline the process by enabling ordering and receipt functions via intranet technology. The following functions have been identified for the prototype implementation:

1. Requester pulls list of supplies.
2. Requester selects items, then specifies quantities on hand and quantities required.
3. Headquarters orders the supplies and updates the order status.
4. Requester receives order confirmation and status.
5. Requester enters receipt of supplies.

Approximately 5,000 users are located in 500 ACME locations nationwide, who enter the system once to twice a week to order, check order status, and confirm receipt. There are more than 5,000 different items stored in the relational database.

Technical Environment

ACME will use a Sun Sparc20 server running Solaris 2.5 with 128MB RAM and a 2GB hard disk to host this application. This server currently maintains the supplies database implemented using an Oracle RDBMS. On the client side, users have desktop PCs running a combination of Microsoft Windows 3.1 and Windows95. ACME has a standard TCP/IP network with a combination of leased WAN lines and LAN lines, providing 10 megabits of bandwidth to the desktop (see Figure 9.1).

Based on this environment, Netscape Enterprise 3.0 server will be used as the HTTP server running on the server machine. On the client side, Netscape Communicator will be used on both the Windows 3.1 and Windows95 platforms. As stated earlier, server-side JavaScript and Netscape LiveWire will be used to develop this application. Figure 9.2 builds on the existing ACME intranet information architecture design to show the addition of the Supplies Ordering application.

Task Flow

Figure 9.3 illustrates the flow of information for the Supplies Ordering Application. In conjunction with the information architecture diagram, the task flow diagram is used to demonstrate and collect feedback from users as part of the design process of the application.

Figures 9.4a through 9.4e show the LiveWire application created based on the preceding design specifications.

This section demonstrates the high level intranet application design process. This shows a simple database application for a typical supplies ordering application. This application was created using JavaScript and LiveWire to connect the Enterprise Server to a relational database. The user interface is constructed of JavaScript and HTML to easily distribute the application to ACME users. Moreover, this demonstrates the ability to quickly develop and deploy applications using the intranet. There is no client software to be installed on the user's desktop and maintenance of the application is centralized. The user interface is simple and leverages the user's familiarity with Web technology. The combination of ease of development, distribution, and usability provide an efficient cost effective application solution.

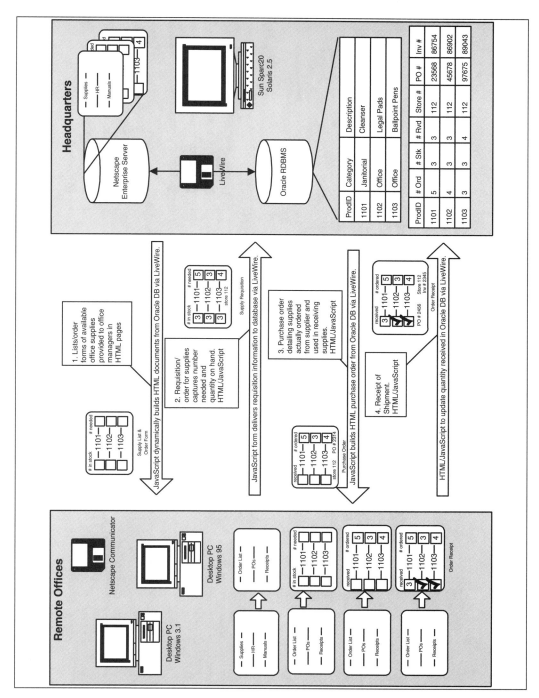

Figure 9.1 Application architecture.

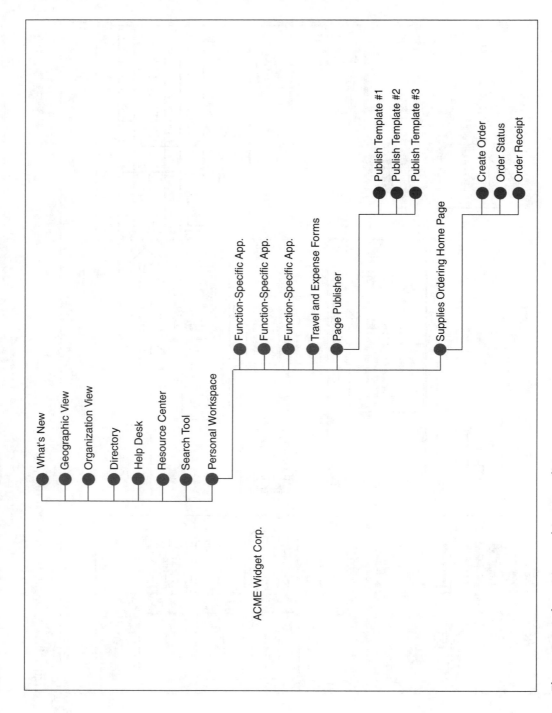

Figure 9.2 Information architecture diagram.

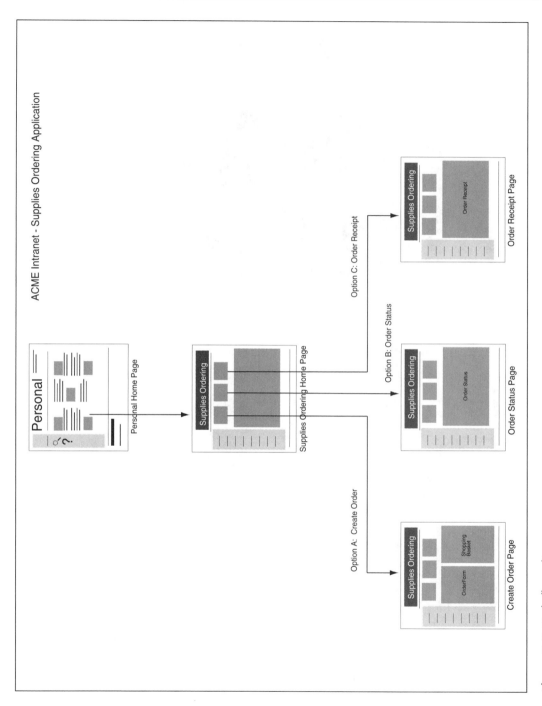

Figure 9.3 Task flow diagram.

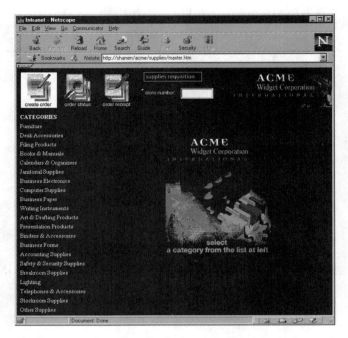

Figure 9.4a Supplies Ordering application (select category).

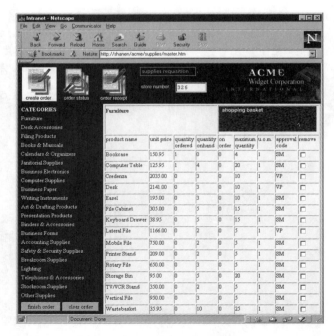

Figure 9.4b Supplies Ordering application (category list).

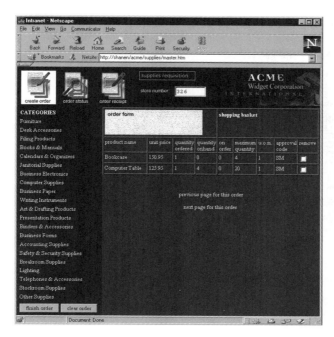

Figure 9.4c Supplies Ordering application (create order).

Figure 9.4d Supplies Ordering application (order status).

Figure 9.4e Supplies Ordering application (order receipt).

10

DEPLOYMENT ISSUES

Bandwidth

Bandwidth is one of the most talked about issues in the intranet deployment process: how much there is, how much is needed now, and how much will be needed in the future. Bandwidth is the single most significant bottleneck to break through when implementing intranet technology. It determines what can be practically sent across the wire in terms of graphics and other "eye candy" that dress up applications; it also has an influence on the architectures that are built for accessing databases and legacy systems. In a perfect world, with unlimited bandwidth, applications would be tremendously dynamic as they interface with back-end systems; users all over the world would experience identical performance using the same hardware; and graphics and colors would proliferate.

In short, the question on everyone's mind is, "How much bandwidth do I need?" And, the answer is always "It depends"—on a number of parameters, the most important of which is what is considered adequate performance by a given organization. The average page size, the number of graphics per page, the size of the largest documents, the number of hits per page, and the overall number of user hits per day on the server all have an impact on performance. The guidelines presented in this book should be considered as a good place to start, but all intranets will go through a growth period during which trial and error lead to the appropriate infrastructure and architecture modifications.

Remote Users

Related to bandwidth restrictions is the problem of how to connect users in remote areas of the world who may have extremely limited methods of connectivity. To solve this problem, the level of service required by remote locations to corporate information must be evaluated. In most cases, limited bandwidth availability requires intranet architectures with a strong replication component to bring the content closer to the users. Some foreign governments strictly control the telecommunications available to companies, which necessitates the implementation of heavy replication.

Internal Resistance

Any new technology is bound to meet with resistance from within the company. Unlike most systems, however, resistance to intranet technology is often most fierce from IT departments, rather than users (as mentioned earlier, the user community is often the first to adopt and promote intranet technology). For IT departments, this paradigm shift is somewhat uncomfortable. Criticism usually comes in the form of complaints regarding the maturity of the technology and the tools available for system administration and development. But the strongest resistance is from those for whom the intranet is their first implementation of client/server technology. Companies that have a long history of mainframe or midrange application environments, such as CICS or Tandem where applications and application control are primarily server-side, have a lot of questions and concerns regarding the "bulletproof" application environment. The fact is, intranet applications handle information in completely different ways from mainframe systems. It is important to acknowledge that although intranet applications do share some similarities to the mainframe environment (using a thin client and heavy server-side processing), they are client/server systems and take advantage of processing on the client machine. This is the aforementioned paradigm shift for IT organizations. Thus, the intranet development environment entails a retooling of the IT department. IT staff must become skilled in HTML, Java, JavaScript, C, and C++, and the introduction of new programming languages always has an impact on an IT department and may require the hiring of additional personnel. Fortunately, the popularity of Web technology has produced a large pool of application developers and system administrators for the Web environment.

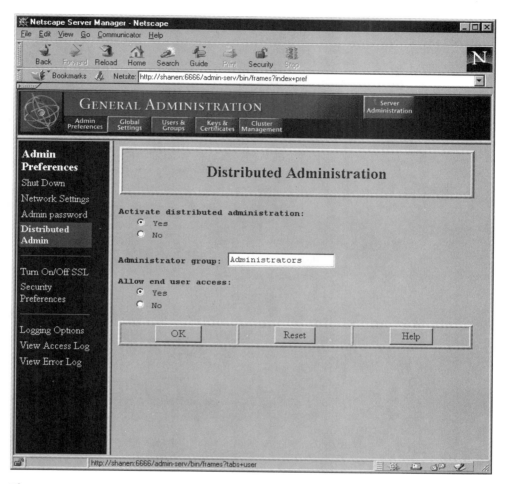

Figure 10.1a Netscape administration server interfaces.

Internal complaints are also often directed at the lack of system administration tools or tools for integrating intranets into the existing maintenance environment. Certainly, this was true of the first generations of intranet servers, but in recent releases, many tools have been developed to address the system administration function, including visual tools for maintaining file system structures and links, tools for integrating with network monitoring tools through SNMP, and tools for publishing and distributing HTML using document management.

This chapter specifically, and this book generally, are intended to present intranet solutions in a favorable light and to describe the benefits of

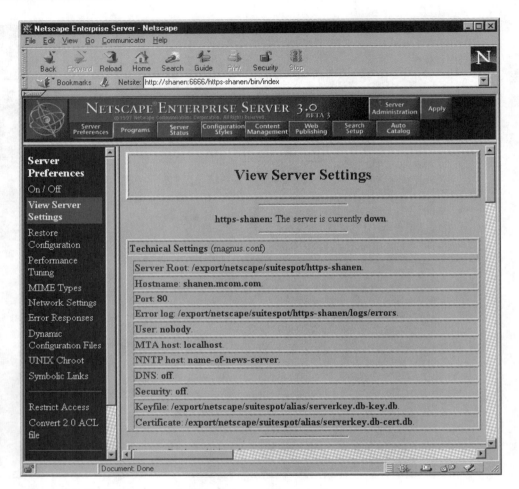

Figure 10.1b Netscape administration server interfaces.

multiplatform, single-source coding for application developers, but it is important to recognize that intranet application development is not a panacea for application development. Full requirements gathering and user testing are still necessary; in fact, all of the challenges of integration and user acceptance exist for application development in the intranet environment.

In some companies, personnel are eager to break out of traditional technology and learn the latest in information processing, and this is the best-case scenario for developing intranets: to integrate employees' industry knowledge with their interest to learn and use new technology. As stated earlier, the most important key to success is to gain support and ownership from the user community and those who will develop and maintain it.

Vendor Support

Essential for minimizing the negative impact of introducing the intranet is fitting into the current application environment, so of course companies have many questions about the integration of Netscape's products with those of competitors. The Internet has established numerous standards bodies, such as the World Wide Web Consortium (W3C), the Internet Engineering Task Force (IETF), and others, which approve a base level of conventions to create standards such as HTML, SMTP, VCAL, and others. Although this does not preclude different manifestations of the standards, it does ensure a low level of communication and interface standardization. Will every Netscape and Microsoft Web product plug and play seamlessly for all applications? Probably not. But there are ways to design applications that are perfectly portable. The best recommendation is to use those tools provided in the application that are based on open standards, such as HTML and Java. Developers should be leery of any application code that requires a plug-in tool or other proprietary components to ensure cross-platform, cross-product applications. ActiveX is a prime example of a development environment that is specific to an operating system. Rooted in Microsoft Windows OLE technology, ActiveX will run natively in Microsoft Internet Explorer as well as Netscape Communicator through a bound browser plug-in. ActiveX, however, makes heavy use of the Windows application environment which makes its applications platform-specific. By comparison, Java code is far more portable than ActiveX, as it is compiled dynamically on an as-needed basis.

Employee Misuse of the Intranet

A common concern of many information technology organizations and executives is the potential for employee misuse of the intranet. These concerns run the gamut from posting inappropriate materials internally to misrepresentation of the company externally on newsgroups, to productivity lost to endless surfing. The solution is often thought to be to limit user access to particular services or specific areas on the Internet. Of course, there are technical ways to limit user access, but the larger issue is purely political. As everyone knows, the misuse of company property by employees is not specific to intranets. All companies rely on a certain level of professionalism and common sense from their employees, as dictated by their company culture. The intranet must be treated no differently in this regard. To maintain a policy of limiting site access, a company would have to first define the term inappropriate and then have a staff of system administrators scouring the Web for potentially inappropriate sites. An obvious alternative is to deny Internet connectivity to the user community; however, it has been proven that access to online information makes employees both better decision makers and more productive. A better alternative is to implement logging of usage on the intranet to protect against misuse, but this, too, calls into question the level of trust that management affords its employees. In many cases, such policies have a negative affect on user willingness to work with the system. To address the problem of posting of inappropriate material, most companies have instituted a publishing process that includes a review process in a staging area prior to release of the information to a production system. The bottom line is, though, no safeguards are foolproof; but remember: policies are followed or ignored by people, not technology.

Conclusion

This chapter is a conglomeration of many of the deployment issues companies experience in the intranet planning process. Many of these issues are not specific to intranet technology, but are important questions for administrators and executives to anticipate and answer early in the deployment process.

Part III

THE FUTURE OF INTRANETS

11

TRENDS AND DIRECTIONS IN INTRANETS

In the face of unprecedented technological developments, CIOs and IT organizations invariably want to know, "What's next?" This chapter identifies some trends in intranet technology. The speed at which the technology is progressing and the way existing technology is being used are both important factors in answering that question. It is undeniable that intranet technology is progressing at a remarkable pace, and as companies fuel the demand, Netscape responds. Overall, the answer to what's next is dependent upon how quickly companies become comfortable with the technology. To reach that stage, more corporate computing must move to native open standards, to start there rather than to convert, to trust the security of the intranet, and to look for ways to leverage open standards in conjunction with existing systems.

Hype Is Hype

Hype is part and parcel of any new technology, and so it is with intranets. Senior IT managers and CIOs will continue to be bombarded with marketing information from competitors keeping "score" in the Web wars. Much of this information is necessarily skewed. The "browser war" is a perfect example of the level of hype surrounding Web technology. But the browser war will pale in comparison to the marketing strategies that will be launched to gain control of corporate IT funding for intranets. As the stakes get higher and existing market share in the area of enterprise computing is challenged, the competition will heat up. Lotus and Microsoft will no doubt move their marketing against the Netscape full-service intranet solution to center stage. In the face of all the "noise," it will become imperative to stay focused on the essential compelling reasons for adopting intranet technology: open standards, cost of ownership, and flexibility.

Already, media hype has led many companies to believe that if they haven't deployed a full-blown intranet they are way behind the technology curve. This is certainly not the case. It is true that most of the companies Netscape Professional Services works with have a Web server and a few browsers on site, but they do not constitute an intranet solution. Even the most technically advanced companies are still working out the technical details and standards of a full-service solution. Further, at the rate of change in Web technology, the most any company can be behind in intranet technology is a couple of months. Where companies do gain ground, however, is in experience and comfort with intranet systems.

From Internet to Intranet

Netscape has gone through a number of phases in meeting consumer demand. The first resulted in Internet browsers that enabled users to surf the Net. The browser push was followed by the rush for servers; then companies began to want a presence on the Web—an external home page. The current phase of demand concentrates on the internal web, the intranet. Naturally, these demands have significantly shaped the functionality of Netscape products and services. In the early days, the professional services area was devoted to one thing: the installation and configuration of Netscape's commercial applications. Customers of the Merchant and Publishing systems needed assistance in getting these products up and running, and so a rogue group of developers was sent on-site to help with the installation.

As the number of products has grown, and companies have begun to focus internally, Netscape Professional Services has become dedicated to providing services to its corporate customers by deploying its SuiteSpot servers to build world-class intranet solutions. Certainly, many customers still need assistance with external sites and configuring the Publishing and Merchant systems, but the demands of the market and the existing external presence of companies has shifted attention to the corporate intranet. It is important to recognize, however, that Netscape products are not specifically external nor internal. Based on the open Internet standards, there are many ways to deploy Netscape technology. For example, many companies with large and complex publishing requirements have deployed the Netscape Publishing system internally. Nor is it uncommon for companies that have large supply inventories for internal use or that employ an accounting system that requires chargebacks to different departments to deploy the Merchant system within the company. All these systems are based on the SuiteSpot servers with extensive integration with back-end databases. For some companies, buying a packaged solution like the Publishing or Merchant systems is a better option than building them from scratch. This often is dependent of the development and support resources available within the company.

The Extranet: From Intranet to Internet

Now that the technology has come inside the company, companies want to know how to leverage the open platform to communicate with customers and partners outside. Fortunately, the technology started on the Internet side and was designed to be scalable at that level of usage. Thus, it is now possible to make some basic assumptions about the general public and companies, which make communications much easier. For example, we can assume that most companies have deployed a TCP/IP network and that many of their employees have access to HTML browsing technology. From there, many companies began to pursue building interfaces using HTML and standard interface tools to open a new level of communication with their customers. Furthermore, the ubiquity of the Internet enables access from anywhere; and the near-term promise of new levels of secure access makes it possible to guarantee customers and partners confidential information through a standard, secure interface. Many companies already use this approach to improve customer service programs. In some cases, it was found that the extranet could greatly reduce the number of resources required to support customers. In addition, groupware tools coupled with secure access enables business partners to communicate and archive information through standard formats and protocols including NNTP (news/discussions), S/MIME (mail), and CAP (scheduling), blurring the traditional harsh lines of the firewall on an application level. If it is assumed that all information and access must be secure, and that all users, internal or external, are required to authenticate themselves upon connection (via certificates and using secure transmission (SSL) for all sessions), the firewall is put in place not to draw the line between the Web technology within the company, but to deny access to other machines and information within the company.

The Networked Enterprise

The Networked Enterprise is Netscape's vision of the next step in corporate intranets. Described in a whitepaper by the same name, the Networked Enterprise is achieved when a company connects segments of the intranet to the intranets of their business partners, thus forming a web of extranets. This enables companies to communicate freely and efficiently with customers, partners, suppliers, and distributors using the same communications technology deployed as part of the full-service intranet. The Networked Enterprise hinges on two very important technological advancements: open standards support and security. Open standards enable companies to share information more efficiently and accurately than ever before. In addition, the support of standards enables *crossware*, or the sharing and deploying of applications across platforms, companies—in short, across everything.

Another important element of the Networked Enterprise is security. Connecting intranets and sharing information require a new level of security and access control, as extranets blur the lines of corporate firewalls by placing more information outside and accessible by business partners via the Internet. This is accomplished through the wide support of standard security technology such as X.509 certificates and the Secure Sockets Layer transmission protocol. More than advances in technology, however, the Networked Enterprise relies on advances in user and management comfort of these standards as the firewalls are torn down.

Moving Away from the Operating System

Just as the first-generation Navigator browser afforded users a standard visual interface to the Internet across multiple platforms, Netscape products will continue to separate users from the underlying operating systems of their computers. Netcaster is a good example of how the importance of information and the independence of location/platform is driving the vision of these products. As users roam from office to office around the building or around the world, they can log in to a PC, Macintosh, or Unix box and access the same information and applications, and not have to understand the underlying operating system commands. Soon, users will not rely at all on the operating system for file management, sharing, or printing. What's more, users will be able to move between locations and systems while maintaining full functionality and access to information without conversion, filters, or gateways. By focusing on information-centric functionality for users, Netscape will continue to release products that will not require the user to leave the intranet or networked enterprise environment to perform all of their tasks.

Objects and ORBs Everywhere

As discussed in the products chapter, IIOP, CORBA, IDL, and object-oriented programming will no doubt become familiar to the application development community in the future intranet and extranet arena. The Netscape ONE platform and the Netscape products individually will become increasingly object-centric, using IIOP and IDL to communicate with one other. As an example, the next-generation Enterprise Server will become an object request broker (ORB) at the core, and all of its currently embedded functions will become objects that it manages. For example, the Web publisher will become its own object and will be invoked by the core ORB when a user requests publishing functions. In this way, applications can be developed as modular objects and incorporated into the Enterprise Service in a similar fashion. This is a drastic change from the use of NSAPI to modify or extend the server, which will result in greater flexibility and functionality in application development.

Similarly, the Netscape Communicator is moving to a more modular and object-oriented architecture for its components. This, too, will allow for greater flexibility in configuration of the client and in client-side application development. Companies are encouraged to investigate the possibilities of utilizing the object request brokers in the Enterprise Server, and the Communicator to develop applications, as well as to build skills within their IT organizations. The first-tier applications using this technology have wrapped existing systems with Java to provide an IDL interface to CORBA-standard ORBs. It is clear that objects, ORBs, IIOP, and IDL will replace NSAPI as the way companies modify and extend the functionality of SuiteSpot servers.

Deployment via Grassroots Efforts

As stated in the introduction to this book, the intranet has, in many cases, turned the tables on the IT department. Individual users and workgroups often are the first to implement intranet technology within the company. These grassroots efforts, usually departmental, utilize Web technology to meet very specific goals for a team of people: to post and share information among the members of the group. The intranet grants them ownership and autonomy in an easy-to-learn, easy-to-use technical solution to their immediate business problems. Often, however, shortly after this type of deployment, the intranet grows to an unmanageable size for the department and the IT pros are asked to take over the support role or to provide more functionality via the intranet. In a large company, this same scenario occurs in multiple departments or groups, and the IT department is bombarded with requests to support a system that they did not evaluate, choose, or design.

This is when a redeployment usually occurs and the IT department establishes standards for the intranet. Often, companies want to define internal standards on hardware, software (operating systems and applications), architecture (network and directory structure), as well as functional procedures for publishing, navigation, and external access. Guidelines for all of these areas are given in this book, but the actual standards implemented within any corporation must always be specific to that entity.

Vertical or Point Solutions

The origin of many intranets is at the departmental level with simple information-sharing applications on the workgroup or team level. As IT departments take over the management of the intranet, it begins to be viewed more as an enterprise tool and as a platform for application development. Moving from the singular application to the desktop is the key sign that the intranet has "arrived" as an enterprise application. The main motivation behind this is to leverage information across the company.

Departmental or workgroup-specific solutions instituted as part of a grassroots effort normally address only the needs of the group for which they were developed. One of the core goals of CIOs is to leverage and share information across departmental divisions and the enterprise. For this reason, part of the redeployment process is to structure the intranet such that the information needs of the smaller groups continue to be met along with those of the enterprise as a whole. This often requires planning in the architecture or placement of the information servers as well as the file system directory structure of each of these servers. The information must be organized so that it is meaningful to the user and can be maintained, yet still has room to grow.

Emerging Corporate Strategies

The second wave of intranet deployment has given companies the opportunity to take a step back and develop strategies for the intranet enterprisewide. These strategies include reengineering communications internally as well as redefining the current organizational systems. The first wave of the intranet swept over on a micro or departmental level, while the redeployment wave has covered the enterprise as a whole. Companies have designed intranet publishing and navigation strategies to supply users with the tools they need to make full use of the extensive information now available. While many companies have achieved great utility in information sharing using the standard intranet functions of information sharing and navigation, more are developing mission-critical applications or integration. This is an important step for Web technology: to move from a complimentary system to the system on which business is done.

Mission-Critical Applications

A mission-critical system is one required to perform a job function; that is, without the system, people could not do their jobs. As stated, the intranet is moving from the status as a secondary or nice-to-have function into the role of a platform on which mission-critical applications are developed and used. A good example of this is the trading systems being developed by many Wall Street brokerage companies. To do business, these companies rely on the speed and dependability of trading systems. Previously, Web technology had been used only for information services; it has now moved into the area of transactions. This is possible thanks to the tools available in the Netscape ONE application development platform, and the maturity of secure, bulletproof application development tools, in conjunction with the capability to write platform-independent, single-source code and to centrally manage and distribute up-to-date application code. Hence, the intranet becomes an application platform rather than just a singular application.

Internal Standards Development

While the intranet has been progressing as an application platform, companies have been developing standards for its deployment and use, primarily to support the intranet on a large scale. These standards include hardware and software specifications as well as application development standards and end-user procedures. As with any system, standards and procedures are the heart and soul of efficient maintenance. Although the promise of running on old iron is appealing from a hardware procurement cost-benefit analysis, many companies are identifying standard configurations in order to lower the number of permutations and ease the burden of support wherever system support is a centralized function. Companies in which system support is highly distributed, and each takes care of his or her own, earn higher return in the platform independence of the Netscape intranet. It is important to establish the lowest common denominator of hardware and software in the distributed intranet architecture, which, in addition to easing support of the intranet, often dictates design decisions. The use of frames, Java, and animated graphics are all considerations heavily dependent upon the client version and sophistication. These features will no doubt be "given" by the time this book is published, consequently, there are sure to be other considerations that will impact development decisions. Consequently, application development teams must be aware of the upgrade decisions being made for the intranet and of all the flavors of clients and servers for which they are developing currently and in the future.

In addition to technical specifications, companies have been instituting procedural standards for their users to both ease administration and give users more flexibility. The first of these procedures is often introduced in the publishing area to answer the questions: "How do I create documents for the intranet?" Where do I put the documents to be published?" "How do I update documents I have already published?"

Converting Documents for the Intranet

Currently, many users create documents using proprietary tools, which must then be converted for display in the Web environment. The most widely used document creation tool set is Microsoft Office. To publish documents created with those tools, users often give their files to the IS department for conversion, clean-up, and posting or publishing. Needless to say, this is a time-consuming and resource-intensive process for distributing information. The alternative is to convert the documents to Adobe's Portable Document Format (PDF) for display in the Netscape Navigator using bundled plug-in technology from Adobe. The PDF format enables the display of documents in their intended format. PDF is based on the PostScript format and therefore is true WYSIWYG technology.

In spite of PDF, HTML prevails as the primary document format on intranets; therefore, the Microsoft Office suite and other popular document creation tools provide conversion tools to translate their proprietary document formats to HTML. In some cases, this is as simple as invoking a Save as HTML command. The downside is that not all proprietary document elements can be converted cleanly to HTML, and the potential exists for data loss in the conversion process. Furthermore, revisions to those documents require the source document, the application in which it was created, as well as the conversion step, before it may be distributed in the HTML version. However, as the HTML specification or document type definition advances, it is approaching parity with some of the proprietary formats. In order to avoid the additional maintenance, many companies are moving to authoring directly in HTML, using the new, more sophisticated HTML editing tools such as the Netscape Composer component of the Communicator (see Figure 11.1). The elimination of the conversion step from the publishing process makes it far more accurate and efficient. Henceforth, users can be certain that what they create will be delivered in an accurate and useful format regardless of platform. The Composer component of the Netscape Communicator gives authors a great deal of control over HTML editing, through visual table editing, absolute positioning, and full rich-text formatting capabilities.

Full-Text Searching to Intelligent Search Agents

As the amount of information on corporate intranets grows exponentially, more sophisticated navigation tools and techniques become imperative. Currently navigation remains largely a pull operation, whereby users seek information, usually by sorting through the hits returned from full-text indexes. But tools are being developed to change this from pull to push as intelligent agent tools are being developed that gather information and bring it *to* the user. Based on a profile constructed by the user, information that is of interest is tagged and brought to the user's attention. An example of this push technology is Netscape's In-box Direct program that sends information to the user's e-mail box

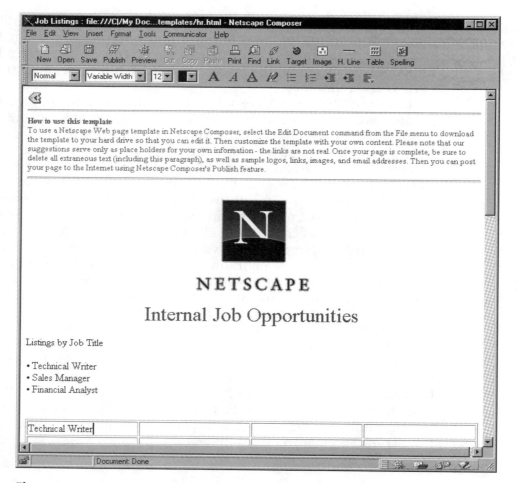

Figure 11.1 Composer Component of Netscape Communicator.

based on a set of criteria set by that user. As with all Web technology, intelligent agents and the push paradigm were first developed for the Internet to help users wade through the huge volumes of information available on the World Wide Web. Now this technology is moving inside the enterprise to help users find information germane to their job function. This is an especially effective and compelling area in which to combine the intra- and internets to form an extranet that delivers pertinent information tailored to users within the company to help them make better decisions.

Many search agents have been engineered to include artificial intelligence logic, which tracks the subject areas most accessed by a user and makes inferences from these patterns to better provide information to the user as it is made available. As patterns change, so does the criteria used by the search agent.

Intranet: From Single Application to Desktop

The intranet started as just another application among the rest of the tools people used to perform their jobs. When users needed information, they launched their browser from the desktop operating system, got what they were looking for, and returned to the desktop. Soon, though, users realized that they were spending a lot of time on the Web and so kept their browser running constantly to have quick access to information. To the rescue comes the Netscape Communicator, and now the intranet has become the desktop. Information is indeed power in the corporate world, and the more pervasive the access to that information, the better. With the Netcaster component of the Communicator, the open desktop of the intranet becomes the hub from which users operate. Now the starting point for computing is the intranet. Other applications are launched and files are managed from the Netcaster/Netscape desktop. This marks a turning point for Web technology. The announcement of Microsoft's Active Desktop also attests to this direction of the intranet and Web technology.

The intranet as the desktop also enables full cross-platform user mobility. Since the desktop environment is based completely on open standards, the desktop itself is not specific to a platform; for example, as a user moves from a Macintosh at home to an office PC running Windows, the desktop is identical, with all of the same preferences and interface commands. This makes the desktop ubiquitous for the user, despite location or hardware.

ROI: Hard Costs to Intangible Benefits

The International Data Corporation (IDC) and other studies done to determine the return on investment of intranet systems have shown unprecedented figures of over 1,500 percent return in as little as three months for some companies. In themselves, these numbers are indicative of the value gained by the open solution as delivered by the Netscape intranet. The best news of all, however, is that this is just the tip of the value that intranets offer. A more incalculable value of these systems lies in the better decision-making ability of employees and the efficiencies gained through synergy among groups.

Security as a Given

To date, security has been a barrier to implementation of the intranet. The fear of sensitive information being broachable by outside intruders has changed to the fear of inappropriate information being accessible to the wrong people within a company. Because of this, intranets are often scrutinized more intently than other enterprise systems. Netscape has responded with tools that achieve a new level of secure computing in enterprise systems. The introduction of the certificate security architecture, secure messaging, and encryption has provided solutions for the tough problems of intranet security. These tools do, however, engender trade-offs. System administration must increase to distribute and maintain certificates; data transmission performance decreases when using dynamic encryption and decryption; and users must be trained to employ certificates. Interestingly, these trade-offs often lead IT departments to rethink their security needs and to inventory the nature of the information in their intranets, as well as to compare the level of security offered by existing mission-critical systems to that of the intranet.

The long and the short of security is that the intranet has surpassed many other enterprise systems. Companies are beginning to realize that security for security's sake is not always the right move. In the end, security is only as good as the end user.

Extranets

The extranet is the Internet and the intranet combined. Still developing, the extranet relies heavily on the security of its components. Companies have used the concept of the extranet in two ways: the internal web (employees) looking out and external web (consumers, patrons, suppliers) looking in. The most popular form of the extranet is to grant simple Internet access to internal users. This broadens the information available to the user community significantly, and therefore usually raises concerns about employee misuse of the extranet. More advanced implementations of the outward-looking extranet make use of the push paradigm of information delivery. A good example of this is to produce competitive watch sites to compile information on competitors' press releases.

Inward-looking extranets allow the general public to look at a subset of information on a company's intranet. Usually in the form of providing customer service information to a broadband audience via the Internet, these systems can save a great deal of time and money by making information from internal systems available externally. This is where security is of the essence, to protect confidential information that may exist on the same system. Perhaps the best current example of an inward-looking extranet are package-tracking systems that enable users to check the status of their packages using the Internet. This has allowed shipping companies to greatly reduce their customer service resources while providing a higher level of service. Netscape, too, has been using the Internet to distribute its products for trial and purchase. The key difference is that the Netscape site is designed as a purely external site, while the shipping companies' sites interface with internal, mission-critical systems.

In the future, companies will find more ways to combine internal and external information. Basic Internet connectivity will become commonplace, more sophisticated compilation of strategic information will become possible, and use of the push paradigm will become more widespread. Inward-looking intranets will be implemented more frequently, exposing more information from inside the company to customers. Netscape Professional Services and Technical Support are already developing sites specific to customers that require client-side certificates for access through the Internet. As the tools for secure access become available, the other uses of the extranet will proliferate. The result will be even greater return on investment in the form of elevated client service through self-serve customer service.

The Internet as Intranet

Companies are increasingly intrigued by the idea of using the Internet as a virtual private network to augment or replace existing WAN networks. The opportunity to grant access through Internet Service Providers to remote users and thus alleviate network support resources is very attractive to downsizing IT departments in large companies. The open standards of Netscape products make for a transparent computing environment for internal and external use. Certainly these benefits are very exciting, but there are concomitant issues to contemplate. First and foremost is the level of performance that can be achieved in the user community through public/shared network lines. The Internet is made up of a wide variety of networking hardware and software products, and each access to it is dynamic, meaning that every access may take a different path to the source of data. For example, on one access to an intranet site, a user may be routed through the University of Wisconsin, on the next through the University of Paris, on a third through numerous locations or "hops." For this reason, it is impossible to predict or promise a specific level of performance to the user community.

And don't forget, the Internet is not owned by a specific vendor or provider, so when difficulties arise, it is difficult to know where to turn. There are those who would counter that the dynamic routing of the Internet offers benefits in terms of failover and redundant paths to their companies. Another obvious issue in using the Internet is security, the barrier most companies cite as the reason for continuing to use leased lines for WAN connectivity. The thought of transmitting proprietary information through a series of public networks is very frightening for corporations. Although transmission and data encryption technologies are becoming more widely available and are infinitely more secure than traditional forms of communication (phone/fax), security remains an unsettled issue for many corporations. Consequently, companies must make choices about the information that resides inside and outside the intranet. Ironically, most leased WAN lines are also shared, often with other corporations, and sometimes direct competitors. So which is safer; leased WANs or the Internet? In many cases, companies require transmission and data encryption to protect data that is transmitted across WAN lines, too. This involves issuing and maintaining certificates for all corporate users. So perhaps the Internet is not less safe than the traditional WAN. In truth, although security is often identified as the culprit, more often, an IT department must guarantee a certain level of performance to its network users and therefore will pay the money to lease a line which is the responsibility of a third party. While most companies have opted to stay with traditional leased WANs, if the Internet does become a popular means of supplying WANs to corporations, serious questions arise regarding the need for upgrading the thousands of networks worldwide to accommodate what would be unprecedented levels of information being transmitted across the Internet.

Conclusion

While some questions remain, it is certain that companies will leverage their intranets and the Internet to communicate via the extranet. This will greatly increase efficiencies in communication and deliver competitive advantage to early adapters.

CHAPTER ![12](chapter marker)

INTRANET APPLICATIONS

Companies always want to know: "What is everyone else doing?" To answer that question, this chapter outlines some of the most common applications for and benefits of the full-service intranet. Enterprise applications, which impact all companies, will be discussed first, followed by some industry-specific examples.

Enterprise Applications

Enterprise applications software (EAS) systems are implemented by large companies to run their back-office operations, such as accounting and employee systems that make up core business functions including general ledger, payroll, materials management, and so on. Vendors of these tools include SAP, PeopleSoft, Oracle, and Baan. Such systems are very complex and require major integration and configuration efforts; as a result, they represent a significant investment in hardware, software, user training, and support resources.

EAS systems are based on client/server architecture and normally are priced on a per-client seat or concurrent user basis. Because these packages are designed to be flexible and configurable to meet the specific needs of all types of companies, the setup and implementation of both the client and server pieces are extremely complex. Hence, users must be trained to work with the system. These applications are often delivered in different forms to perform different roles in the company; for example, the interface functionality that enables executives to access general ledger information is very different from the functionality needed by order-entry clerks. Thus, the configuration, distribution, and maintenance of multiple-client interfaces and training of functional user groups must be tailored to each and every implementation.

Benefits of Intranet Interfaces to EAS Systems

❑ Lower licensing costs.

❑ Lower training costs.

❑ Ease of use and maintenance.

Many companies have integrated intranet technology with enterprise applications to mitigate the expense of deployment and maintenance of these systems. Rather than configure and distribute multiple-client interfaces, these companies develop intranet interfaces to the enterprise applications using the open standards of the Netscape ONE development environment. This architecture involves adding a third tier to the client/server architecture (enterprise application server, Netscape Enterprise Server, and Netscape Communicator). Doing so eliminates the need to distribute and manage the EAS client on the user's desktop, and makes configuration of the client flexible in such a way that only those functions needed by a given group of users are enabled.

This architecture, however, seriously impacts EAS vendors, because the intranet interface can be developed so that it requires only one client session (the Enterprise Server connection) to serve many users. This challenges the per-seat licensing structure used by many EAS vendors. No doubt vendors will eventually address this issue by changing the licensing structures of their products or by offering their own intranet clients, but to date, many companies have benefited tremendously using intranet interfaces to their EAS systems. Furthermore, a leaner intranet EAS client often reduces or eliminates the need for specialized training for user groups by leveraging the ubiquity of the Web interface and simplifying and streamlining the presentation of the EAS application. Finally, using intranet technology eliminates the distribution and maintenance requisites of the numerous and complex EAS clients throughout the organization by centralizing the intranet application code on the Enterprise Server.

Employee Self-Service Applications

EAS systems are frequently extended to create what are called employee self-service applications, which often are among the first intranet applications developed within a company. These applications are usually used in the area of human resources to register benefits and update benefits information. Traditionally, registering for benefits and payroll took an employee several hours in an orientation session, filling out paper forms and submitting them to the human resources department, where they were keyed into a benefits system and then sent to providers. The same was true for filing claims or making changes to demographic information. For questions regarding benefits eligibility, start dates, and changes to demographic information, employees had to contact the human resources department help desk. The purpose of employee self-service is to make this information available to employees via the intranet, so that all enrollment and claim filing can be done online from the desktop. The employee can access the status of his or her benefits enrollment process and find answers to many commonly asked questions.

These systems are also a great place to post policy and procedure documents, enable registration to 401K and employee stock purchase programs, and provide access to insurance beneficiary information. In this way, the employee self-service application becomes a one-stop shop for employee payment and benefits information.

Employee self-service has proven to greatly reduce the burden on the human resources department, as well as to improve the benefits decisions made by employees. Because these systems can provide a great deal of information to the user as he or she completes the forms—such as what all of the choices mean—the benefits are chosen with better understanding and accuracy. As discussed in the next section, benefits providers are some of the strongest proponents of these systems, as they provide them with more control over the format in which their enrollment and claim data comes to them. Figure 12.1 gives an example of an employee self-service application.

Industry Examples

Unquestionably, all companies can benefit from the integration of intranets, enterprise applications, and information sharing, but the dynamics and structure of different industries leads to specialized uses and varying benefits of intranet technology. This section describes how com-

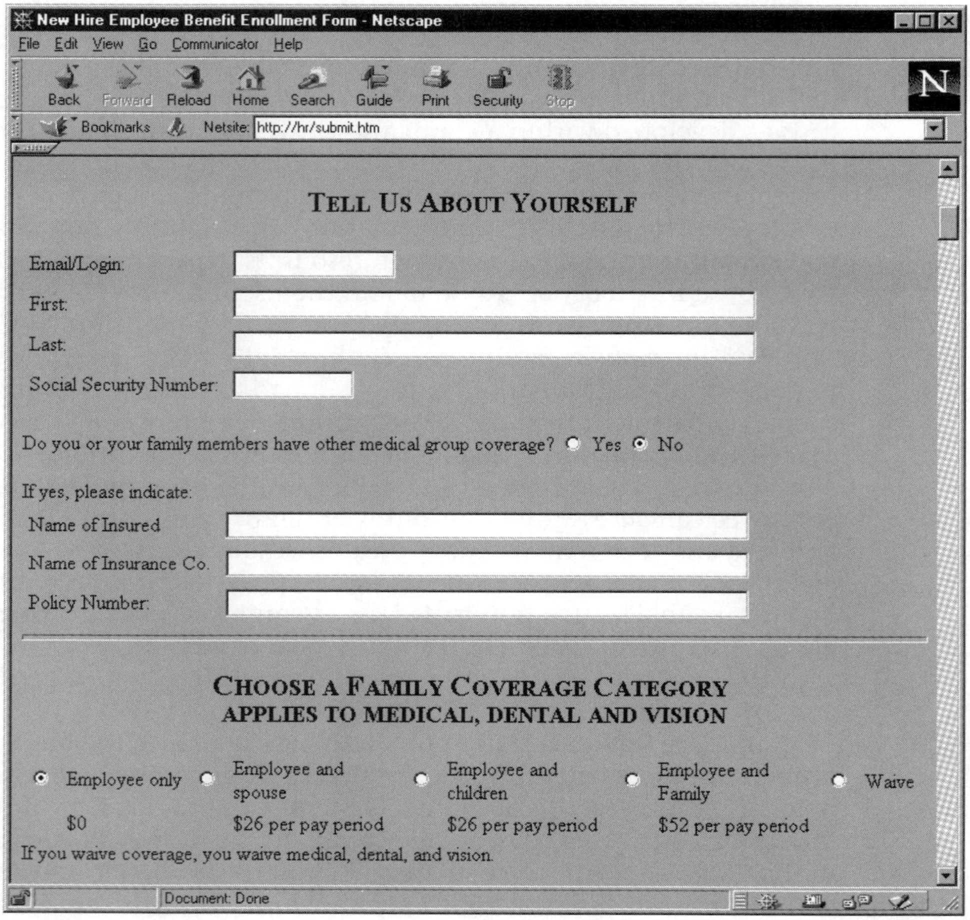

Figure 12.1 Employee self-service application.

panies in a variety of industries have leveraged the benefits of intranet technology, based on experience in the field.

Health Care

On the receiving end of the aforementioned employee self-service applications are the health care providers. Clearly, companies in this industry can benefit enormously through the implementation of intranets and extranets. The motivations for employing Web technology in this area are mixed, surely managing patient records and processing claims electronically result in both efficiencies and, ultimately, better health care. In general, there are two overriding goals: to reduce the amount of paper documentation associated with health care services, and to make the process more efficient for both patients and health care providers.

To meet these goals, intranets introduce platform-independent products and open standards to an extremely diverse computing environment. The health care industry, perhaps more than others, demonstrates the viability of the cross-platform nature of Internet technology. In order to exchange and track personal health care information, systems must traverse doctors offices, hospitals, health care providers, employers, and insurance companies all with a high level of security to protect personal information. Traditionally, each of these entities ran its own internal systems and exchanged information through export from the systems to disk, tape, or hard copy. For the most part, this meant that patient and claim information existed on "islands," which made it difficult or impossible for information to be maintained consistently. More important is that much of this information is very personal and thus restricted under law from release without written permission of the patient, who often is not aware of the information that is available or where it exists.

Obviously, there are many legal and procedural barriers to achieving consistent patient information, not to mention someone to take responsibility for maintaining full medical history documentation. Consequently, many insurance companies are pursuing solutions based on intranet technology to take advantage of the platform independence, ease-of-use and security to help them better track medical histories, exchange information and make transactions electronically, and to provide better medical care—all of which saves everyone time and money.

Financial Services

It hardly need be said that the lifeblood of the financial services community is information; world events, business news, and rumors about the economy all affect investor perceptions and drive the ups and downs of the financial world. It is no surprise, then, that many companies in this industry are the front-runners in finding new ways to access and exchange information. The open standards and platform independence of the intranet have raised to new levels the amount and type of information available to the investor community, so to stay ahead of their customers and competitors, financial services companies must find ways to mange and exchange information. Of particular interest is transferring very specific information to their employees to help them make better decisions faster. For example, intranets are used extensively by financial services companies to distribute internal research information to their employees. Intranets are also combined with Internet access to form extensive extranets for these companies. Of particular value to the financial community was the introduction of push technology with Netscape Netcaster, which enables a tailored, dynamic information stream to users. Several financial companies have developed internal Netcaster channels for their traders to provide up-to-the-minute information from internal research departments and external news feeds.

Pharmaceuticals-Biotechnology

The heavily regulated pharmaceuticals industry has found many uses for intranet technology, particularly for help in collecting and distributing documentation to support the research claims and production processes of their products. The Food and Drug Administration requires companies in this industry to follow strict documentation rules for the research and production processes. For example, the FDA can demand at a moment's notice that a pharmaceutical company produce any and all documents generated during the research and production processes of a drug to demonstrate adherence to the government's standards.

Obviously then, such documentation must be readily available to everyone from the CEO of a company to the maintenance engineers on the production floor. Typically, the documentation and validation departments distribute and collect thousands of paper documents during the life cycle of a single product, and drug and biotech companies spend millions of dollars every year to manage this paper shuffle. Intranets have come to the rescue of many of these companies, which have implemented extensive intranets with a combination of desktop and production floor kiosks for the distribution of standard operating procedures to its employees. The centralized management made possible by an intranet greatly increases the control and accuracy of these documents, and makes them much less resource-intensive to assemble. This has streamlined the document distribution process and improved its accuracy. The result is that product research and production times have been shortened, leading to improvements in the time to market.

Telecommunications

Telecommunications companies more than any other industry have demonstrated the scalability of intranet technology. Both internally and externally, these companies have extended their intranets to tens of thousands of users. The most popular application has been to develop customer service systems to help their employees answer customer questions and inform them of new services. Telecommunications companies have, of course, been closely involved in the development of Internet products and services since they fill the role of Internet service and content providers for the consumer market. To no one's surprise, they have also been the largest implementers of intranet technology.

Oil and Gas

Geographically diverse, oil and gas companies have traditionally had problems communicating efficiently within their organizations. The distributed nature of intranet technology has enabled them to implement a full-service intranet environment using the low-bandwidth network connections and limited infrastructure available in remote areas of the world. This has improved communication within the research and exploration departments of these companies.

Conclusion

This chapter gives brief examples of intranet applications in several industries. It is clear that all industries can benefit from intranet architecture to improve communication infrastructure.

CHAPTER

<img>13</img>

STEPS TO DEPLOYMENT

The remainder of this book serves as a checklist of next steps to take in the intranet deployment process. These comprise decisions and plans that will ease the deployment process and best leverage the guidelines outlined throughout this book.

1. *Decide what the intranet means to your organization.* As stated, you now know the intranet means many things to many companies, therefore, the most important decision to make for your company is where the intranet lies on the technology spectrum. Is it a communications tool à la the telephone and fax machine, or a full mission-critical transaction processing system? The definition will vary by application and information area, so it is important to understand the role intranet technology will play within the organization today and in the future. This premise will dictate much of how the system infrastructure and security architecture will be designed. Further, the positioning of the intranet will determine the amount of effort required to sell this solution internally.

2. *Develop an intranet deployment strategy.* After determining how to position the intranet within the company, the next step is to identify the order and time frame in which the intranet will be deployed. Some companies want to start with the standard of communication and information sharing services to concentrate

on the publishing and document distribution aspects prior to application development. For other companies, application access is seen as the central use of intranet technology. For this reason, it is important to establish the order in which the intranet user services and the network services required to support those user services will be distributed. This order will dictate the skill sets, resources, and policies needed prior to the actual deployment.

3. *Develop intranet standards and policies.* Standards and policies are often overlooked during the planning phase of intranet deployment, which is a mistake, because they can be very valuable as the intranet grows within the organization. The following are important questions to answer regarding support and maintenance of the system:

   ❑ Will the IT organization support only a specific "approved version" of the client and server software?

   ❑ Will beta software be allowed in the production environment?

   ❑ Will applications developed outside the IT department be supported?

   ❑ Will the IT department be responsible for content conversion/maintenance?

Most companies adopt a common desktop environment supported by the IT organization, to outline the specific version of products supported. The output of this step is a list of specifications for the client and server platforms supported in the intranet. This enables the IT department to focus on the functionality of the selected versions and develop enterprise applications based on those specifications.

4. *Define configuration requirements.* After outlining the order of user and network service deployment, it is important to prepare estimates for the hardware and software required for the implementation. This involves identifying the lowest common denominator for client and server platforms within the company, which will in turn dictate the software versions and application development tools appropriate for the initial deployment. It is imperative to also consider planned upgrades for client, server, and network infrastructures, and their time frames relative to the intranet deployment. Some important questions to answer here are:

   ❑ What is the lowest common denominator for client and server machines?

❑ What is current network bandwidth available to different locations within the company?

❑ What infrastructure upgrades are planned, and in what time frame?

Using the answers to these questions and the guidelines in this book, standard configurations should be identified and implemented as the intranet grows.

5. *Plan for an iterative system deployment.* The organization should regard the intranet as a dynamic system, because applications and information will be developed and revisited many times as new products are made available and the intranet evolves to better serve the organization. Compared to traditional systems, the intranet has many built-in mechanisms for upgrading itself; consequently, the overall investments in system deployment, application development, and system administration are much lower in general. The result is that the intranet is more responsive and can better meet user requirements with lower maintenance costs. Indeed, ease of iteration is a key strength in deploying intranets and intranet applications.

6. *Start simple, but start.* The overriding message in this book is start the deployment process. Many companies procrastinate, waiting for promised features in new releases of the product, or because of minor deployment issues. The fact is, paradise will always be just one version away, and there will always be excuses not to begin to deploy the intranet today. The most successful intranets to date are those that have been around the longest, those that have been used and shaped by users and administrators, that have been tuned after the process of trial and error. Intranet and Internet technology is evolving so quickly that iteration is endemic to their deployment. Supporting it requires constant updates and changes by users and system administrators alike. Often, Netscape Professional Services is brought into an organization to start the process by a CIO who recognizes the need to move forward, but faces resistance in the ranks. The first task of any intranet deployment, therefore, is make sure that the technology gets into the hands of the system administrators and users quickly, for then, the most progress can be made in determining the services users need and want, and how these services will be supported.

Appendix

Intranet Workshop Guide

Step 1: Planning the Intranet

An intranet workshop is a two to three day working/planning session held with client management and key client personnel to define the project, its customers, its scope, and its goals. The objectives are to define the project and gain a clear understanding of its scope. This appendix outlines a sample agenda from a planning session, beginning with the questions to be addressed.

1. Define the Project

    What is the scope of the project?

    - ❏ Number of users.
    - ❏ Volume of information.
    - ❏ Departments.
    - ❏ Functional areas.
    - ❏ Applications.
    - ❏ Future plans.
    - ❏ Criteria for completion.

2. Identify Customers

   A customer is anyone affected by the project work.

   - ❑ Participants in the work.
   - ❑ Recipients of the work.
   - ❑ Maintainers of the work.
   - ❑ Defenders of the work.
   - ❑ Users of the work.
   - ❑ Owners of the work.
   - ❑ Buyers of the work.
   - ❑ Managers of the work.

3. Identify Customer Expectations

   Client expectations define the criteria for success.

   - ❑ What expectations of Netscape Communications do you have for this project?
   - ❑ What goals would you like the project to achieve?
   - ❑ What are the expected results of this project?

        Schedule.

        Budget.

        Applications.

   - ❑ Compare the current environment to the perceived future environment.

        Functional.

        Technical.

4. Identify Customer Issues

   Identifying and understanding the customers' questions, concerns, and issues early in the workshop ensures resolution and establishes a comfort level with the solution.

   - ❑ What are your concerns about the system?

        Technical.

        Functional.

        Political.

   - ❑ What can be done to address these concerns?

5. Answer customer questions

Customers often have many questions and concerns about implementing a new and innovative business solution. It is important to establish a comfort level with the proposed solution.

- ❏ What is the solution?
- ❏ What will it take to achieve this solution?
- ❏ How will this affect my business?
- ❏ Is this the right solution for my company? Why?
- ❏ How will I train the users?
- ❏ How will I gain acceptance of the system?
- ❏ Why is this solution better than others?
- ❏ Will this solution really work for me?
- ❏ What are my competitors doing?
- ❏ How long will it take to implement this solution?
- ❏ How will I maintain and update this solution?
- ❏ How long will this solution be valid?

Deliverables

The preliminary project plan and architectural design intranet are important document deliverables from the workshop phase of the intranet planning process.

1. Preliminary Project Plan

A preliminary project plan establishes a list of next steps for adopting an intranet solution.

- ❏ Outline the steps of a prototype phase.
- ❏ Identify resource requirements.
- ❏ Describe subsequent phases of an intranet implementation.

2. Preliminary Architecture Design

A preliminary architecture outlines high-level recommendations for hardware, software, and networking requirements of the intranet solution.

- ❏ Software packages required (by function).
- ❏ Server hardware needed.

❑ Networking upgrades needed.

❑ Readiness assessment of existing infrastructure.

❑ Impact of solution on existing infrastructure.

Prototype: Developing the Intranet

The prototype is a microcosm of the full solution, and is used to demonstrate the feasibility of the intranet in the customer's environment, without incurring a major investment.

Objectives

1. Validate the Architecture

   The prototype demonstrates the proposed architecture to support an intranet solution.

   ❑ Provides proof of concept of intranet technology.

   ❑ Demonstrates support of intranet technology within the customer's infrastructure.

2. Demonstrate the Technology

   The prototype demonstrates intranet technology in the customer's environment and allows for early client involvement in the development of the intranet solution. It serves as a sample of how the technology could be used, and is an introduction rather than an invasion of the intranet.

   ❑ Introduces the technology.

   ❑ Demonstrates sample business process functionality.

   ❑ Induces client participation in the development process.

3. Gain Management Support

   The prototype opens a forum in which management and users can experience intranet technology in their workplace and later, extrapolate its benefits for specific business processes.

   ❑ Builds confidence in client management and users.

   ❑ Establishes a comfort level among client skeptics.

❑ Opens a forum for detailed requirements analysis.

❑ Serves as a precursor to full implementation.

Deliverables

The deliverables of the prototype phase are a working prototype of an intranet application to produce user feedback about the system and identify/expose needed improvements/adjustments to the existing system infrastructure and implementation plan.

1. Intranet Prototype

   The prototype employs the technology identified in the workshop phase and uses "real" client documents and business processes. It is tailored to the individual client to gain support and understanding of the solution.

   ❑ Employs recommendations from workshop findings.

   ❑ Demonstrates client documents and business processes.

   ❑ Develops support and understanding of the system.

   ❑ Provides input to the configuration of the full implementation.

2. Revised Architecture

   The prototype process generates detailed information about the infrastructure at the client site. This information must be reflected in the architecture design drafted in the workshop phase. The revised architecture design will serve as the road map for the technical implementation of the intranet.

   ❑ Detailed hardware/software requirements.

   ❑ Detailed network recommendations.

   ❑ Detailed impact analysis of intranet solution.

3. Revised Implementation Plan

   As with the architecture design, the prototype will result in deeper insight to project goals. For this reason, the preliminary project plan is revised and expanded at the end of this phase to better prepare for the implementation step.

   ❑ Outline the steps of the implementation phase.

   ❑ Identify detailed resource requirements.

   ❑ Design a detailed workplan for the implementation phase.

Implementation: Deploying the Intranet

Implementation is the deployment of intranet technology to the user community. It is the culmination of the planning and development phases, and thus requires continuous user interaction.

Objectives

The objectives of the implementation phase are the building of the intranet and preparing users to be effective within the system.

1. Build the System

   Building the system means constructing the system architecture, configuring the client and server tools, and designing applications that meet the needs of the customer.

   ❑ Construct the system architecture.
   ❑ Configure the client and server tools.
   ❑ Develop applications.

2. Train the Users

   Preparing the client personnel to use the system is an extremely important step in the deployment process. It is essential that the user community embrace the intranet solution in order for it to be a success.

   ❑ Involve users early in the process.
   ❑ Understand the needs and concerns of users.
   ❑ Explain the impact of the solution on specific jobs.
   ❑ Work with the users to develop new procedures.

Deploy the Solution

Deploying the solution involves making the necessary tools available to client personnel. At this stage, the intranet solution becomes realized by the client and the greatest impact of change occurs.

1. Plan for System Maintenance

   The longevity of the intranet solution depends upon the ongoing maintenance of the system. For this reason, it is crucial that system maintenance requirements be addressed in the deployment of an intranet.

❑ Identify resource requirements for system maintenance.
❑ Document system administration procedures.
❑ Train system administrators.
❑ Develop plans for future system directions.

Deliverables

1. World-Class Intranet Solution

   The final deliverable of this process is a world-class intranet solution.

   ❑ Trained and efficient users.
   ❑ Satisfied client management.
   ❑ Demonstrated value.
   ❑ New Netscape business partners.

Sample Workshop Agenda

Day 1

Project Overview

❑ Vision.
❑ Project history.

   Current initiatives
   Time line

❑ Expected results of planning session.
❑ Current Environment.

   Demonstration

Intranet Overview

❑ Full-service intranet.

   User services
   Network services

Functional Requirements

- ❏ Information sharing and management.

    Corporate communications

    Content publishing

- ❏ Communication and collaboration.

    Messaging

    Groupware

- ❏ Navigation.
- ❏ Application access.

    Employee self-service applications (examples)

    401K

    Benefits

    Insurance

    Access to PeopleSoft/SAP/Oracle financial

    Other applications

Technical Infrastructure Overview

- ❏ Server.

    Hardware

    Operating systems

    Software—applications

- ❏ Desktop.

    Hardware

    Operating systems

    Software—applications

    Lowest common denominator

- ❏ Network.

    Protocols

    Architecture and topology

    Bandwidth and utilization

    Planned upgrades

Technical Requirements

- ❏ Replication.
- ❏ Security.
- ❏ Directory Services.
- ❏ Management.

Personnel Overview

- ❏ IT resources.

  Administration skills
  Development skills
  Placement of resources

- ❏ User community.

  Application skills
  Maintenance skills

Detailed Requirements

- ❏ Functional requirements.

  Applications
  Database access
  Others

- ❏ Technical requirements.

  WAN connectivity
  Satellite issues/concerns
  Others

- ❏ Analysis prototype environment.

  Demonstration
  Architecture review
  Application review

Netscape Product Overview

- ❏ Clients.

  Communicator
  Netcaster

❑   Servers.

> Enterprise
>
> Media
>
> Messaging
>
> Collabra
>
> Calendar
>
> Proxy
>
> Directory
>
> Certificate
>
> Catalog

❑   Tools: Netscape ONE and SuiteTools.

> JavaScript—LiveWire
>
> Java—Symantec Café
>
> Net Objects Fusion
>
> Net Dynamics
>
> Mapping tools to applications

Day 2

Preliminary Architecture Design

❑   Prioritization of full-service intranet.

❑   Network services.

> Directory
>
> Security
>
> Replication
>
> Management

❑   User Services.

> Information sharing and management
>
> Communication and collaboration
>
> Navigation
>
> Application access

Required Software

- ❑ SuiteSpot server placement.

    Enterprise

    Messaging

    Collabra

    Proxy

    Directory

    Certificate

    Catalog

- ❑ Client distribution.

    Communicator/Navigator

Required Hardware

- ❑ Hardware Servers.

    Configuration

    Placement

- ❑ Impact on existing infrastructure.

    Bandwidth estimation tools

    Network upgrades

Preliminary Project Plan

- ❑ Rollout schedule.
- ❑ Resource requirements.
- ❑ Training requirements.

    System administration

    End user

- ❑ Subsequent phases of project.
- ❑ Applications.

Wrap-up

- ❑ Identify outstanding issues.
- ❑ Action plan.
- ❑ Next steps.

Bibliography

Marc Andreessen and The Netscape Product Team. *The Full-Service Intranet.* (Mountain View, CA: Netscape Communications Corporation), 1996.

Marc Andreessen and The Netscape Product Team. *The Networked Enterprise.* (Mountain View, CA: Netscape Communications Corporation), 1996.

Ian Campbell. *The Intranet: Slashing the Cost of Business.* International Data Corporation (http://www.idcresearch.com), 1996.

Bill Bercik & Jill Bond. *Inside JavaScript.* (Indianapolis, IN: New Riders), 1996.

Ryan Bernard. *The Corporate Intranet.* (New York, NY: John Wiley & Sons, Inc.), 1997.

William R. Cheswick & Steven M. Bellovin. *Firewalls and Internet Security.* (Reading, MA: Addison-Wesley), 1994.

George Eckel & William Steen. *Intranet Working.* (Indianapolis, IN: New Riders), 1996.

Tim Evans. *Building an Intranet.* (Indianapolis, IN: Sams.net), 1996.

Forrester Research, Inc. *The Full Service Intranet.* (http://www.forrester.com), 1996.

Mellanie Hills. *Intranet Business Strategies.* (New York, NY: John Wiley & Sons, Inc.) 1997.

Tim Ritchey. *Java!* (Indianapolis, IN: New Riders), 1995.

Darrel Sano. *Designing Large Scale Web Sites: A Visual Design Methodology.* (New York, NY: John Wiley & Sons, Inc.), 1996.

Ed Tittle & James Michael Stewart. *Intranet Bible.* (Foster City, CA: IDG Books Worldwide), 1996.

Index

Page references in italic type indicate illustrations. Netscape intranet products are generally indexed *without* "Netscape" as a modifier. For example, look up Enterprise Server instead of Netscape Enterprise Server.